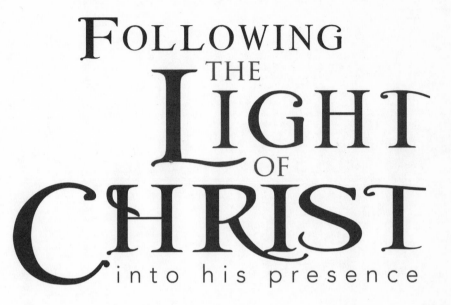

FOLLOWING
THE
LIGHT
OF
CHRIST
into his presence

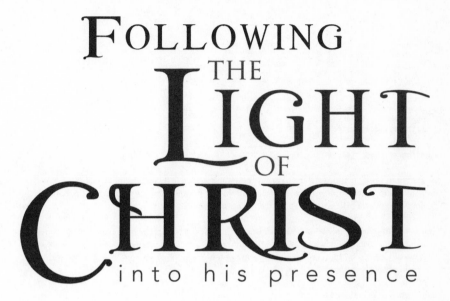

FOLLOWING THE LIGHT OF CHRIST

into his presence

JOHN M. PONTIUS

CFI
Springville, Utah

© 2011 John M. Pontius

ISBN 13: 978-1-55517-643-3

Published by CFI, an imprint of Cedar Fort, Inc., 2373 W. 700 S., Springville, UT 84663
Distributed by Cedar Fort, Inc. www.cedarfort.com

THE LIBRARY OF CONGRESS HAS CATALOGED THE THIRD EDITION OF
FOLLOWING THE LIGHT OF CHRIST INTO HIS PRESENCE AS FOLLOWS

Pontius, John M.
Following the light of Christ into His presence / by John M.
Pontius.-- 3rd ed.
p. cm.
Includes bibliographical references.
ISBN 1-55517-643-7 (pbk.: alk. paper)
1. Jesus Christ--Mormon interpretations. 2. Jesus Christ--Presence. 3. Holy Spirit. 1. Title.
BX8643.J4 P66 2002
230'.9332--dc21

2002151393

Cover design by Brian Halley
Cover design © 2011 by Lyle Mortimer
Edited and typeset by Heidi Doxey

Printed in the United States of America

10 9 8 7 6 5 4 3 2 1

Printed on acid-free paper

One of the grand fundamental principles of "Mormonism" is to receive truth, let it come from whence it may.
(Smith, *Teachings of the Prophet*, 313)

Author's Note

I owe a profound debt of gratitude to the Lord for His love and marvelous gospel. It is my deepest-held hope that this book, in some way, furthers His latter-day work, and brings all who read it closer to those inspiring promises discussed herein.

Books by John M. Pontius

Following the Light of Christ into His Presence

Millennial Quest Series:
The Spirit of Fire
Angels Among Us
Angels Forged in Fire
Angels and a Flaming Sword, Part 1
Angels and a Flaming Sword, Part 2

We Three Kings
The Triumph of Zion

Brother Pontius may be contacted through his website and blog:

www.Followingthelight.org
http://Unblogmysoul.wordpress.com

Contents

Foreword

The contents of this book constitute the thinking and opinions of its author, and should not be regarded as official Church doctrine. The author lovingly acknowledges the preeminent stature of the Holy Scriptures, and voice of the Brethren in proclaiming church doctrine.

Most of what you will read is the result of the author's personal experiences in the gospel. The Holy Spirit will testify to all who humbly read this work that which is of eternal significance to them.

I owe a profound debt of gratitude to the Lord for His love and marvelous gospel. It is my deepest-held hope that this book, in some way, furthers His latter-day work, and brings all who read it closer to those inspiring promises discussed herein.

I, like Nephi, have been born of goodly parents, and much, if not all, of the deep and abiding faith I feel in the Lord, I owe to their powerful examples in my youth.

I am especially blessed to be married to Terri Jeanne, the love of my life and eternal friend. She has taught me the most important thing I know, which is what it is like to be loved without condition.

Introduction

Every journey begins with a single step. No matter how distant or near the destination, that first step is not optional. To fail to begin is to fail the entire journey.

With the process of obtaining the greater latter-day blessings and the stature of righteousness, that first step is learning to hear and then to obey the voice of revelation in one's soul. There is no other first step. There is no other process. There is no other path.

The purpose of this book is to make personal revelation easy to recognize and to implement in your life. There truly is a way. It is not complicated, nor is it intended for prophets and apostles alone. Anyone can learn to hear the voice of the Holy Spirit and to walk the path of righteousness to its glorious end.

Now we live in a dispensation of the gospel whose primary objective is to build a society worthy to dwell in the presence of our returning Christ. When we actually understand what we are being asked to do, it is a calling and obligation that may seem beyond our capacity. But it is not. There is a sweet and empowering pathway directly before us, which each of us can identify and walk.

The process is actually very simple. When we take the Holy Spirit as our guide, we allow Christ to become our shepherd. Then He begins to change us. This is the empowering aspect of the Atonement. He not only causes us to see our potential, He vastly upgrades it. He doesn't just forgive us of our sins, He shields us against them. He doesn't just give us a glimpse of the glorious blessings in store; He enables us to obtain them.

Every time we yield our will to Christ's, something divine happens—we become more and more like him.

When you read the scriptures and survey the lives of the noble and great ones of previous gospel dispensations, you are not reading the lives of the extraordinarily talented. You are reading the lives of the extraordinarily obedient. They all started with no greater advantage or genius or strength than most of us.

This book is written with the hope of helping us reach our fullest potential in righteousness. These principles will enable us to walk in constant revelation and to know the correct choice in every decision that matters to our exaltation.

This book is like the owner's manual we were sent to earth without. Within it is the grand key to finding the straight and narrow path. It is a mystery revealed, a door opened, a divine gift. Within, you will find the key to receiving answers to your prayers, daily guidance, personal revelation, prophetic understating, power in the priesthood, rebirth of the Spirit, your calling and election, and much more.

CHAPTER ONE

Personal Revelation

THREE PILLARS OF TRUTH

There are three supreme truths upon which our salvation rests. They form the foundation of all gospel truths. It is impossible to be exalted without understanding and applying all three truths. All three must be equally understood and implemented, or the structure topples. Remove any one of them, and exaltation simply becomes impossible.

First, God, our Heavenly Father, is a perfected and exalted man, a personage of flesh and bone. As we are now, so once was He. As He is now, so we may become. He offers us the ultimate attainment in eternity—to become like Him and share His eternal glory. He is the author of the great plan being carried out by His beloved Son.

Second, Jesus Christ is the savior and redeemer of mankind. Through His Atonement, all mankind may be saved by obedience to the laws and ordinances of the gospel. He is the great exemplar, and has shown us the way to exaltation through His own life here on earth. He is the source of all light and truth. His is the only name given under Heaven whereby men may be saved. To enter the celestial kingdom and its attendant glories, we must become His spiritual offspring, His sons and daughters. After having been proven worthy, sanctified, born again, and after having our calling and election made sure, we may, in time, be ushered into His presence during this life. This blessing is intended for all faithful, and is not reserved for prophets only.

Third, the light of Christ emanates from our Savior, is administered by the Holy Ghost, and is revelation which constitutes the conscience of man. The Holy Ghost, acting in the capacity of the Holy Spirit, is the primary means by which Jesus Christ accomplishes His Father's work among men. Through priesthood ordinances, and by obedience to the promptings of the Holy Spirit, one may receive the constant companionship of the Holy Ghost, which constitutes being born again. This spiritual rebirth burns out the impurities, refines, perfects, sanctifies, effects a remission of sins through the Atonement, and works a mighty change in the soul of man. This mighty change is the *only* way one can achieve the perfection of character required to become like Him. This process is the only way whereby we can be exalted.

As Latter-day Saints, we understand the first two truths with great clarity, but falter somewhat on the third. For this reason it has been my intent to focus on this pillar of truth throughout this book.

THE VISION OF THE TREE OF LIFE

The Lord gave us a detailed description of the course required to achieve spiritual greatness in the vision of the tree of life. A study of this vision will reveal everything a person needs to know on this subject. It is often misinterpreted, with additional meanings attached. The message is very specific, and is intended as a guide in our earthly journey.

Nephi describes their departure into the wilderness, and then makes this astounding statement.

> And it came to pass that I, Nephi, . . . also having great desires to know of the mysteries of God, wherefore, I did cry unto the Lord; and behold He did visit me. (2 Nephi 2:16)

Nephi's soul was surely bursting with joy as he sat to record the events of his life, and the object, the purpose for his writing, was to teach others how they might also attain the great blessings and joy which he had attained, including standing in God's presence. We can well surmise that the Savior's love permeated Nephi's soul and filled him with a glowing, irresistible desire to teach us what he knew. He had seen in vision that his own posterity would dwindle in unbelief for centuries, and had obtained the promise that the people of this latter-day dispensation would take his words to his posterity. Nephi wasn't just writing to record his life, he was writing to save his family.

He knew the way because he had walked it faithfully and unerringly until he had stood in the presence of the Lord and received this sweet promise, and many others, from the Savior's own lips. He knew it was the only way, and had watched his brothers wander forbidden paths and perish. The thought that his own family might likewise wander foolishly unto destruction undoubtedly wracked his soul with torment.

Nephi next records the tremendous vision of the tree of life which his father beheld, and which Nephi later sees and interprets. The Lord caused this vision to be included in scripture because it has tremendous value. It must be understood in its entirety for us to benefit from what it is teaching. A blurry understanding of portions of this vision will obscure its overall message.

This vision is a beacon to spiritual seekers. It identifies the light which will dispel the darkness obscuring the way home.

Nephi wrote it for those of his posterity aimlessly wandering in spiritual twilight among shadows and false images. It is for those who understand truth but have yet to chart a determined course of righteousness. It is for anyone who knows there is more, but does not know how to pierce the heavens and claim the promises. It is for all those who would be the elect of God, if they only knew how.

This vision is an allegory to teach us what we may achieve in this life, and how to accomplish it. Each part of this vision is symbolic of some part of our earthly journey.

Nephi's joy was in his Savior, and the Savior's love radiated through him like a lighthouse on a desolate hill to illuminate the way for millions of travelers in the barren wastes of spiritual twilight. This vision is the spiritual road map the Lord gave Nephi to hold up to those struggling thus along the way home. The message and promise of the vision of the tree of life pertain primarily to *this life*. It is a message that all who seek eternal life must understand and apply in their lives.

Lehi's dream was of a vast and dreary wasteland in which he wandered until he beheld a spectacularly beautiful tree of exquisite whiteness whose fruit was most delicious and precious to the soul. After partaking of the fruit, Lehi sought his family that he might share the precious fruit with them. He succeeded in enticing all but Laman and Lemuel to come and experience the joy of partaking with him.

After his family had partaken, Lehi beheld a straight and narrow path leading to the tree. He also saw a rod of iron running along the length of the path. A river of filthy water flowed beside the path and swept away many of those who lost hold of the rod of iron. The path and rod were occasionally obscured by thick mists of darkness, which made it necessary to hold tightly to the rod of iron to keep from becoming lost from the path.

He also observed that there were many other forbidden paths leading in unknown directions, away from the tree. After Lehi and his family had partaken of the fruit, they looked around and saw a great and spacious building on the other side of the river. The building appeared to be floating in the air.

> And it was filled with people, both old and young, both male and female; and their manner of dress was exceedingly fine; and they were in the attitude of mocking and pointing their fingers towards those who had come and were partaking of the fruit. And after they had tasted of the fruit they were ashamed, because of those that were scoffing at them; and they fell away into forbidden paths and were lost. (1 Nephi 8:27–28)

THE TREE

Nephi's account of the tree of life begins by the Spirit of the Lord showing him the tree that his father had seen.

> And the beauty thereof was far beyond, yea, exceeding of all beauty; and the whiteness thereof did exceed the whiteness of the driven snow. (1 Nephi 11:8)

Nephi next requests to be shown the interpretation and meaning of the tree. The Spirit of the Lord answers his request in a most unusual way by showing him "a virgin, most beautiful and fair above all other virgins" (1 Nephi 11:15). Then the angel asks, "Knowest thou the condescension of God?" (1 Nephi 11:16). Nephi responds that he knows God loves His children but does not know the meaning of all things. The messenger explains: "The virgin whom thou seest is the mother of the Son of God, after the manner of the flesh" (1 Nephi 11:18).

Immediately, the vision expands to show the virgin carried away in the spirit and then bearing a child in her arms. Nephi is then triumphantly told:

> Behold the Lamb of God, yea, even the Son of the Eternal Father! (1 Nephi 11:21)

The angel asks again, "Knowest thou the meaning of the tree which thy father saw?" (1 Nephi 11:21). At this point Nephi knows what the tree represents. The written description of his vision and conversations with the Spirit of the Lord leaves us wanting to know how he arrives at his answer. Yet his answer is powerful and specific:

> Yea, it is the love of God, which sheddeth itself abroad in the hearts of the children of men; wherefore, it is the most desirable above all things. (1 Nephi 11:22)

In seeing the nativity of our Lord, Nephi undoubtedly was filled with an understanding of the tremendous love required on the Lord's part to cause Him to leave His throne (condescend) to be born in the flesh. Further, Nephi was taught how this love spreads abroad in the hearts of the children of men. He undoubtedly felt that love, felt the power and majesty of it, felt the soul-refining fire it is, felt the eternal worth of souls, and felt the deep compassion it engenders within the recipient. His whole being was filled with such unspeakable joy that he could only exclaim, "It is the most desirable above all things!" (1 Nephi 11:22). The Spirit of the Lord, who could utter nothing but pure truth, exclaims in harmony, "Yea, and the most joyous to the soul" (1 Nephi 11:23).

It is important at this point to state the obvious. The tree of life represents the love of God. It does not represent the celestial kingdom. It does not represent eternal life, calling and election, or any other spiritual gift or reward. It represents only the love of God.

It is apparently tempting to editorialize on this great vision and ascribe expanded meanings. Yet, this vision was given with specific intent, to deliver a tremendous message and instruction for those who can understand its import. It is so potent that attempting to add anything actually dilutes it. The power is thus lost in favor of a truism lacking the soul-saving message. Who are we to instruct the Lord or assume we know better what is most joyous to the soul? Attaching other meanings to the tree voids its power and invents other blessings that have not been promised.

The prophet Moroni, nearly a thousand years later, would teach this message:

> And now I know that this love which thou hast had for the children of men is charity; wherefore, except men shall have charity they cannot inherit that place which thou hast prepared in the mansions of thy Father. (Ether 12:34)

The tree of life in Nephi's vision represents His love for us, which is charity, the most desirable above all things, and the most joyous to the soul. For emphasis I repeat: Charity is the love of God *for us*, not the other way around.

If an angel of the Lord appeared to you and emphatically informed you that something was the most desirable and precious thing that could be attained in this life, and that it was readily available, would you not pursue that thing with great vigor and determination? Is it possible to read such promising words, such wonderfully potent language, and ignore its message? The effect that charity has upon the soul is the greatest of all feelings in this life; it is the loveliest, the most joyful, and the most delightful. There is nothing to compare with its joyous effect upon the human soul.

Note Elder McConkie's definition of charity:

> Above all the attributes of godliness and perfection, charity is the one most devoutly to be desired. Charity is more than love, far more; it is everlasting love, perfect love, the pure love of Christ which endureth forever. It is love so centered in righteousness that the possessor has no aim or desire except for the eternal welfare of his own soul and for the souls of those around him. (McConkie, *Doctrinal New Testament Commentary*, 2:378)

Charity is a gift of the Spirit, bestowed as a result of personal righteousness. To attain a full measure of charity is to become like unto Christ, to become purified even as He is pure.

> Wherefore, my beloved brethren, pray unto the Father with all the energy of heart, that ye may be filled with this love, which he hath bestowed upon all who are true followers of his Son, Jesus Christ; that ye may become the sons of God; that when he shall appear we shall be like him, for we shall see him as he is; that we may have this hope; that we may be purified even as he is pure. Amen. (Moroni 7:48)

In this light, it makes better sense that the great reward the tree represents, is to be infused with charity, that which is greatest of all, and most joyful to the soul.

> And above all things, clothe yourselves with the bond of charity, as with a mantle, which is the bond of perfectness and peace. (D&C 88:125)

This divine bestowal of charity is so important to our spiritual journey that we cannot be exalted without it. It is not an optional achievement.

> Wherefore, there must be faith; and if there must be faith there must also be hope; and if there must be hope there must also be charity. *And except ye have charity ye can in nowise be saved in the kingdom of God*; neither can ye be saved in the kingdom of God if ye have not faith; neither can ye if ye have no hope. (Moroni 10:20–21; emphasis added)

Hear Nephi's words and those of the Spirit of the Lord: "It is the most desirable above all things. . . . Yea, and the most joyous to the soul!" (1 Nephi 11:22–23).

Charity comes into one's soul in increasing amounts as we grow spiritually. When the rebirth occurs, the Holy Ghost blesses the recipient with charity. Charity continues to grow ever after, filling the soul with an increasingly greater endowment of this divine attribute until the person becomes like unto God. Charity forms the joy in the human soul experienced by the righteous and those sealed up unto eternal life.

It is also wonderful to note that the fulfillment of this vision of the tree of life, which is to partake of the precious fruit of charity, is to be achieved in this life. There is no mention of death, resurrection, or eternal worlds. Indeed, Lehi called earnestly to his mortal family, most of whom came and partook of the fruit, but his rebellious older sons rejected the call, both in the dream and in real life.

Since charity is that which is most desirable and joyous to the soul, then the question begs to be answered by the earnest soul, "How may I attain this charity of which the Spirit of the Lord speaks?" To this question the answer shines like the morning sun, "Learn the lesson of the tree of life." It has no other purpose than to teach exactly how to arrive at that glorious tree and partake of the precious fruit. To learn the lesson of the tree of life, we must accurately understand each part of the vision.

THE ROD OF IRON

> I beheld the Son of God going forth among the children of men; and I saw many fall down at his feet and worship him. And it came to pass that I beheld that the rod of iron, which my father had seen, was the word of God. (1 Nephi 11:24–25)

Again, the Spirit of the Lord instructed Nephi with imagery, and he learned much more than what he recorded for us to read. What he saw with his eyes was only part of the message. The rest of what he learned came as bursts of understanding, which revealed to his heart the meaning of the rod of iron.

Whatever the rod of iron represents, it caused the people to fall down and worship the Lord, and is specifically the "word of God." It is tempting to assume that this refers only to the holy scriptures and inspired writings of the prophets, and move on to the next subject. However, consider the imagery of the vision. The rod of iron ran beside the straight and narrow path. Its most important feature is that any person who grasps it, and does not let go, will arrive at the tree of life. There can be no exception. This is a universal law because the truths of the gospel are universal, and all who obey will succeed. It is unthinkable that someone could firmly grasp the rod of iron and end up at some destination other than the tree of life.

Let us consider for a moment what the rod of iron and the "word of God" represent in Lehi's dream. We'll start with the Bible. How many people have loved the Bible, even made life-long studies of it, and yet failed to savor the fruits of the tree of life? Multitudes have wandered amiss, even quoting scripture while wielding the sword in awful carnage. The Bible thus fails the test, not because it is not inspired scripture, but because it simply is not what the Lord was symbolizing for us in the rod of iron.

Consider the Book of Mormon. Has any person read the Book of Mormon, steadfastly believed in it, and yet failed to pluck the precious fruits? Of course. There are many who have similarly failed. We all know of people who have considerable faith in the Book of Mormon's truths, who are spiritually stagnant. The Book of Mormon, the Doctrine and Covenants, Pearl of Great Price, conference talks, and every other written source of truth similarly fail the test. They simply do not guide all of the people who love and use them to the promised blessings. Again, this is not because these writings lack spiritual veracity or fall short in any way. They just are not what the Lord was representing with the imagery of the rod of iron.

In The Church of Jesus Christ of Latter-day Saints we are uniquely blessed with multiple sources of truth. The "word of God" takes many valuable forms, all of which are indispensable in our lives. The scriptures are the standard of truth and the yard-stick by which all doctrine is measured. The voices of the living prophets are God's mind and will to the church. There could not be a true church without a living prophet's divinely inspired guidance. Personal revelation (among other things) is the divine witness whereby we are able to recognize the scriptures or the words of the latter-day prophets as the "word of God." Without the inspiration of personal revelation, we would not have a testimony of any form of the "word of God" (Moroni 10:5).

There should never be a circumstance when any of these three conflict. Particularly in the case of personal revelation, we must measure, and judge the validity of what we receive by these other two sources. If we find we have received a prompting that conflicts with either of these other two, it should be abandoned immediately as being incorrect. Any person who achieves a full and profound measure of personal revelation will be in full harmony with the brethren, and with the scriptures.

This book deals specifically with personal revelation, and for that reason focuses upon achieving a greater measure of that source of truth. Personal revelation is the means whereby we are able to embrace the scriptures as the word of God. It is the reason we know we have living prophets, and as we will discuss throughout this book, it is the means whereby Jesus Christ guides us moment by moment. However, nothing said is intended to promote personal revelation as a substitute for the others, or as a superior form of the "word of God." All three are vitally essential, and none can take the place of the other.

Possessing the scriptures without having (or recognizing the existence of) living prophets is largely responsible for the turmoil we see in the modern Christian world. The lesson of the people of Zarahemla in the Book of Mormon is partly what happens to a people who do not have the scriptures, and among whom no prophet is called. Yet, they undoubtedly had personal revelation available to them to the extent they were worthy of it, and still they forgot God entirely (see Omni 1:17).

When Mosiah, himself a prophet, came among them, he brought the scriptures, as well as the voice of revelation, and they turned unto God and repented of their apostasy. Perhaps this

11

gives us a vision of the symbiotic role these sources of the "word of God" play in our lives.

Having the scriptures *and* a living prophet among them in the person of Jesus Christ, and yet being devoid of the power of personal revelation, is the condition into which the Jews plunged themselves, and which made it possible for them to crucify their own Savior.

This is also the great tragedy of our time. With all God has done for us, having the scriptures in perhaps the most complete form they have ever existed, having living prophets among us, still the vast majority of the world chooses to walk in darkness. Why? Not because there is anything wrong with the word of God, but because they choose to ignore that spark of revelation in their souls which would, and actually does, point them to the restored gospel and the truths made available in the scriptures and by living prophets. Without that essential element of divine inspiration, the power of all other sources of truth invariably goes unheeded.

PERSONAL REVELATION

Personal revelation is surely the word of God in its purest and simplest form: unfiltered, unedited, untranslated, pure, intimate, specific, and direct. It is the essence of faith, hope, charity, and prophecy. Even in its least significant forms, it unerringly points to the true north of light and truth and leads us away from evil and darkness.

Any person who grasps hold of personal revelation as his or her rod of iron, never letting go, obeying every prompting, will walk unerringly through the mists of satanic darkness and arrive at and dine upon the fruits of the tree of life.

Such a person will also recognize and rejoice in all other sources of the "word of God."

This has always been true and always will be. It will never fail—indeed it cannot fail. It is the spiritual rod of iron that withstands the buffetings of everything Satan can muster against it and still it guides those who cling to it to the precious fruits, without fail. Additionally, all whose lives are guided by personal revelation are led to fall down and glorify God, as Nephi indicated they would.

We know personal revelation is essential to our exaltation, and all true seekers struggle to receive it. At times, however, it seems as if the heavens are made of stone, and the silence is deafening. We struggle with prayer and satisfy ourselves that the silence means "no," when in reality it means we have not learned to receive answers to our prayers. We wade through life's trials seemingly alone, desperately needing divine guidance and, failing to pierce the heavens, we content ourselves by assuming that only the prophets do it differently. We puzzle out our problems in our minds, arrive at a conclusion, and pray for confirmation. When we hear nothing, we take it for divine indifference and permission to proceed with our plans. We pride ourselves on having received guidance, when in fact we have not and are only groping in the darkness, pursuing our own agenda instead of the Lord's.

The truth of the matter is that the Lord wants to guide us in our lives, and actually does so. The problem is we fail to hear most of what He says. Only an occasional shout from the heavens gets through, while the quiet whisperings of truth remain unheard.

Personal revelation is mother's milk to the spiritual and manna to the righteous. To those spiritually reborn it is as natural as speech and as beautiful as choirs of angels. It is neither difficult nor sporadic, and is available to every man, woman, and child who lives.

Personal revelation begins as our conscience, and if we learn to give heed to it, it expands greatly after the gift of the Holy Ghost is given. It is neither reserved for the perfected nor is it only for times of great crisis.

Revelation is, however, very demanding. Even the most seemingly insignificant communication from the Lord must be acted upon courageously and without complaint, or the heavens remain silent for a time. The Lord does not take revelation lightly, and neither must we. If we attain unto this precious gift and follow it meticulously, it will lead us to the precious fruits of the tree of life and far beyond. If we fail to do so, we shall forever remain in spiritual mediocrity.

The purpose of this book is to help us recognize revelation, and how to make it grow into a life-giving force in our lives. It is essential that we first learn to recognize and obey that which we already have before we can expect to be given anything greater. We will discuss how to do all these things after we finish discovering what the remainder of the vision of the tree of life symbolizes.

THE STRAIGHT AND NARROW PATH

In Nephi's vision the straight and narrow path leads to the tree of life. It is often assumed that the straight and narrow path represents the gospel and its teachings. This is a true statement, but lacks completeness. Recall that the path is bordered and literally defined by the rod of iron, which represents personal revelation. Personal revelation is specific, individualized instruction on how to arrive at the tree of life. Therefore, it would be more accurate to say that, in addition to the gospel requirements, the straight and narrow path represents the course of life each individual must walk in order to arrive at the tree and partake of the precious fruit.

To walk the path is to follow the true course in life as the Lord directs through the Holy Spirit. It is straight, because it is the shortest distance between where we are and the blessings of the fruit of the tree of life. It is narrow, because the Lord does not allow us diversions and side trips on forbidden byways, nor does He allow us to *almost* walk the path. We are required to walk it with every footfall placed precisely where it belongs. Every prompting of the Spirit obeyed is a tighter grip on the rod of iron, and a new step correctly placed on the straight and narrow path.

THE MISTS OF DARKNESS AND BUILDING

The mists of darkness Nephi saw represented the temptations of Satan, which blind the eyes and harden the hearts of men. They obscured the way in various places along the path, making it impossible to walk by sight. The mists of darkness are more than isolated temptations. They are complex, intelligently organized, maliciously constructed barrages of opposition, which are impossible to penetrate with the understanding of man. To remain on the path the travelers had to retain a firm grip upon the rod of iron. Lehi describes the mists of darkness as "exceedingly great" (1 Nephi 8:23), so everyone who had commenced upon the path, but had not seized the rod of iron, wandered off and were lost.

Our own journey is exactly this way. We cannot walk by sight. This means that it is impossible to figure out everything we must do by using our intellect. The journey is specifically designed to force us to rely upon the word of God in its many forms, especially personal revelation, to guide us through times of confusion and darkness. It is also noteworthy that there are certain times when the path was not obscured by the mists of darkness. During these times we recover, and prepare for further travels. We must beware during easy times, for it is tempting to become lax and release our hold upon the rod.

Since the rod of iron represents the light of personal revelation, it becomes obvious that the purpose of the mists of darkness is to obscure personal revelation, and thus entice us into wandering off the path. Satan cannot cause revelation to cease, but we can. When we disobey the promptings of the Holy Spirit, the heavens remain silent for a time, and the evil one has scored a small victory.

> And that wicked one cometh and taketh away light and truth, through disobedience, from the children of men. (D&C 93:39)

The building was filled with the rich and powerful people of the world. It represented the vain imaginings and pride of worldly success. Throngs of people were pressing forward, struggling to enter the building. Once they gained entrance to the building, they turned and pointed and mocked those who were trying to find their way along the straight and narrow path. This building was floating above the ground, suggesting that it was not a real building, nor a real prize. It lacked substance and solidity, its pleasures temporary and insubstantial.

The river of filthy water represented the depths of hell, which was the awful reward of those who chose to abandon the path once they had started upon it. Notice, it was in close proximity to the path, meaning those most likely to fall in and be lost were those upon the path. People wandering the other byways were not as threatened by the river of filthy water, and the condemnation it represents.

In order to understand the rod of iron, which represents personal revelation, it is important to understand where it comes from and who is speaking to us. Every prompting which we receive to do good, to turn away from evil, and to be Christlike in our acts, comes to us through the light of Christ.

Chapter Two

The Light of Christ

The light of Christ is many things. It is the power that keeps the sun burning, keeps the planets in their orbits, and gives life to all living creatures. It is the order of the universe, that which we call nature, and the power by which God governs (D&C 88:7–13). It is a free gift to His children. But, most importantly for our purposes, it is the light of our understanding, and the source of our conscience.

> And the Spirit giveth light to every man that cometh into the world; and the Spirit enlighteneth every man through the world, that hearkeneth to the voice of the Spirit. And every one that hearkeneth to the voice of the Spirit cometh unto God, even the Father. (D&C 84:46–47)

Every person born into this world receives a birthday gift from his or her loving Heavenly Father. Through the Atonement of Christ, Father gives each child a precious gift of Light. This light serves as a guide, a teacher, and a voice of truth. It is commonly called the conscience, and is felt by everyone. It is constant, unerring, and persistent. It can only be extinguished by repeated abuse, but it can be extinguished. Most important of all, it *is* revelation.

The conscience of man constitutes our first and most important contact with the divine.

THE HOLY GHOST AND THE LIGHT OF CHRIST

The Holy Ghost is the means by which Jesus Christ communicates all truth to mankind. The light of Christ emanates from Christ and is disseminated to us through the Holy Ghost. This function of the third member of the Godhead is commonly referred to as the Holy Spirit (as an example, see Mosiah 3:19). It is also appropriately called the light of truth, the voice of Christ, the voice of truth, the spirit of truth, the word(s) of Christ, His voice, my voice, the voice of the good shepherd, the Spirit of Christ, the Spirit of God, the Spirit of the Lord, and the light of Christ.

All spiritual gifts come through the Holy Spirit, which is the Holy Ghost acting in his role as the light of Christ (see Moroni 10:1–34).

> Moroni says that the gifts of God come from Christ, by the power of the Holy Ghost and by the Spirit of Christ. (Moroni 10.) In other words, the gifts come by the power of that Spirit who is the Holy Ghost, but the Spirit of Christ (or light of Christ) is the agency through which the Holy Ghost operates. (McConkie, *Mormon Doctrine*, 314)

The Holy Spirit, which begins as our conscience, is a free gift to all mankind. It has power to warn, entice, enlighten, and urge to obedience. It will expand its mission to become a teacher of great eloquence as we give heed to its guiding voice. Prior to the ordinance of bestowing the gift of the Holy Ghost, the Holy Spirit is limited in its mission. It can only expand to a given level, and therefore, a person must receive the gift of the Holy Ghost in order to progress further. After the gift of the Holy Ghost is given, the Holy Spirit expands and amplifies its role, administers the spiritual gifts, and begins the process of purging the dross and unrefined from the soul as we give heed to its voice. Sanctification begins as the Holy Ghost, acting in his role as a revelator and purifier, becomes our occasional companion prior to the rebirth.

Even in its most powerful role, the Holy Spirit remains a still small voice. It rarely exceeds a quiet whisper, and even profound truths come silently and require faith to hear and obey. It requires much experience and righteous obedience to develop faith in the still small voice of the Holy Spirit.

It would be easy to get confused if we assume all "promptings" have launguage, words, or audible voices. Promptings generally are impressions that lack an actual voice, and most often do not employ language. The phrase "still, small voice" labels it as inaudible. "Still" means without sound, subdued, hushed. "Small" describes something tiny, in no great amount, of minor weight or consequence, easy to overlook.

The operation of the Holy Spirit should not be confused with that of the Holy Ghost. When the Holy Ghost speaks in His role as a revelator, the message is much easier to understand. The Holy Ghost communicates in a more powerful way, which enlightens the soul with poignant truth. When we are so blessed to enjoy profound revelation and glorious manifestations, these also come through the Holy Ghost. This type of grand communiqué becomes an abundant part of our lives only after we have learned to faithfully follow the lesser gift of the guiding voice of the Holy Spirit.

Prior to this, the Holy Ghost only speaks on inspiring occasions, and for a special witness, such as when we first gain a testimony that Jesus is the Christ. We will discuss and document these principles as we continue.

The Holy Ghost is also called the Holy Spirit, or other terms which apply to the light of Christ, due to the fact that the operation of the agency of the Holy Spirit, and that of the Holy Ghost, becomes nearly indistinguishable as one grows nearer and nearer to perfection. The Holy Ghost is also correctly called the Comforter, the Holy Spirit of promise, the Spirit of Truth, and the Spirit of God.

For the sake of clarity throughout this book, the term "Holy Spirit" refers to the Holy Ghost acting in His assigned role as the light of Christ. Whenever the term "Holy Ghost" is used, reference is being made to the third member of the Godhead speaking in His role as a revelator. The scriptures and most other texts do not confine themselves to this definition, and often use these name-titles interchangeably. We will only do so for clarity.

Even after the rebirth, when the Holy Ghost has become our constant companion, most truth and guidance is communicated through the Holy Spirit, and as such, remains a still small voice.

Consider the impact of this truth. Your conscience is revelation to you as surely as if the Lord sent an angel to your bedroom with a flaming sword.

The truths communicated to you by your conscience come from Jesus Christ, are administered by the Holy Ghost, and are revelation.

No longer may we brush aside the still small voice and go our own way without knowing we are disobeying revelation from Jesus Christ. If Jesus Christ called you on the phone and asked you to go help your spouse with the dishes, wouldn't you immediately go from the phone to the sink? Or would you return to your TV show and shrug it off with little or no thought? If a telephone call from Jesus Christ would impress you, then why not His voice in your spiritual ear, whispered from the eternal realms? Are we more impressed with electronics than we are with revelation?

Consider again the words just quoted above:

> And every one that hearkeneth to the voice of the Spirit [which begins as the conscience], cometh unto God, even the Father. (D&C 84:47)

Application of this principle precedes the promise of eternal life. In other words, we must first learn to hearken to the voice of the Holy Spirit before the greater blessings are bestowed.

This is a grand key. It is a mystery revealed, a door opened, a divine bequest. It is the key to receiving answers to your prayers, daily guidance, personal revelation, prophetic understanding, receiving power in the priesthood, the rebirth of your spirit, your calling and election, and much more.

If all of God's people applied this truth, we *would* be Zion, and pillars of fire would blaze above the temples of God!

The Spirit of the Lord is talking to us constantly, and we have only to lift our heads from the confusion of the world to hear Him and be inspired and led. This promise is profound. If we learn to hearken to His voice, we will be guided back into the presence of God.

Elder Faust expressed it this way:

> Lehi, teaching his son Jacob, declared: "Men are that they might have joy." To achieve this objective, we must "give ear to the voice of the living God." I wish to testify as a living witness that joy does come through listening to the Spirit, for I have experienced it. (Faust, "Voice of the Spirit," 7)

Notice that Elder Faust is referring here to the Spirit as "the voice of the living God."

THE LIGHT AND THE LIFE OF THE WORLD

When Jesus appeared in glory to the ancient Nephites, He introduced Himself with words chosen to teach the most important truth we can understand about Him and what He has done for us. After first declaring Himself to be Jesus Christ, he announces:

> And behold, I am the light and the life of the world; and I have drunk out of that bitter cup which the Father hath given me, and have glorified the Father in taking upon me the sins of the world, in the which I have suffered the will of the Father in all things from the beginning. (3 Nephi 11:11)

Notice, He first wants us to understand that He is the light and life of the world. All else He has done is secondary to this great accomplishment, yet we scarcely understand what He means by so declaring Himself. Abinadi adds to our understanding with these words:

> He is the light and the life of the world; yea, a light that is endless, that can never be darkened; yea, and also a life which is endless, that there can be no more death. (Mosiah 16:9)

Christ is the life of the world because of the Creation and Resurrection. Not only did He give life unto every living creature, both in the Creation and in sustaining life as we know it, but He has provided a means of resurrection which will bring endless life to all His creations.

But even this great gift is secondary to the great gift of light. Christ is an endless light that can never be darkened. John the Baptist gave us this great testimony of Him:

> I saw his glory, that he was in the beginning, before the world was; Therefore, in the beginning the Word was, for he was the Word, even the messenger of salvation—The light and the Redeemer of the world; the Spirit of truth, who came into the world, because the world was made *by* him, and in him was the life of men and the light of men. (D&C 93:7–9; emphasis added)

He is an endless light because He was the light in the beginning, before the world was and will continue to be throughout eternity. He was in the beginning the Word, even the messenger of salvation. John explains what being the Word means by further describing Him as "The light and the Redeemer of the world, the Spirit of truth." The Spirit of truth is the Holy Spirit—the Spirit of Christ, which is the conscience of man. This is one of our Savior's greatest gifts to us—that He is the light of our conscience. And, it truly is a gift; we have done nothing in this life to earn it.

It is of such great worth to us that without it none of Father's children would find their way home, and thus the Atonement would become a moot and meaningless accomplishment, for no one would be able to take advantage of it.

Without the Light or the Word of truth, which permeates our souls, we would have no sense of right and wrong, no higher understanding, no sweetness of soul, no spiritual refinements, no urging to pray, no goodness, no progression, and no ability to choose between right and wrong. All the works of God would have been frustrated without the Holy Spirit to entice us to do righteously, and in opposition to that, the enticements of the evil one.

> Wherefore, the Lord God gave unto man that he should act for himself. Wherefore, man could not act for himself save it should be that he was enticed by the one or the other. (2 Nephi 2:16)

Without the existence of these two opposites in our lives, the world and all things in it:

> It must needs have been created for a thing of naught; wherefore there would have been no purpose in the end of its creation. Wherefore, this thing must needs destroy the wisdom of God and his eternal purposes, and also the power, and the mercy, and the justice of God. (2 Nephi 2:12)

Is it any wonder that John refers to Christ as the "Messenger of Salvation"? (D&C 93:8). Is the message of salvation dispensed to any person in a different way? Even when the words come from an inspired teacher or divinely appointed text, it is the Holy Spirit—the light of Christ which bears witness, and thus infuses the truths into the soul. Without this divine witness, there would be no believers. No—not one.

Consider how vast and significant His work is to us.

During all the history of mankind, in the soul of every person who has ever lived, He has whispered unending and unerring messages of truth, hope, and guidance. No man, woman, or child has ever lived who did not hear His sweet voice. Never was there a people or a time when this was not so. He has always spoken.

His was, and is, the most momentous task ever undertaken—to teach every living being the truth, to oppose every thought and action that comes from the evil one, to endure with great long-suffering and patience the endless disobedience mankind inflicts upon Him.

It is small wonder that He first proclaims Himself the Light of the world, and all else thereafter. It is small wonder He calls Himself the Fountain of All Righteousness (see Ether 12:28 as an example). Is it any wonder He laments so often that He is a Light shining in darkness, and in spite of His love and gracious work, most people choose darkness, comprehending Him not?

> For verily I say unto you that I am Alpha and Omega, the beginning and the end, the light and the life of the world—a light that shineth in darkness and the darkness comprehendeth it not. (D&C 45:7)

There is great meaning in the injunction He has given that we should become children of light. Consider the following verses, for they amplify our understanding of what the Savior meant by these words.

> While ye have light, believe in the light, that ye may be the children of light. (John 12:36)

For ye were sometimes darkness, but now are ye light in the Lord: walk as children of light. (Ephesians 5:8)

Ye are all the children of light, and the children of the day: we are not of the night, nor of darkness. (1 Theselonians.5:5)

Therefore, gird up your loins, that you may be the children of light, and that day [the second coming] shall not overtake you as a thief. (D&C 106:5)

THE FUNCTION OF THE CONSCIENCE

The conscience has three primary tasks: first, to give every person the knowledge that God exists; second, to instill the concept of right and wrong in the soul; and, third, and perhaps most important, to guide each person to the gospel of Jesus Christ where he or she can receive the Holy Ghost and thus continue his or her journey home. (see McConkie, *Mormon Doctrine*, 447)

It does not matter if a person is a Buddhist, Jew, Baptist, or Latter-day Saint. It does not even matter if the person is an atheist. If they hear and obey that still small voice they will not long remain an atheist, nor will they long remain outside The Church of Jesus Christ of Latter-day Saints, for that spark of divine contact will lead them home as quickly as they can find the courage to obey it.

If people listen to and obey their consciences, the day will come when they open their doors and see the missionaries of the restored gospel standing there. That same voice which warned them against stealing a candy bar when they were six years old will inform them that these are true messengers. As they read the Book of Mormon, that same voice that whispered to them that Jesus is the Christ will whisper again that this, indeed, is His scripture. As they are challenged for baptism, in spite of fear, in spite of persecution, in spite of feelings of unworthiness, in spite of their hearts banging loudly in their chests, they will know they must be baptized.

How beautiful is the plan—how simple, how sublime, how unerring, how tremendously fair and just. No wonder all will bow the knee and acknowledge that Jesus is the Christ and all His judgments are just. All people live their lives exposed to saving revelation! This continues right up to the point that they receive exaltation or turn off their sources of revelation through abuse and neglect.

Every person who is baptized into The Church of Jesus Christ of Latter-day Saints is given the gift of the Holy Ghost. In addition to this gift being the promise that they may eventually enjoy the constant companionship of the Holy Ghost, it is also the right to have greater contact with the same gift they already have.

> Now I say unto you, if this be the desire of your hearts, what have you against being baptized in the name of the Lord, as a witness before him that ye have entered into a covenant with him, that ye will serve him and keep his commandments, that he may pour out his Spirit more abundantly upon you? (Mosiah 18:10)

The conscience is the voice of Jesus Christ acting in His role as the Holy Spirit! After we receive the gift of the Holy Ghost, we continue to enjoy the same voice of the Holy Spirit. It remains a still small voice, but the messages it delivers are now amplified and enlarged. It is the same sweetness, the same comfort, the same quiet warnings and urgings, except now those sweet promptings become more informative and more urgent. They teach, expound, direct, inspire, and uplift. When obeyed, the Holy Spirit quickly transcends the "don't, stop, that's good, that's bad," language of the rudimentary conscience to become a teacher of great eloquence.

This increased access to the Holy Spirit should not be confused with the actual reception of the Holy Ghost or with revelation from the same. The Holy Ghost reveals with unmistakable power and authority. Although we may receive occasional revelations from the Holy Ghost, He generally reserves His messages until we have fully availed ourselves of the preparatory gift of the still small voice.

Each prompting becomes an eternal stepping stone; each revealed directive constitutes a celestial boost heavenward; each truth building on the last, lifting with loving care. Each prompting obeyed qualifies the obedient for more and greater revelations. Each prompting disobeyed causes the disobedient to plateau and then sink.

The only thing that can stop a person endowed with continuous revelation is an unwillingness to obey. A person stalled on a spiritual plateau must analyze his life and consider what it is he is unwilling to do. It will usually be amazingly small, yet soul stretching. It may be an unwillingness to tell your wife that you are sorry. Perhaps it is an unwillingness to do home teaching or visiting teaching. Maybe it is a rebellious attitude toward priesthood leaders, reading the scriptures, or saying family prayers. It may be drinking tea or smoking cigarettes. Maybe it is a nagging feeling that you need to go talk to the Bishop about the senior prom or that last business trip. Perhaps it is your tendency to stretch truth or push the wrong buttons on the cash register. Perhaps it is never-acted-upon feelings of lust or mismanagement of your body. It may be as simple as an unwillingness to turn off the TV, as urgent as going on a mission, or as dangerous as adultery.

If you prayerfully examine your life, you will quickly find it. There is something stopping you, and God will give you the power to remove it, if you let Him.

The Holy Spirit often prompts us to do something other than what we were planning. Satan may tempt us to counsel the Lord out of it. If prompted to fast, we might be tempted to remind the Lord that "It's a work day, Lord. You know everyone will wonder why I'm not eating. Lord, you understand how difficult it is to work hard and not drink water. Lord, you know I feel like I'm coming down with a cold. Lord, you must be mistaken, I don't need to fast. Fast Sunday was just last week, Lord."

Satan often attempts to use logic to negate the promptings of the Spirit and consequently cheat us out of blessings. If we obey Satan's promptings, we counsel the Lord out of a tremendous opportunity, and our disobedience shuts the heavens for a time.

Perhaps the hardest thing to learn about personal revelation is that it begins as the voice of the conscience. Every person knows what it is like to be prompted by their conscience to *not* do something. Fewer ever recognize the promptings to *do* something. It is the positive promptings that are the beginnings, the seeds of revelation. Just like the conscience, they come without fanfare or heralding trumpets. No angels songs, no glorious lights from heaven, no burnings in the bosom, or visions of eternity occur; just a still small voice. The only way you know it is actually revelation is that it prompts you to do something good, such as to say your prayers, to do some kindness, to share, to give, to expand and grow.

John Taylor related this exchange with the Prophet Joseph Smith:

> I well remember a remark Joseph Smith made to me upwards of forty years ago. Said he, "Elder Taylor, you have been baptized, you have had hands laid upon your head for the reception of the Holy Ghost, and you have been ordained to the holy Priesthood. *Now, if you will continue to follow the leadings of that spirit, it will always lead you right. Sometimes it might be contrary to your judgment; never mind that, follow its dictates; and if you be true to its whisperings it will in time become in you a principle of revelation, so that you will know all things.*" (*Journal of Discourses*, 19:153–54; emphasis added)

Hearing and obeying the voice of the conscience/Holy Spirit is the most important and powerful step you can take toward beginning your spiritual journey in earnest.

Little progress can be made without it. These promptings are not limited to church subjects. They prompt us to do correctly in all aspects of our lives which bear upon our growth. Anything that will move you closer to God, that will bless you and those around you, that will build faith in the Lord's voice may be the subject of these revelations. You may be prompted to pack up your tents and depart into the wilderness or to pick up your socks. You may be prompted to help your wife with the dishes or to stop at the scene of an accident and give a priesthood blessing.

Why would the Lord send you a revelation to pick up your socks? It is because even in something this small there is a right and a wrong outcome. If our spiritual hearing is so dim that we cannot be directed in very small things, how will He ever direct us to pick up our tents and save our families, as he did Lehi? We must first be obedient in small things—greater things come later. He will not elevate us to the profound until we advance beyond elementary obedience.

There are many aspects of life that play powerfully upon us but that may actually have little bearing upon our exaltation. Some of these may be where we work or where we live, as well as whether or not we move, go on vacation, buy a new car, get fired from our jobs, or contract some life-threatening illness. In some people these things may bear upon their exaltation, and not in others. In cases where they have a neutral impact upon our growth, they will probably not be the subject of whisperings of the Spirit. It is almost a paradox that the Spirit may whisper to us about picking up our socks but if something like finding a new job is not salient to our salvation, the Holy Spirit may be silent.

Faced with little or no guidance in these demanding affairs of life, we may feel directionless and alone. In these things we must pray with faith, seeking the Lord's guidance in matters that can't be measured on the scales of right and wrong.

Faith tells me that having once exercised our best judgment in these matters, the Lord delights in having us pray unto Him concerning them. When a righteous individual petitions the Lord for blessings in these types of affairs, He blesses them according to their righteous desires, whether that desire is for guidance in making the decision, or for a specific outcome.

> O Lord, thou hast given us a commandment that we must call upon thee, that from thee we may receive according to our desires. (Ether 3:2)

> Yea, humble yourselves, and continue in prayer unto him. Cry unto him when ye are in your fields, yea, over all your flocks. Cry unto him in your houses, yea, over all your household, both morning, mid-day, and evening. Yea, cry unto him against the power of your enemies. Yea, cry unto him against the devil, who is an enemy to all righteousness. Cry unto him over the crops of your fields, that ye may prosper in them. Cry over the flocks of your fields, that they may increase. (Alma 34:19–25)

However, sometimes, things bear upon our exaltation in a way we cannot guess. Years ago I had the pleasure of sharing the gospel with a brother and sister who had been inactive all their lives. They were both older and retired when I came to know them. One evening we were discussing this very subject when this good brother told me the following story.

"I have been a well driller all my life. One of the worst things that can happen when drilling a well is to have the drilling tool get stuck down the well. If this happens it is difficult, if not impossible at times, to retrieve the tool. As long as the rig keeps running this rarely happens, but if it runs out of gas it can get stuck. Years ago, I began to recognize that I always had an impression a few minutes before the rig was going to run out of gas. I learned that if I got up right then and dumped gas in, that it never ran out. If I ignored it, I almost always lost an expensive drilling tool. This certainly didn't have anything to do with my growth or exaltation, so do you think this was the Holy Spirit?"

I thought for a moment, then asked him. "You became familiar with these impressions, with this voice, did you not?" He nodded. "Can you feel it tonight, and what is it communicating to you?"

He pondered this for a brief time before tears welled up in his eyes. He replied in an unsteady voice: "It is telling me the Church is true, and that I need to get my life in order. I guess in the long run, it has had a significant bearing upon my exaltation. Over the years I have come to trust that voice, and I know it is speaking the truth tonight. It has taken the Lord a lot of years to soften me up, hasn't it?"

In those things that bear upon our growth, the Holy Spirit whispers truth, sometimes for years, until the intended message is finally heard. In his case the intended message wasn't "add gas now!" It was, "hear my voice, and know that I am God." It took years, but he finally understood. He changed his life and the course of his whole family before he died a few years later.

As we begin to recognize the voice of the Spirit and obey each prompting, we qualify for revelation of increasingly greater importance and magnitude. In time we become pure and holy, ever vigilant, and valiant in obedience. Each obedience calls forth greater revelations and faith, until He can command us to move yonder mountain, and we will simply turn and repeat the words of the Master, order it to depart—and it will.

Joseph Smith, the Prophet of the Restoration, expressed this truth in this way:

> We consider that God has created man with a mind capable of instruction, and a faculty which may be enlarged in proportion to the heed and diligence given to the light communicated from heaven to the intellect; and that the nearer man approaches perfection, the clearer are his views, and the greater his enjoyments, till he has overcome the evils of his life and lost every desire for sin [which occurs at the rebirth]; and like the ancients, arrives at that point of faith where he is

wrapped in the power and glory of his Maker, and is caught up to dwell with Him. (Smith, *Teachings*, 51)

The biggest problem is learning to hear. The biggest challenge is learning to obey.

Every prompting is an opportunity. Each has a purpose and a promise, and it requires faith to obey. It is fear and lackluster faith that cause us to disobey. If you receive a prompting to bear your testimony to your boss at work, you might fear the possible ramifications of obeying. If you have not experienced the inspiring and life-changing blessings that always come from obeying divine direction, then you may well succumb to your fear and not obey. If you have faith that has grown into a powerful, motivating force in your life because of your past obedience, then when such a prompting comes, you would welcome it joyfully as a sign that your boss is finally ready to hear your testimony. Fear, after all, is the opposite of faith, as much as disbelief or faithlessness. It is fear that keeps us from manifesting what faith we have. Most often, what we fear is minute; that is, it is fear of small things like being embarrassed, hungry, tired, or some other inconvenience.

The following true story may help illustrate this principle.

One Sunday morning a few years ago I sat down to eat breakfast. Just as the fork was inches from my mouth, the Spirit prompted that I needed to fast. I slowly lowered the fork and pushed the plate away. I explained to my wife why I was not going to eat breakfast. I retired to the bedroom and knelt in prayer. The still small voice, not much more than an impression, told me that I would be giving a priesthood blessing today and needed to prepare.

I went to church fasting, excited to be preparing for this blessing. While I was engaged in one of my duties, a member of the bishopric walked up to me and asked if I would accompany him to the hospital to give Brother Jones a blessing. I said I would love to, and would meet him in the foyer in just a moment. I hurriedly finished and went to the foyer with considerable anticipation. He was nowhere to be found. The Bishop informed me he had taken someone else to give Brother Jones a blessing. I was saddened, yet the Spirit whispered comfort and patience to my soul.

As I was about to leave following Sacrament Meeting, a young man walked up to me and introduced himself. He was new to the ward and had waited uncertainly in the chapel until almost everyone had gone. He told me his wife had been very ill with the flu for five days now. He said that he probably should have taken her to see a doctor, but they couldn't afford it. He asked if I would come give her a blessing. The Spirit confirmed that this was the blessing I had been prepared to give, and I said I would love to.

As I drove to their apartment, I prayed, thanking the Lord for the opportunity to serve Him and His children. I pondered how carefully I had been prepared and asked Him if there was a special blessing this young sister needed. The Spirit answered there was. I was to rebuke the illness and command her to be made well immediately. This came as a surprise to me. Yet, I knew that this was the blessing He had ordained for her, and that I had been prepared to deliver it.

I found a faithful priesthood holder to assist, and we arrived at their home to find her in bed. Her face was as white as the sheets upon which she was lying. I sat beside her and felt the Spirit confirm her worthiness. My companion anointed her with oil. I laid my hands on her head and gave her one of the shortest blessings I have ever given. I simply rebuked the illness and commanded her to be made well instantly.

I lifted my hands from her head and looked at her face.

She continued to look close to death. I waited for several minutes, and still she appeared the same. I knew what the Lord had commanded me to do, and it never occurred to me that it might not take place. The only question in my mind was what the Lord's interpretation of "immediately" was. A few minutes after the blessing we began to excuse ourselves, and as we were opening the front door to their very small apartment, she arose and walked past us into the kitchen. I could hear the refrigerator door opening and several cupboards open and close. Moments later she emerged with a roll in her teeth and both arms laden with food.

She smiled at us; the color had returned to her face.

Mumbling around the roll in her mouth, she asked if we would like to eat something with her. She set her lunch on the table and sat down with purpose.

"I just can't believe how hungry I am all of a sudden. I haven't eaten anything for almost four days, and I'm just starved! Would you please excuse me while I eat?"

We shook their hands and left. She was totally healed.

As I reflect on this event, I ponder not only the wonderful blessing, but how much would have been missed if I had not been able to stop that fork. Would the Lord have sent someone else? Would she have gone without the blessing because I wouldn't obey? I don't know. But, I do know how richly blessed this young couple was because of obedience to the Spirit and a single bite of food not taken.

Helaman illustrates this in beautiful language when he said:

> Nevertheless they did fast and pray oft, and did wax stronger and stronger in their humility, and firmer and firmer in the faith of Christ, unto the filling their souls with joy and consolation, yea even to the purifying and the sanctification of their hearts, which sanctification cometh because of their yielding their hearts unto God. (Helaman 3:35)

Yielding your heart unto God and, at least in this case, yielding your fork unto God are exactly the same thing. How do we yield? By hearing, stopping, and obeying.

Why would this cause us to grow firmer and firmer in the faith of Christ? Because seeing the fruits of obedience time after time builds an unshakable confidence in the whisperings of the Holy Spirit. You only need to see one person instantly healed to feel a deep conviction that God honors His word and those who obey Him. All these blessings begin when we recognize and obey the voice of the Lord through the Holy Spirit.

As one learns to identify and obey the voice of the Holy Spirit this question frequently arises: "Does the Holy Spirit guide us in all things? Will He tell me what to fix for dinner and help me with other such decisions I must make?"

The answer is no. We must learn to make decisions, and to direct the mundane affairs of our lives. This is a vital understanding because the scales of eternity are being tipped according to which voices we choose to obey. If we can be deceived into following the wrong voice, then we can be delayed in our growth, even possibly kept outside the Kingdom of God.

The Evil One would be delighted to have us following his direction, thinking we are obeying the Lord. If we do not carefully discern the sources of the voices we choose to obey, we may well be choosing evil, even while we are trying to be obedient. Do not expect the Lord to direct you in all things. He does not interfere in events and decisions that have neither a right nor wrong outcome.

We may expect the Holy Spirit to direct us any time there is a choice to be made between right and wrong, or good and evil. Since all good comes from God and all else comes of evil, the Holy Spirit's divine task is to guide us in making all such decisions. Once fully attuned to the voice of the Lord, you will be surprised and delighted at how many decisions you make that actually bear upon your exaltation and are, therefore, subjects for divine guidance.

In the following section, we will discuss at length how to determine which voice is His and which is not. There is a tendency among some to want to be directed and prompted in every thought and action. Because of their desire to be thus guided, they cease to distinguish clearly between the voices, and begin to obey every thought that enters their minds. They thus become like ping pong balls in a wind storm, unmercifully tossed and blown about by the winds of deception. In time, it becomes obvious that they have been deceived and injured, and they abandon all promptings in favor of that which eyes can behold and fingers touch. Satan thus cheats them out of the glorious reward of obedience to the voice of the Lord. For this reason we must be very particular about which voice we obey. In time, with experience, and with the gift of discernment, the sweet voice of the Spirit becomes familiar and easily identified. Until then, we must take heed, lest we obey the wrong master.

THE VOICES

It is one thing to say we must follow the voice of our conscience, which is the voice of the Lord within us. It is quite another to be able to clearly distinguish it from the other voices we hear. Toward that end, let us cast some light upon the other voices.

Elder James E. Faust had this to say about the voices we hear:

> But we hear other voices. Paul said, "There are . . . so many kinds of voices in the world." (1 Corinthians 14:10) that compete with the voice of the Spirit. Such is the situation in the world. (Faust, "Voice of the Spirit," 7; ellipses in original)

There are three main sources of voices in a healthy mind. The first is the voice of your own mind. You hear yourself think. You talk with yourself, discuss things with yourself, argue with yourself, berate, praise, and jabber with yourself all day long. This voice is distinguishable because it is unsure, or in other words, it questions things, and is seldom definite or decisive. It almost always asks questions. "What was that? Who said that? Why did you say that? What does it mean? Do you suppose? What would happen if? I wonder?" Even when it is emphatic, it leaves open the possibility of change. "I'm definitely going to bed now—Okay?"

"I'm going to town—if the car will start." You will notice that this voice usually takes the personal case; "I think I should fast today." The Holy Spirit would have said, "Fast today."

The second voice comes from Satan's realm. It is unlikely that we receive much attention from the king of that kingdom personally. Rather, we deal with his minions, his messengers, and his tempters. These beings have been in the business of tempting mankind as long as the earth has existed, perhaps longer. They are undoubtedly very skilled and highly motivated. Each has probably tempted thousands of people like us. They have spent thousands of years in intimate contact with mortals. They have much more experience with tempting mortals to sin than we could possibly have in resisting it. They know the subtleties and tricks necessary to entice and trick us into failing. They undoubtedly specialize in their work, meaning that certain of them specialize in anger, marital infidelity, family disharmony, murder, drugs, illness, depression, hate, or a million other maladies, sins, and vices. Once successful, they linger year after year with those they afflict.

When we hear a voice from this source, it will be cleverly disguised and enticing. It will appeal to the natural, carnal, sensual, and devilish side of us. There is real intelligence in the message and malice aforethought. They plan and plot against us, and their messages are carefully chosen.

> The adversary tries to smother this voice [of the Holy Spirit] with a multitude of loud, persistent, persuasive, and appealing voices: murmuring voices, conjuring up perceived injustices; whining voices, abhorring challenge and work; seductive voices, offering sensual enticements; soothing voices, lulling us into carnal security; intellectual voices, professing sophistication and superiority; proud voices, relying on the arm of the flesh; flattering voices, puffing us up with pride; cynical voices, destroying hope; entertaining voices, promoting pleasure seeking; commercial voices, tempting us to "spend money for that

which is of no worth" and our "labor for that which cannot satisfy." (2 Nephi 9:51), and delirious voices, spawning the desire for a "high" . . . [which is] death-defying experiences for nothing more than a thrill. (Faust, "Voice of the Spirit," 7)

A prompting from this source will nearly always be stated as an absolute. "Don't let him get away with that. You're too tired to pray. You deserve better. Pay him back. No one will notice. It should be yours anyway—just take it. She's your wife—not your mother. Football only happens once a year, the church can get along without you for one Sunday. She wants you—its only natural. He loves you more than your husband, how can you not love him back?"

These promptings will *always* lead us away from the truth. They prompt us to disobey, to not pray, to abandon church assignments and family responsibilities, to commit sin and walk in forbidden paths. They do not limit themselves to voices alone. They can draw from the trash stored in our minds to dredge up memories that will either lure us away from purity and virtue or keep our minds harrowed up with vivid memories of our sins—even after we have repented of them.

The evil ones cannot read our minds or hear our silent prayers. Yet it seems they hear what the Holy Spirit says to us, for they respond immediately. When the Holy Spirit prompts, "Say your prayers," you immediately hear something like, "Don't say prayers, you're too tired."

> Yea, I tell thee, that thou mayest know that there is none else save God that knowest thy thoughts and the intents of thy heart. (D&C 6:16)

They cannot force us to do anything, unless we yield to them, and they value our inability to see them. They can tell when a temptation excites or repels us. They are most successful in half-light, half-truths, and half-hearted people. Their tools are limited, but they use what they have with great effect. They have destroyed millions of souls, and you are simply the next on their list. They are confident, efficient, successful, and they hate us with unimaginable intensity. From their perspective, they are engaged in an all-out war against us. Our perspective barely includes a realization they exist, and certainly no thought of a war with them. It is no wonder they win so frequently. Yielding to the enticings of Satan's minions will have the opposite effect of yielding to the enticings of the Holy Spirit. Any time we receive a prompting to do wrong, or disobey, it comes from Satan's realm.

One of their weaknesses is that they can rarely voice just one lie. While the Holy Spirit generally prompts us only once, the tempters often voice many objections to each prompting. The Holy Spirit may prompt us to call everyone to family prayers. Thereafter, the evil ones suggest many reasons why we should not obey. "Everyone is tired. They will complain. You don't feel like it. The wife is already in bed. It's late. It's useless. You can do it tomorrow." This is actually one of the ways we may discern the voices. The Holy Spirit whispers truth, and thereafter, the opposition tirades against it.

The third source of information in our minds is the voice of the Lord through the Holy Spirit. It begins as the conscience, the light of Christ, and is a free gift. In its most rudimentary stages it is a quiet urging to choose right, to abandon wrong choices, and to seek greater truth. This voice grows in content and quality as one heeds its direction until it becomes a significant guide and measure of truth. Following baptism and the bestowal of the gift of the Holy Ghost, the Holy Spirit assumes greater power and authority, and though remaining a still small voice, it becomes a comfort, guide, and source of great strength as we learn to obey it.

This voice always entices us to do good, to believe, serve, pray, and repent. It often prompts contrary to where you were headed. If you were just settling into the Super Bowl on Sunday morning, it would tell you to go to church. If you were already on your way to church, it would prompt nothing, but would give a feeling of comfort and satisfaction.

The voice of the conscience is easy to recognize because it is the *only* one of the three that prompts to do good. These promptings come as absolute statements. The Holy Spirit would say, "Fast today." Your mind would have said, "I wonder if I should fast today," or "Perhaps I should fast." Any time you have a prompting to do good, it has come from God.

We have been talking a lot about promptings. Perhaps even the term needs clarification. A prompting is information that originates outside one's mind. The Holy Spirit prompts to do good, the devil prompts to do evil. Our minds consider and analyze the promptings and make decisions concerning them. These promptings all appear, and sound, exactly like our own thoughts. The only way to differentiate between them is the way we have already discussed. Good comes from God. Evil comes from the adversary. Questions and analysis come from within. It really is just that simple.

It is worth noting that a prompting carries less weight than a commandment. To be prompted by the Holy Spirit is to receive a divine urging, or enticement, similar to a strong suggestion.

> Wherefore, the Lord God gave unto man that he should act for himself. Wherefore, man could not act for himself save it should be that he was enticed by the one or the other. (2 Nephi 2:16)

We are continually being enticed (as opposed to being commanded) by the Holy Spirit to do good, to choose right, to seek righteousness, and to come unto Christ.

> Wherefore, all things which are good cometh of God; and that which is evil cometh of the devil; for the devil is an enemy unto God, and fighteth against him continually, and inviteth and enticeth to sin, and to do that which is evil continually.

But behold, that which is of God inviteth and enticeth to do good continually; wherefore, every thing which inviteth and enticeth to do good, and to love God, and to serve him, is inspired of God. (Moroni 7:12–13)

To hear and obey all such promptings is to act of our own free will, to respond by choice to the voice of truth. To be obedient to the voice of God is to be anxiously engaged in righteousness of our own free will.

For behold, it is not meet that I should command in all things; for he that is compelled in all things, the same is a slothful and not a wise servant; wherefore he receiveth no reward. Verily I say, men should be anxiously engaged in a good cause, and do many things of their own free will, and bring to pass much righteousness; For the power is in them, wherein they are agents unto themselves. And inasmuch as men do good they shall in nowise lose their reward. (D&C 58:26–28)

This verse asserts that the power is in us, in that we are agents unto ourselves. We have agency because we have choice. We have choice because we are continually presented with right and wrong between which we must choose (Moroni 7:12–13).

Being enticed in all things does not relieve us of the necessity of making decisions great or small. One of the fears occasionally voiced is that in becoming fully obedient, we will become robots, or non-thinking servants who mindlessly act out the role proscribed by a demanding inner voice. Some worry that we will no longer need to think of solutions to our problems nor meet growth-promoting trials. They fret that we will actually lose our free agency by committing ourselves to complete obedience.

If anything, becoming fully attuned with the voice of the Holy Spirit gives us greater choices and opens the doors to greater decisions. It makes thinking clearly vitally important, and mindless obedience a seductive trap. It makes us examine our thoughts, our motives, and our values. It makes decisions appear where none existed before. As an example, if one has never bothered to really study the scriptures, but has habitually turned to worldly entertainments instead, then suddenly hearing the Holy Spirit urging us to study the scriptures opens the door to a challenging decision: to obey or disobey, to yield or rebel, to stand still or move ahead, to grow or stagnate. To choose obedience in every such case is to open the door a crack wider, to increase our spiritual stature, and to qualify ourselves for further and greater revelation. Who can doubt that such greater things will demand even greater decisions, and more powerful obedience?

All truth comes from God, and the primary means by which we come to recognize truth is through the Holy Spirit. It is truth that sets us free, hence the greater our endowment of truth, the greater our freedom.

> And ye shall know the truth, and the truth shall make you free. (John 8:32)

Freedom comes through truth and obedience thereto. Bondage occurs from falsehoods and disobedience. In reality, we realize these fears (of becoming mindless robots responding unthinkingly to demanding voices) when we turn from the Holy Spirit and become a captive of the devil and his enticements, and the will of the flesh through which he has great power to tempt and entrap.

> Wherefore, men are free according to the flesh; and all things are given them which are expedient unto man. And they are free to choose liberty and eternal life, through the great Mediator of all men, or to choose captivity and death, according to the captivity and power of the devil; for he seeketh that all men might be miserable like unto himself. And now, my sons, I would that ye should look to the great Mediator, and hearken unto his great commandments; and be faithful unto his words, and choose eternal life, according to the will of his Holy Spirit; And not choose eternal death, according to

the will of the flesh and the evil which is therein, which giveth the spirit of the devil power to captivate, to bring you down to hell, that he may reign over you in his own kingdom. (2 Nephi 2:27–29)

There are differing opinions regarding the frequency of promptings and the subjects upon which the Holy Spirit actually prompts. While the discussion is wholesome, it is perhaps unnecessary. We must all individually develop our relationships with deity and our levels of association with the Holy Spirit. At different times in our lives those levels of association will vary up and down. It may actually be that all viewpoints of the discussion are at times valid. The one point which is not debatable, in my opinion, is this: regardless of how frequently the Holy Spirit prompts, when it does speak, it is incumbent upon us to be obedient. Let each person decide when, and to what degree, the Holy Spirit blesses his or her life with truth, but let us take whatever we have and become flawlessly obedient. This will be sufficient to move us along the straight and narrow way.

An instructive insight into the way the Lord sometimes guides completely and then other times leaves us to our own means to find a solution to our dilemmas is found in the experience of the brother of Jared.

You will recall that the Lord commanded the brother of Jared to build eight barges, wherein his people were to cross the great ocean. They labored diligently to construct the barges. After the task was completed, several problems became obvious. The barges were sealed tight, and they would have neither air nor light. It would be a long voyage, and both would be vital to their survival. The brother of Jared again approached the lord.

It is interesting that the Lord gave the brother of Jared the solution to the air problem by instructing them to make a hole in the top and the bottom of each barge (Ether 2:19–21). However, He left the problem of light for the brother of Jared to solve, though He did give him some guidelines.

And the Lord said unto the brother of Jared:

> What will ye that I should do that ye may have light in your vessels? For behold, ye cannot have windows, for they will be dashed in pieces; neither shall ye take fire with you, for ye shall not go by the light of fire. For behold, ye shall be as a whale in the midst of the sea; for the mountain waves shall dash upon you. Nevertheless, I will bring you up again out of the depths of the sea; for the winds have gone forth out of my mouth, and also the rains and the floods have I sent forth. And behold, I prepare you against these things; for ye cannot cross this great deep save I prepare you against the waves of the sea, and the winds which have gone forth, and the floods which shall come. Therefore what will ye that I should prepare for you that ye may have light when ye are swallowed up in the depths of the sea? (Ether 2:23–25)

The brother of Jared withdrew to consider what to do.

He eventually came up with an inspired solution and set out to put his plan into effect.

> And it came to pass that the brother of Jared, (now the number of the vessels which had been prepared was eight) went forth unto the mount, which they called the mount Shelem, because of its exceeding height, and did molten out of a rock sixteen small stones; and they were white and clear, even as transparent glass; and he did carry them in his hands upon the top of the mount, and cried again unto the Lord. (Ether 3:1)

In response to the brother of Jared's desires, and his incredible faith, the Lord stretched forth His finger and touched the stones one by one so that they gave forth light for the journey. What is most enlightening about this account is that the Lord solved part of their dilemma forthright, literally commanding them to cut holes in the barges, and left the other part awaiting a solution of their own formulation.

It is of little doubt that the solution the brother of Jared eventually conceived and presented before the Lord was inspired, meaning that the Holy Spirit aided in the conception and execution of the plan. Had the solution been in any way flawed, it would not have been rewarded with such a glorious outcome. Since all good things come from God, if the brother of Jared's plan was good, then it also came as a byproduct of divine inspiration. His great faith in bringing this proposal before the Lord came in part because he felt the witness of the Holy Spirit that his plan was good, correct, and acceptable to the Lord. Without this essential knowledge, or if he had doubted the Lord would be pleased with his proposed solution, his faith would have been tainted and thus it would have prohibited such a glorious response.

It is also of little doubt that it stretched him to the limits of his faith to arrive at this solution, which proved to be bold but completely satisfactory to the Lord. The end result this fantastic exercise in faith had upon the brother of Jared was to actually bring him into the presence of the Lord, and to open the door to fantastic blessings no mortal man had previously earned (Ether 3:9–13). It is manifestly apparent that his blessings were far greater when he was not given an easy answer to his dilemma.

This experience of the brother of Jared also highlights the difference between being commanded by the Lord, and being prompted by the Holy Spirit. The commandment demands obedience, with little need for anything else. The prompting entices and guides, making the exercise of thought, logic, and intellect of great importance to arriving at the appropriate solution. It also makes obedience to what guidance the Lord does allow us in these times doubly important. Since this latter process is much more difficult, and much less obvious, it is this process upon which this book focuses.

The Lord surely uses similar methods to stretch our growth, at times feeding us freely from the fountains of truth, solving our problems, drying our tears, opening doors for our deliverance. At other times, with equal love, and perhaps even to our greater blessing, He withholds detailed guidance, answers to our sorrows, and solutions to our complicated lives. At these times we are left to feel after him, to listen intently to the quiet whisperings of truth, to seek with prayers and fasting, to strain our faith to its limits. It may well be that these times bless our lives even more richly, as with the brother of Jared's case.

A personal experience during the preparation of this book seems to illustrate this same principle. After the manuscript had been completed, obstacles arose which made publication seemingly impossible. Prior to this time I had received some detailed guidance both from inspired leaders and from the Spirit. But when this situation arose, the heavens seemed silent. After diligent prayer and fasting, the Spirit seemed to whisper, "Be faithful, be fearless, be patient." It calmed my soul but gave me no more idea how to deal with the problems at hand than before. I resolved myself to obedience.

It was actually harder than if I had been directed to do some great task. Being faithful has always been second nature to me, and being fearless was possible with the help of the Lord, but being patient was like asking the wind not to blow. Childishly, I wanted a solution, and I wanted it immediately. It felt like I had been orphaned, and I labored, thought, contemplated, and struggled in almost complete confusion. No amount of reasoning provided a workable solution, yet I was (mostly) patient, and the blessings flowed in response.

During those months it seemed as if I was completely without guidance, left to puzzle everything out in the face of impossible obstacles. Yet, when the solutions came, they came not as a result of any intellectual triumph on my part, but as a direct result of being faithful, fearless, and patient. It was a difficult time, but so, so sweet a blessing in the end.

Often, we receive promptings that cannot be measured by the standard of right and wrong. A prompting to ask for a priesthood blessing is easily identifiable as a prompting from God. A prompting to sell the house and move to Alaska is neither obviously good nor evil, and consequently may be confusing. We are blessed with a way to distinguish even these promptings using the same standard of good and evil. The way is open to those who have so ordered their lives that they can call upon the Lord for a confirmation by the Holy Ghost.

If our full intent is to be obedient to all promptings, and our hearts yearn to do whatever He commands us, then we may approach the Father with this humble and powerful request. "Father, I have received a prompting to sell the house and move to Alaska. I will do anything thou commandest me, and I rejoice in obeying thee. For this purpose, I require a confirmation of this prompting, that I might obey thee, and not be confused by voices which are not thine." If this is a true prompting, and your heart is pure in your desire to obey, you will immediately be blessed with a confirmation and a feeling of peace. You may begin packing your coat and fishing rod. If you receive nothing, or have a flood of thoughts and conflicting emotions, drop the issue immediately. Consider the following verse:

> But, behold, I say unto you, that you must study it out in your mind; then you must ask me if it be right, and if it is right I will cause that your bosom shall burn within you; therefore, you shall feel that it is right. But if it be not right you shall have no such feelings, but you shall have a stupor of thought that shall cause you to forget the thing which is wrong; (D&C 9:8–9)

This scripture teaches both how to determine the will of the Lord in the absence of a prompting, and how to determine what is true in the face of conflicting or confusing promptings. If we have received no prompting we can recognize on the subject, then "study it out in your mind" would imply the need to make a rational decision and present that decision before the Lord for confirmation. It has been incorrectly assumed by some that this is the only way we may receive divine direction. We should rejoice that it is only *one* of many forms of personal revelation.

The greater question to be studied out may be, "If this decision I am making is important enough for the Lord to guide me through it now, why did I not hear, or feel, the guidance of the Holy Spirit concerning it already? Is my life in order? Have I lived such that I can hear the still small voice? If I have failed to hear the promptings, am I worthy to receive an answer now? If the response I hear is silence, have I been answered, or has my unworthiness kept me from being blessed with guidance?"

If you have taken the Holy Spirit to be your guide, and have therefore been prompted, then "study it out in your mind" means to study each prompting to determine its source, and thus discover the will of the Lord.

> Wherefore, I beseech of you, brethren, that ye should search diligently in the light of Christ that ye may know good from evil; and if ye will lay hold upon every good thing, and condemn it not, ye certainly will be a child of Christ. (Moroni 7:19)

Moroni is literally begging us to search diligently that we may know good from evil. This search certainly includes promptings that are of both good and evil origin. He further promises that if we will lay hold upon every good thing, that is, if we will humble ourselves and be obedient in every righteous prompting, we will certainly be children of Christ. In those cases where we cannot decide the source of the prompting, we may ask for confirmation.

Once prompted by the Holy Spirit, there is no wisdom in analyzing the facts and making a decision based on logic, and asking the Lord if that decision is correct. The heavens often remain silent on this type of inquiry since you are leaning to your own understanding, even though you have already been instructed by the Lord. If we trust the Lord with all our hearts, we will not feel a need to double check His guidance against our own wisdom.

Trust in the Lord with all thine heart; and lean not unto thine own understanding. In all thy ways acknowledge him, and he shall direct thy paths. Be not wise in thine own eyes: fear the Lord, and depart from evil. (Proverbs 3:5–7)

It is not unusual for people to receive a prompting and then when obstacles arise later on, to question whether the prompting was correct. The tendency here is for people to then ask again and again in prayer for permission to do what they wanted to do in the first place, even though they knew the original prompting had set their feet and heart upon the true course.

One principle will serve your life well if your faith is sufficient to receive a prompting and understand its divine source—it is the principle that if something was true on Tuesday, it is still true today.

Years ago I had a good friend who managed a thriving little business. The owner of the business grew old and offered my friend the opportunity to buy the business for a considerable sum of money, which he did.

One Sunday I saw my friend in High Priest's Group with a sad expression on his face. After the meeting I asked him what he was troubled about. He told me his business was struggling and he was faced with huge expenses to expand, or to watch his business falter. He said, "I'm beginning to doubt that buying the business was the right thing to do."

I asked him, "When you were considering buying the business didn't you pray about it?"

"I sure did," he replied.

"What was the answer you received?"

"It was a dramatic answer. I *knew* it was the right thing to do," he assured me.

I looked at him closely. "If it was true then, it is still true today."

His face relaxed. He straightened his shoulders and smiled. "Of course it is," he replied. He went on with faith in his earlier revelation and made his business even more successful in a short time.

If your life is in order, and you have otherwise attuned yourself to the voice of the Spirit, then seeking the Lord's divine approbation in a decision is wholesome and delightful to Him. But, once the Lord has revealed our path, it is not wisdom to doubt what we once knew to be true.

If a person has abandoned the path of light, and now in a moment of crisis and pain begs Him for guidance, the heavens may well remain silent. This silence is not a heavenly shrug of indifference, but divine disapproval and an indication of a need for repentance. But, what was once true remains true. Doubt today cannot change what was true and precious yesterday. The full blessings of the gospel and the Atonement of Christ are still within your reach.

This is not to say that silence from the heavens is always a sign of unrighteousness. The Lord deals with us in His own way and according to His own timetable. Sometimes the answer is "No," and this is best expressed through silence. There may be uncountable reasons why we may experience a period of divine silence, none of which arises from unrighteousness on our part. However, if we have abandoned the path of righteousness, silence will almost certainly result for a time. His love has not changed for you. What was true many yesterdays ago is still true today. Come home, come home and be healed.

This principle of understanding the source of your promptings is perhaps the most important truth you can learn to begin living by personal revelation. You cannot progress far without this knowledge.

If you cannot distinguish between good and evil promptings, you will always be surrounded by conflicting voices and confusion. Your life will lack purpose and direction, and you will blow to and fro upon the winds of mediocrity. As soon as you identify the voice of the Holy Spirit in your mind, you can begin obeying, and doubt and confusion will melt away. Your obedience will call forth greater revelations, and your life will take on the mantle of divine direction.

Consider the words of Moroni on this subject:

> For behold, my brethren, it is given unto you to judge, that ye may know good from evil; and the way to judge is as plain, that ye may know with a perfect knowledge, as the daylight is from the dark night. For behold, the Spirit of Christ [the conscience] is given to every man, that he may know good from evil; wherefore, I show unto you the way to judge [which promptings come from the Lord, or from another source]; for every thing which inviteth to do good, and to persuade to believe in Christ, is sent forth by the power and gift of Christ; wherefore ye may know with a perfect knowledge it is of God. (Moroni 7:15–16)

Any prompting to do good, to fast, to pray, to help, to bless, to be kind, to express love, to obey a commandment, to worship, to serve; all these, and a million more like them, come from God. You can know with an absolute knowledge, nothing doubting, that these promptings are revelation. They can no longer be ignored with impunity.

Recognizing the three voices and their various sources helps in deciphering the complex conversations we hear in our minds. When you understand who is saying what, you need not be confused any longer about what to do.

Almost every prospective missionary hears, "Go on a mission;" "Take the scholarship, skip the mission;" and "I wonder what I should do?" Notice the three voices. The Spirit says, "Go," the adversary says, "No," and your mind says, "I'm confused." Now that you know from whom the messages are originating, you can change your question from, "I wonder what I should do?" to, "I wonder if I will do what the Lord wants and go serve a mission?"

How often have you said or heard something similar to this: "On the one hand, I feel like I should quit my job and stay home with the kids. On the other hand, I'm afraid what would happen to our finances. What should I do?" Or, "The thought of an abortion makes me sick, but it's my body, and I can do what I want with it. What should I do?"

Can you distinguish the three voices in these exchanges? If you can do the same in your own life, you will have found the rod of iron. If you can always choose what is right, you will have your hand firmly clasped upon it. You will have renewed your journey unto the tree of life with great purpose. The mists of darkness may still blind you from time to time, but they will no longer have power to deceive you, and your feet will walk unerringly upon the straight and narrow path to exaltation.

Elder Faust explains it this way:

> First, if we are to survive, we must exercise our moral agency wisely. Amaleki tells us how we can select the proper channels: "There is nothing which is good save it comes from the Lord: and that which is evil cometh from the devil" (Omni 1:25). Every moment demands that we choose, over and over again, between that which comes from the Lord and that which comes from the devil. As tiny drops of water shape a landscape, so our minute-by-minute choices shape our character. Living the eternal gospel every day may be harder than dying for the church and the Lord. (Faust, "Voice of the Spirit," 8)

Moroni also gives us these powerful directions and wonderful promise:

> Wherefore, I beseech of you, brethren, that ye should search diligently in the light of Christ that ye may know good from evil; and if ye will lay hold upon every good thing [including promptings], and condemn it not, ye certainly will be a child of Christ. (Moroni 7:19)

We have the gift. It is fully operative in the lives of all who have not blunted it by sin and neglect. The Lord chose to mingle this great gift with the voices of opposition to grant us agency, and to teach us to choose righteously. Moroni counsels us to search diligently in the light of Christ. In other words, pay diligent heed to the promptings we receive; carefully search out that which is truth and revelation, and once found, lay hold upon it with great firmness. If we lay hold upon every good thing (including good promptings), and act obediently to it, we will certainly become a child of Christ. If we walk by revelation, we will walk after the manner of happiness all the days of our lives.

> We will not be able to travel through life on borrowed light. The light of life must be part of our very being. The voice we must learn to heed is the voice of the Spirit. (Faust, "Voice of the Spirit," 8)

THE WORD OF CHRIST

The scriptures refer to the "words of Christ." This phrase is commonly interpreted to mean the scriptures and other inspired writings. However, the words of Christ also come from the light of Christ, which fills the soul of those willing to listen and be led by the Holy Spirit.

Note the words of an Apostle of the Lord:

> God's voice and his counsel come from the light of Christ and by way of his prophets; the devil's enticements are whispered into the minds of men from an evil source and are taught by false prophets. (McConkie, *Millennial Messiah*, 70)

We are commanded to give diligent heed to the words of Christ and live by every word that proceeds forth from the mouth of God. That is, in addition to written words of the prophets, we must hear and obey every word spoken to us by the Holy Spirit, for every word it speaks is the voice of Christ.

> And I now give you a commandment, to beware concerning yourselves, to give diligent heed to the words of eternal

life. For you shall live by every word that proceedeth forth from the mouth of God. For the word of the Lord is truth, and whatsoever is truth is light, and whatsoever is light is Spirit, even the Spirit of Jesus Christ. (D&C 84:43–45)

This principle of hearing and obeying the Spirit of Jesus Christ, which is the Holy Spirit, is so profound that every person who gives heed to its divine message will receive eternal life with Heavenly Father.

And every one that hearkeneth to the voice of the Spirit cometh unto God, even the Father. (D&C 84:47)

Conversely, everyone who will not receive and obey His voice will be counted among the unrighteous—regardless of whether or not they belong to His true church. Those who refuse to obey the voice of Christ are counted as wicked, and under sin and darkness.

And whoso receiveth not my voice is not acquainted with my voice, and is not of me. And by this [that they obey His voice] you may know the righteous from the wicked, and that the whole world groaneth under sin and darkness even now. (D&C 84:52–53)

Consider the power this understanding gives to this statement by Alma:

For behold, it is as easy to give heed to the word of Christ, which will point to you a straight course to eternal bliss, as it was for our fathers to give heed to this compass [Liahona], which would point unto them a straight course to the promised land. (Alma 37:44)

Alma is saying that the word of Christ, or personal revelation, which begins as our conscience and matures thereafter, is like the Liahona, which God gave to Lehi's family to guide them in the wilderness. There is a divinely ordained parallel here that can give us greater understanding on the workings of the Spirit of Christ.

If we assume the words of Christ exist only in scriptures, this parallel loses impact and becomes easily dismissed. When one knows this scripture is teaching about personal revelation, then it becomes a pearl of great price, a gem of wisdom.

Recall that the Liahona was given to Lehi as a compass, to point the way they should travel through the wilderness. It operated according to the "faith and diligence and heed" (1 Nephi 16:28–30) that they gave to its direction. When they sinned, or ignored the compass, it ceased to work for a time. The direction it pointed changed according to the will of God. The Liahona also had writings upon it, which were made new from time to time, and taught about the ways of the Lord.

> And there was also written upon them a new writing, which was plain to be read, which did give us understanding concerning the ways of the Lord; and it was written and changed from time to time. (1 Nephi 16:29)

Consider how powerful this parallel is, and apply it to your own life. Personal revelation is mostly quiet, a still small voice that merely points the way in the wilderness of our lives, similar to the Liahona's spindles quietly pointing the way for Lehi. Occasionally, the Holy Ghost reveals something that is most plain and easy to understand about the ways of the Lord, much the same as the writing on the Liahona. Furthermore, Alma attests that it is as easy for us to give heed to this inner compass (of personal revelation), as it was for Lehi to give heed to the Liahona. And, if we do follow it diligently, it will point us "a straight course to eternal bliss" (Alma 37:44). He doesn't stop there. He wants to make sure we understand this parallel, so he continues:

> And now I say, is there not a type in this thing? For just as surely as this director did bring our fathers, by following its course, to the promised land, shall the words of Christ, if we follow their course, carry us beyond this vale of sorrow into a far better land of promise. (Alma 37:45)

Besides emphasizing that the Liahona was a type, or parallel with personal revelation, he wants us to understand that following this inner compass is absolutely sure. It cannot fail.

By emphasizing personal revelation, we do not deemphasize any other source of truth. Certainly the scriptures and the voice of our beloved prophets are vitally involved in our spiritual journey, and when accompanied by the witness of the Holy Spirit, are in themselves a powerful "Liahona."

Scriptures have been misinterpreted, even modified by evil men. Highly placed leaders have fallen, but the Holy Spirit has never led a soul amiss, neither will it ever. If we believe the "words of Christ" or the "rod of iron" refers only to holy writ, the message is lost, because alone, written words lack the witness of the Spirit. Without personal revelation, they fail the test of absoluteness. The only unerring measure of truth we have is also the purest.

Only personal revelation, which begins as the promptings of the Holy Spirit, has the promise of being absolutely sure. Whosoever yields to them will unfailingly arrive at this "far better land of promise" of which Alma testified. Consider also that Lehi already had the scriptures. The Brass Plates actually contained more than the Old Testament does today, yet it was not enough to bring them safely home. Lehi needed a source of revelation that was personalized and daily modified to meet their needs. Such is also our case. Although we have the scriptures, we need the daily guidance of the Holy Spirit to find our way in our own wildernesses. Alma then offers this caution in words that cannot be misinterpreted:

> O my son, do not let us be slothful because of the easiness of the way; for so was it with our fathers; for so was it prepared for them, that if they would look they might live; even so it is with us. The way is prepared, and if we will look we may live forever. (Alma 37:46)

As a matter of fact, it is so easy that anyone, that is *anyone*, who tries it, will find it to be true. It is so easy to do that it may almost seem too simple. It may seem as if God should be making it more dramatic, that a trumpet fanfare or bright pillar of light should accompany personal revelation. The fact is that the inner compass begins as a still small voice that enters the mind barely distinguishable from everyday thoughts and prompts us to do what is right. Yielding to its direction will quickly transform it into a teacher and guide of significant power. Alma gave these additional teachings on how this inner compass works:

> And it did work for them according to their faith in God; therefore, if they had faith to believe that God could cause that those spindles should point the way they should go, behold, it was done; therefore they had this miracle, and also many other miracles wrought by the power of God, day by day. (Alma 37:40)

And thus it is with us also. If we believe God is able to direct us via this "still small voice"—that he will lead us every step of the way—He will cause personal revelation to become the compass in our own wilderness travels. Then we will not only have the miracle of personal revelation, and the comfort and security of knowing we are following His divinely-inspired course for our lives, but we will be led to rejoice in many other miracles, day by day.

Finally, this solemn warning is given against ignoring the inner compass:

> Therefore, they tarried in the wilderness, or did not travel a direct course, and were afflicted with hunger and thirst, because of their transgressions . . . as our fathers were slothful to give heed to this compass . . . they did not prosper; even so it is with things which are spiritual. (Alma 37:42–43)

Even so it is with us. When we are slothful in giving heed to our inner compass, we are afflicted with spiritual hunger and thirst, and physical pain and sorrow; we stall out and stagnate in our growth. We are not able to walk a direct course back to God, no matter how badly we may want to. It is impossible to find our way without personal revelation.

Brigham Young lay ill at Winter Quarters. At noon on February 17, 1847, he dreamed he went to see Joseph Smith. Brigham related the following poignant conversation with the prophet.

> Joseph stepped toward me and looking very earnestly, yet pleasantly, said, "Tell the people to be humble and faithful, and be sure to keep the spirit of the lord and it will lead them right. Be careful and do not turn away the still small voice; it will teach them what to do and where to go; it will yield the fruits of the kingdom. Tell the brethren to keep their hearts open to conviction, so that when the Holy Ghost comes to them, their hearts will be ready to receive it. They can tell the Spirit of the Lord from all other spirits; it will whisper peace and joy to their souls; it will take malice, strife, and all evil from their hearts, and their whole desire will be to do good, bring forth righteousness and build up the Kingdom of God. Tell the brethren if they will follow the Spirit of the Lord they will go right. . . . Tell the people to be sure and keep the Spirit of the Lord and follow it, and it will lead them just right." (Preston Nibley, *Exodus to Greatness: The Story of the Mormon Migration* [Salt Lake City: Deseret News Press, 1947], as quoted in Yorgason, *Spiritual Progression*, 16)

When this truth—that the Holy Spirit is indeed the voice of Jesus Christ—rises like the morning sun across the dark horizon of our mortal journey, we will be empowered to put off the natural man and become saints through the Atonement of Christ.

THE NATURAL MAN

Our fallen nature makes us want to release our hold on the rod of iron and do what is pleasing to the flesh, rather than what is pleasing to God. Because of the effect of the fall, we are by nature disobedient.

> And Satan came among them saying: I am also a son of God; and he commanded them, saying: Believe it not; and they believed it not, and they loved Satan more than God. And men began from that time forth to be carnal, sensual, and devilish. (Moses 5:13)

To be carnal means to have as our primary reason for living to satisfy the cravings and lusts of the flesh. People whose main motivation for living is physical thrills, physical pleasures, food, sex, or other appetites, fit into this category.

To be sensual means to have as a primary reason for living the urge to titillate and please the senses. Persons who excessively value sensations, thrills, bodily pleasures, and things which can be experienced with the five senses, are sensual.

To be devilish is to seek the same thing which the devil seeks, which is to control and dominate others; it is to take away others' free agency as much as possible and supplant it with one's own will. Persons who focus on control, power, wealth, praise, honors, politics (as a means to power) and other such lusts, have a devilish nature. All three of these negative attributes combined constitute the nature of fallen man.

King Benjamin had this to say:

> For the natural man is an enemy to God, and has been from the fall of Adam, and will be, forever and ever, unless he yields to the enticings of the Holy Spirit. (Mosiah 3:19)

Every man and woman born into the world begins life as a natural man. This is our heritage, and it's inescapable. The natural man is every person in and outside the Church who has yet to implement the lesson of the tree of life. It is those who seek after, yearn for, love, enjoy, dream of, are motivated by, and work for the material things of this world as their main object in living. To the natural man, his career and possessions are most important, though he may loudly proclaim that "family comes first."

The natural man evidences his unsancitified state through his actions. Any person who is a social climber or who is career-oriented, politically centered, or any of a thousand world-applauded attributes, is a natural man or woman. Does this cause you concern? Is it wrong to be career-oriented? The answer is no. It is not wrong, in fact, it is quite natural. However, the primary objective of this life is to abandon what is natural in favor of that which is spiritual. As long as we are acting naturally, we are being natural men. Once we transcend the natural by yielding to the entic-ings of the Holy Spirit we will still have careers, we just won't be career-oriented. We will have become spiritually oriented.

The natural people of this world are the geniuses, the fools, the good, the bad, and the indifferent. The definition is all-inclu-sive, and excludes only those who have taken the Holy Spirit to be their guide.

If this strikes one as wrong, it is because one does not yet understand the power of the change that occurs when we tran-scend the natural man and become spiritual beings. All these things listed above, which the world applauds, become of little interest or value after the mighty change. Everything, including one's wealth, career, possessions, honors, and authority, becomes secondary. As long as a person cannot distinguish between a natural man and a spiritually reborn one, that person has not the power to transcend his or her fallen nature. If the differ-ence escapes us, or if we insist on thinking that we can have all the natural-world benefits and goals and still become spiritually sanctified people, we have been deluded.

> No man can serve two masters: for either he will hate the one, and love the other; or else he will hold to the one, and despise the other. Ye cannot serve God and mammon. (Mat-thew 6:24)

It is time for Latter-day Saints to quit being spiritually complacent, and become Saints in these the Latter-days. Awake! Awake! Arouse your faculties. No person in all the history of the world has successfully served God and the world. Mighty King David could not. Even Solomon, with all his wisdom, could not. Why then, would one of us think we can?

The willingness to sacrifice all our natural possessions and place them on the altar comes with exposure to the Holy Spirit. Don't become concerned if you cannot yet do it. Just be aware that eventually you must, and let the Holy Spirit guide you and purify you until you can. The change is powerful, and can purify anyone.

The parable of the ten virgins (Matthew 25:1–13) teaches a powerful lesson and echoes a solemn warning to those who have been given the gift of the Holy Ghost. You will recall that ten virgins went out to await the coming of the Bridegroom that they might go with him to the wedding feast. As they waited, they slept until the cry arose that the Bridegroom was coming. They arose to trim their lamps, but the five foolish virgins' lamps had gone out, and they were left in darkness. The five wise virgins had brought extra oil. The foolish five begged for oil, but there was none to give, and they departed in search of oil. While they were gone, the Bridegroom came, and they missed their chance. When they knocked at the door of the wedding feast they were told to go away, for they were unknown and unwelcome.

A virgin is one who is pure and unsullied by the world. They are those who have diligently kept themselves clean. They are the faithful, and the good. They are members of the church who actively pursue their assignments, pay their tithing, and raise their families in righteousness. They are you and me, and most everyone you sit next to in church. Still, half were turned away because they did not have oil in their lamps and were walking in darkness. They were not turned away because they were impure, they were turned away because, without the Holy Spirit, they were unprepared to meet the Lord.

And at that day, when I shall come in my glory, shall the
parable be fulfilled which I spake concerning the ten virgins. For they that are wise and have received the truth, and
have taken the Holy Spirit for their guide, and have not been
deceived—verily I say unto you, they shall not be hewn down
and cast into the fire, but shall abide the day. (D&C 45:56–57)

Notice that those who are the wise virgins have all received
the truth, and were not deceived. They are not only members of
His true church, they have received the truth. They accept something which the foolish five do not recognize as truth. Whatever
it is, it has taught them how to take the Holy Spirit to be their
guide. This is what the foolish five do not know, and for which
they will be turned away. The wise virgins will have learned the
lesson of the tree of life, which taught them how to take the Holy
Spirit to be their guide. They will have firmly clasped the rod of
iron, and will not have been deceived.

The foolish virgins have been deceived! What is the deception
which has cost them so much? It includes the lie that one can succeed spiritually without taking the Holy Spirit to be your guide.
This is obviously what the foolish five believed, and what cost
them their place at the wedding feast. They thought that being a
virgin alone was enough to exalt them.

This single lie breaks out into many ugly half-truths. Among
them are these: that we must, of our own strength, and by our own
efforts (works), overcome all our sins, obey every commandment,
and when we are finally perfect, the Lord will apply the Atonement, and we will be exalted. It is that baptism alone constitutes
the rebirth of the Spirit. The lie wants us to believe that casual performances and halfhearted obedience will exalt us. It is that being
a member of His true church (being a virgin) is in itself enough. It
persuades that being married in the temple, without further justification and sanctification will give us claim to the promises. It
is that "All is well in Zion, yea Zion prospereth," when in fact, all
is *not* well in Zion. Zion is under attack. It is circled about by its

enemies, and their war is being successfully waged while we swagger about securely unaware that we are under siege.

FASTING

Proper fasting is a principle of the gospel that can force the carnal part of our nature to yield to the spiritual. As such it has the power to pierce the opposition of the flesh and call forth spiritual power. Most importantly, it is a principle that involves obedience for which the Lord blesses us. It is unthinkable that a person could accomplish powerful spirituality without a mastery of this principle.

There are four general types of fasts.

The first is the monthly fast we are asked to participate in on Fast Sunday. The reason it is least powerful is because we are commanded to do it. Obeying a commandment has certain blessings attached, but doing the same thing without being commanded has greater rewards. Of course fasting on Fast Sunday can be very powerful, and just because it is the least powerful of those listed should not deter a person from participating. When done properly, fasting on Fast Sunday is of great benefit spiritually.

The second type of fast is one motivated by need. These types of fasts are entered upon to bolster faith, enhance priesthood power, calm the troubled soul, or assist in making an important decision. They are soul-healing and of great worth. They are more beneficial than the habitual fast, yet are motivated by need, which may be selfish in origin. Sometimes we are petitioning the Lord for something that is not within His wisdom to give us. When we fast to receive a blessing because of need, it may run opposite to His will and cannot be answered the way we wish.

The third kind of fast is one that we do because we have been prompted by the Holy Spirit. These fasts are always powerful.

We do them because God has prompted, not because of a standing commandment. The Lord has a specific purpose for this type of fast, which usually becomes apparent by the end of the fast. Such a fast calls forth great blessings, and is an opportunity not to be missed. The prompting to fast is always a quiet urging, and requires faith and obedience to yield to it.

When this prompting comes, an opportunity lies before us. Perhaps we will need special spiritual attuning to bear our testimony that day. It may be that we will be giving a priesthood blessing. Perhaps He is preparing us to receive a gem of knowledge essential for our progression. He could be preparing us to receive revelation concerning some facet of our premortal calling. Maybe some trial looms ahead, and we need extra strength or comfort.

Whatever the reason may be for the Lord's prompting us to fast, failure to obey will leave us unprepared and less able to accomplish His work, thus depriving us and others of special blessings.

The fourth kind of fast is a fast of thanksgiving. This type of fast also originates by a prompting from the Spirit. It is fasting of an extraordinary type. It calls forth great blessings, and fills the soul with joy and relief. This type of fast is peculiar to the spiritually reborn, and is often the way in which unspeakable gratitude is expressed. During this type of fast no request is made of the Lord. Its only purpose is to express love and gratitude.

All of these types of fasts enlarge the soul when done with proper care. No matter what the motivation for the fast, it needs to be done correctly to be effective. Here are a few simple steps to help in fasting effectively:

1. Consider the fast a forty-eight-hour spiritual exercise; twenty-four hours of preparation and twenty-four hours fasting. Plan it several days in advance if possible. Inform the Lord of your intent to fast, and

ask Him to guide and bless you in your efforts. Decide the exact time you will begin and end the fast. Arrange your affairs accordingly. Please note that occasionally the Spirit will prompt us to begin a fast immediately, in which case there will be no opportunity to prepare. Obedience is always the correct response.

2. Cleanse your tabernacle. The day preceding your fast, do what you can to eliminate worldly assaults on the spirit. Stay away from TV, movies, novels, parties, jokes, unsavory company, and evil influences of any kind. If necessary, absent yourself from the vicinity of such interference. Prepare through praying and discussing with the Lord what you plan to do. Ask Him what you should expect in response. Ask Him to reveal if what you are asking for is in harmony with His will.

3. Fast for twenty-four hours. This includes complete abstinence from food and water. If you are physically handicapped and cannot fast, pray and ask the Lord what he will accept from you as your fast. There is something which is acceptable. He may accept going without food but still drinking water. He may recognize a twelve-hour fast, or even a twenty-four-hour scripture study.

4. During your fast, avoid anything that detracts spiritually. Keep yourself wholesome. Do not watch TV. Select your music carefully—much of it is spiritually bereft. Think pure thoughts, and engage in pure activities. If you are fasting at work, arrange your affairs as favorably as possible. Do not tell people you are fasting. Pray as often as you feel prompted.

5. Begin and end your fast with prayer. Thank the Lord for this opportunity to fast. Ask Him to fill your soul with the object of your fasting. Then, be quiet and

listen. Wait upon the Lord. In your mind, focus on the image of the Father smiling at you. In this image, place yourself on the same elevation, in the same room, kneeling before Him.

6. Break your fast without engorging yourself. Eat moderately and with thanksgiving.

A note of caution may be in order concerning establishing a habitual weekly fast. Fasting is a powerful tool, and when directed by the Holy Spirit will dramatically improve your spirituality. The prime directive is to be obedient to the voice of the Lord. We should not establish a routine fast unless led to do so by divine instruction. The problem is that a routine fast is just that—routine. It loses its power with time. I know people who have fasted weekly for years and have yet to accomplish what they are so diligently fasting for. The key to spiritual excellence is not fasting, it is obedience to the promptings of the Holy Spirit.

When done correctly, fasting will have a powerful effect upon your ability to receive personal revelation.

PRAYER

Prayer is both a joy and a struggle. Everyone who has attempted mighty prayer has at some time felt awkward about it. Even when we know the correct procedure, and understand Heavenly Father's love for us, it seems at times as if the heavens are a stone wall. Prayer is often sweet and natural, and at other times, as remote as speaking a foreign language. The reason for this is that prayer *is* a foreign language. It does not come easily to the natural man. It is the Spirit of the Lord that teaches both how to pray and for what we should pray. The nearer we approach the time when we may claim the title of "saint", which implies a rebirth of the spirit and a transition to being a spiritual person, the greater our prayers become.

If you could analyze your praying, you would recognize that the times when prayer comes most easily are when you are feeling spiritual and devotional. The times of struggle are during periods of spiritual alienation or stagnation.

The way to powerful prayer then, becomes the very path that leads to all other spiritual blessings as well. It is that path which Nephi beheld leading unto the tree of life, the path to spiritual perfection, and eventual exaltation.

Prayer infuses into the soul exactly the same way that faith does. It comes because of the presence of the Holy Spirit. The greater our endowment of the Holy Spirit, the greater will be our prayers, our faith, our hope, and all other spiritual blessings.

No man can teach you to pray. Men can only teach you how to string the words together, and stringing words together is not effective prayer. Only the Holy Spirit can teach you how to pray. If it is your desire to truly pray, you must yield yourself to the enticings of the Holy Spirit and learn to receive personal revelation.

To those who are approaching the tree of life, or who already rejoice in its fruits, prayer is the breath of life. It is as natural as thinking, as easy as speech, and as precious as life itself. The righteous pray constantly. Prayer is that by which every action is measured. They pray every moment. Their very lives are a prayer. They pray on their knees, in their cars, at work, at home, in their beds, and anywhere else they find themselves. Their prayers are unrepetitious and unrehearsed, and flow forth naturally and seemingly without effort. Few of their prayers are formally framed, but are rather an outpouring of love that adheres to no structure. How did they learn to pray this way? The Holy Spirit, which they have learned to hear and obey, simply filled their souls with the gift of prayer. It is indeed a gift, and there are few gifts of the Spirit sweeter.

Becoming a Saint

There are many powerful discourses in the Book of Mormon. Perhaps the greatest on the subject we are pursuing is in the discourse of the elderly King Benjamin to his people shortly before his death. King Benjamin was a prophet of God, and had served his people faithfully all his life. Most importantly, he knew first-hand the requirements for becoming the Elect of God. He was instructed by an angel of the Lord to deliver a mighty sermon to teach his people how to become Saints of God.

He first taught them about their relationship with God, the Atonement of the Savior, and the nature of man. He then, in a single verse, teaches them the entire gospel of exaltation, and how to be born again:

> For the natural man is an enemy to God, and has been from the fall of Adam, and will be, forever and ever, unless he yields to the enticings of the Holy Spirit. (Mosiah 3:19)

The natural man is an enemy to God because God has a single purpose in our lives: "To bring to pass the immortality and eternal life of man" (Moses 1:39). From your perspective, you are the most important person on this planet—and correctly so. If you fail, for you at least, the work of God has been frustrated. Anyone who frustrates the work of God is, by definition, His enemy.

The natural men and women of this world will remain in that unredeemed state forever and ever unless they learn to yield to the enticings of the Holy Spirit. Forever and ever is a long time. It includes this life, the next, the judgment, the assignment to kingdoms, and beyond. This is a permanent state, unless we choose to yield to the enticings of the Holy Spirit. In other words, it does not change at death, the resurrection, or any other time. We will, forever and ever, be counted an enemy to God.

How does the Holy Spirit entice us? As we have discussed several times, we are first enticed by our consciences. That which we call a conscience is the light of Christ. That still small voice which urges us to do good and to believe in Christ comes from God, and is revelation to us. (Moroni 7:16). We often refer to the still small voice as the Holy Spirit. Learning to yield to the Holy Spirit is the grand key to righteousness and personal revelation. This small voice of truth will expand and intensify as we school ourselves to obey (which is to yield to its enticings), until we are born again, have our calling and election made sure, and much, much more.

King Benjamin continues:

> And putteth off the natural man and becometh a saint through the atonement of Christ the Lord (Mosiah 3:19)

These words amplify our understanding of what a saint is to be, and how to become one. We are, after all, The Church of Jesus Christ of Latter-day Saints, and of all people should understand how to become saintly.

It is true that the simplest definition of a saint is one who has joined Christ's true church, yet this includes many who cannot, by any stretch of the imagination, be considered saintly. Like so many words we use, "saint" also has a more perfect meaning, one which implies valiant obedience, singleness of heart and purpose, purity of spirit, and spiritual greatness. King Benjamin was applying this latter definition when he taught that a saint is one who has taken the Holy Spirit to be his or her guide, who has put off the natural man by yielding to the Holy Spirit, and who has applied the healing blood of the Atonement of Christ through faith, repentance, baptism, and reception of the Holy Ghost.

SAINTLY ATTRIBUTES

Following this, King Benjamin records a list of attributes of those thus spiritually endowed. This is not a list of required attitude changes. They are not further requirements heaped upon the

69

weary traveler. It is a gift list! These are God's gift to those who put off the natural man through the rebirth and become saints through the Atonement. They will be so filled with the purifying fire of the Holy Ghost that they will be cleansed, refined, and purified.

> And [they will] become as a child, submissive, meek, humble, patient, full of love, willing to submit to all things which the Lord seeth fit to inflict upon him, even as a child doth submit to his father. (Mosiah 3:19)

President Brigham Young described the attendant refinements this way:

> How shall I know [if the mighty change] has occurred? By the Spirit that shall come upon you through obedience, which will make you feel like little children, and cause you to delight in doing good, to love your Father in Heaven and the society of the righteous. Have you malice and wrath, then? No, it is taken from you and you feel like the child in its mother's lap. You will feel kind to your children, to your brothers and sisters, to your parents and neighbors, and to all around you. You will feel a glow, as of fire, burning within you; and if you open your mouths to talk you will declare ideas which you did not formerly think of; they will flow into your mind, even such as you have not thought of in years. The Scriptures will be opened to you, and you will see how clear and reasonable everything is which this or that Elder teaches you. Your hearts will be comforted, you can lie down and sleep in peace, and wake up with feelings as pleasant as the breezes of summer. This is a witness to you. (*Discourses of Brigham Young*, selected and arranged by John A. Widstoe [Salt Lake City: Deseret Book Co., 1954], 331, as quoted in Yorgason, *Spiritual Progression*, 114)

This submitting isn't a brow-beaten humility. The Lord only *inflicts* upon us His divine guidance. The course He leads us to walk will include instruction, training, lessons to learn, and to the extent we need it, pain, sorrow, and suffering.

The importance of this statement is that one of the changes wrought in the soul of man by the Holy Ghost at the rebirth is a powerful willingness to submit—to obey. It is obedience out of love and faith, and knowledge that this course of life will lead us safely and most efficiently back into His presence.

It isn't *natural* for any person to be as a child—submissive, meek, humble, and patient, let alone full of love, but it is *spiritual*. This is the way Jesus Christ is, and as we draw nearer and nearer to Him, we experience this tremendous change within, which infuses these powerful attributes upon the soul of the recipient. The change is sweet, healing, and joyful.

This powerful change is so startlingly real, so magnificently potent, so wonderfully life-enriching, that it is called the "Mighty Change" in the scriptures. This powerful upgrading of the soul calls forth great spiritual blessings and liberally bestows the gifts of the Spirit upon the recipient. It is to experience the rebirth of the Spirit.

There is a divinely-ordained process to prepare for being born again. It is a pathway we are familiar with, though we may not have realized where it was taking us.

CHAPTER THREE

Preparing for the Rebirth

FAITH IN CHRIST

Faith is always centered in Christ. Since the Holy Spirit's primary mission is to bring to us the truths and light of Christ, faith in Christ always results from the companionship of the Spirit. Thus, yielding to the enticings of the Holy Spirit will bring with it an increase of faith.

Faith is the first principle of the gospel because it is the foundation of all spiritual truths, and the place at which spiritual progress begins. It is the clay from which a testimony is molded, and the first building block of a righteous-seeking soul.

Joseph Smith, the great Prophet of the Restoration, taught that faith is: "The first principle in revealed religion, and the foundation of all righteousness. Paul said, 'Now faith is the substance (assurance) of things hoped for, the evidence (proof) of things not seen.' (Hebrews 11:1)" The prophet then goes on to explain, "From this, we learn that faith is the assurance which men have of the existence of things which they have not seen." (Smith, *Lectures on Faith*, 8)

Alma adds to this by affirming:

> Faith is not to have a perfect knowledge of things; therefore if ye have faith ye hope for things which are not seen, which are true. (Alma 32:21)

Faith does not bring a perfect, irrefutable knowledge. It is essential to our progression that we not know perfectly until we have learned to submit ourselves to His guidance and have become like He is. Faith comes as a result of contact with the Holy Spirit, which descends upon us because of obedience. This divine contact brings us faith, hope, and all other spiritual gifts. These gifts purify and refine. As spirituality grows, we are further refined, and we become more and more like Him. When we have finally arrived at a point where we are ready to know with an absolute surety, our faith is so strong that it is a small step from faith to knowledge, and we are as nearly like Him as we can become in this life. When we have become so purified by the companionship of the Holy Ghost that we have become like Him, then we will be ready to be in His presence. Once we have entered His presence, our faith in Him will become dormant. It will no longer even be possible to have faith in His existence, because faith will have been replaced with absolute knowledge.

It is the uncertainty of faith that motivates us to seek further and greater blessings. Believing, but not knowing for sure, teaches us trust in Christ. We can't know the outcome of our obedience beforehand. But we do learn by repeated experience that the Lord always blesses us when we obey. He never sends on a mission we are not equipped to complete. He never asks us to do the impossible. It is not possible for God to give us a goal we could never reach. "All things are possible to them that believeth" (Mark 9:23).

Jesus Christ is faithful to deliver, and quick to honor those who love and obey him.

Not knowing of a certainty also gives us both the opportunity to fail—and a pathway to succeed. The very definition of agency is that we always have two paths to choose from—right and wrong, good and evil, virtue and vice (see 2 Nephi 2).

An absolute knowledge would effectively end our agency because we would have no reasonable choice. Only the spiritually suicidal would choose to disobey such knowledge.

The English language does not give us appropriately different words for intellectual faith and faith as a gift of God. Intellectual faith is nothing more than a strong belief. While it is possible to believe something so strongly you are willing to die for it, such belief is not faith. One can believe a stone statue is God, and be willing to die for it, but this is not faith. This type of belief is a logical conclusion and has no saving power. It comes as a result of the churnings of the human mind.

True faith, that which has power to heal, comfort, exalt, and raise the dead, is a gift of God and fills the soul with power and spiritual motivation. Faith comes from the Holy Spirit as a result of righteous obedience to the still small voice of the Holy Spirit. Since it is a gift from God, it only remains as long as we continue within the influence of the Holy Spirit. Hereafter, we will only be discussing faith which is a gift of God.

We can only have saving faith in that which is true, which means that we can only have faith to the extent that we possess truth. It is impossible to have true faith in a falsehood.

> *Faith and truth cannot be separated; if there is to be faith, saving faith, faith unto life and salvation, faith that leads to the celestial world, there must first be truth.* (McConkie, *Mormon Doctrine*, 262; italics in original)

> *Faith is a gift of God bestowed as a reward for personal righteousness.* It is always given when righteousness is present, and

the greater the measure of obedience to God's laws the greater will be the endowment of faith. (McConkie, *Mormon Doctrine*, 264; italics in original)

Faith is not naturally found in the natural man. It is an attribute of God, and is transmitted to His children as a refinement to their souls by the Holy Spirit. Faith will only remain as long as the recipient remains in contact with the Holy Spirit. Faith enters the soul of man and emanates outward from him. It is like the light shining from an electric lightbulb. That light remains and shines forth only as long as it is connected with the source of its power. Disconnect that power, and there will be an immediate loss of light. For a Latter-day Saint, faith and testimony are nearly synonymous terms. Faith is a revealed assurance that Jesus is the Christ, and testimony is a revealed knowledge which adds to that faith the additional truths of the restored gospel.

Faith and testimony will continue to flow from the Holy Ghost and grow inside one's soul, unless that person severs or limits in some way, his link with the source of those gifts. The most common cause of stagnant or diminishing faith is an unwillingness to obey some law or prompting.

There is an additional aspect of faith that is experienced only by those who have taken the Holy Spirit to be their guide, and who faithfully live by its guiding voice. The Holy Spirit communicates the mind and will of Jesus Christ to those who listen. As we obey the voice of the Lord, we receive a tremendous witness that everything He sends us forth to do works miracles in our lives, and in the lives of others. We learn to trust and rely on His guidance. We learn that He *always* honors those who obey Him. We are prospered and blessed without exception and filled with blessings overflowing.

Continual obedience allows us to acquire confidence in the Lord, and in His loving care and guidance, until our witness becomes profound and unshakable. This is an aspect of faith experienced by those upon the straight and narrow path. It is faith in the voice of God. It is this confidence in Christ that makes us mighty in His service, and like Enoch, able to move mountains at His command. It is this faith that yields power in the priesthood and propels the obedient into a world of powerful service experienced by but few of his children. They join Abraham, Esther, Enoch, John the Beloved, Mary, the mother of Christ, the three Nephite Disciples, Lehi, the brother of Jared, Joseph Smith, and a host of others, in works of great power and eternal worth to the Kingdom.

There is much that a faithful servant can accomplish by the workmanship of his own hands, but consider what greater things that servant can do when the Master's own voice has sent him forth with specific instructions. The servant takes on the mantle of the Master; his acts become the acts of the Master, and his voice, the voice of the Master. It was in just such a state of powerful investiture of authority that Moses divided the Red Sea, and the brother of Jared called forth the finger of God, and all others of His servants wrought miracles in His holy name. If we also wish to serve with equal power and effect, then we must also become equally obedient to the voice of the Master. It is the very purpose of the restored gospel to bestow these gifts upon all who seek them. The nearly incomprehensible joy of this truth is that it is as profoundly available to us, as it was to Moses.

OPPOSITION IN ALL THINGS

As previously stated, the blessings of faith and testimony continue to grow until we cease to be obedient either to the written commandments, or to His guiding voice. If we find ourselves suffering from a famine of faith or testimony, it is because we have severed our link with the source of those gifts through our disobedience. If this is the case, then we have succumbed to the opposition in our lives. We have turned our eyes away from the promised reward of righteous obedience to the Master of our souls, and focused on something more worldly and closer at hand, something more pleasing to the basic part of our nature.

Lest we become judgmental of our neighbors, or unduly harsh on ourselves, let us observe here that opposition is an ordained principle of the divine plan, and not necessarily a result of sin or disobedience. While trials do occur because of transgression, it is more often the case that they occur because of our inability to recognize the promptings of the Holy Spirit. We aren't being disobedient, so much as being blind (or deaf as it were), and bumping into things which hurt. By not hearing the warning voice we unavoidably blunder into painful obstacles. In fact, the purpose of the pain is to inform us that we have strayed from the straight and narrow path. Again, it is probably not so much because of sin, as because of foolishness.

Even when we are faithfully walking the straight and narrow path we are given obstacles and trials to overcome. We must remember that Father has a single purpose in our lives, which is to bring us to exaltation. Anything which moves us nearer to that goal is valuable, even pain and suffering. From His divine perspective, worldly possessions, jobs, careers, health, happiness, even life itself, is expendable if the outcome is exaltation. After we share His divine viewpoint, we will shout praises to His holy name for His wisdom and love. Until then, we see through a glass darkly, and our trials seem immense.

The best way to ease life's trials is to take the Holy Spirit as our guide. The trials still come; it is just that with the Lord's guidance through the Holy Spirit, we will know how to handle them. We will learn the lessons quickly, and each trial will end sooner, the relief will be sweet, and the strength gained will be exalting. With the Holy Spirit filling our bosoms, we will also be able, in a limited way, to share God's perspective on life, and we will view our trials differently.

The most difficult and devastating way to deal with

opposition is to press forward with all the suborn vigor we possess, without the guidance of the Holy Spirit. The opposition will arise according to divine law, and without guidance, we will be battered and buffeted, confused, weakened, and disillusioned. Righteousness will not seem to be worth the price required to gain it. In fact, powerful righteousness cannot be achieved this way, and the price is too high, because we simply are incapable of paying it.

This law of opposition, which means that everything good we attempt will be opposed, is an ordained and essential part of the plan. Consider these very important scriptures:

> For it must needs be, that there is an opposition in all things. If not so, . . . righteousness could not be brought to pass . . . Wherefore, the Lord God gave unto man that he should act for himself. Wherefore, man could not act for himself save it should be that he was enticed by the one or the other. (2 Nephi 2:11, 16)

Without opposition, the plan of exaltation would not work. Righteousness could not be brought to pass. This opposition was of necessity in all things (2 Nephi 2:11). In order for agency to operate properly we must be enticed proportionately by good and evil. We know that guidance is also available in all things—otherwise the balance between good and evil would be lost. The difference between the two is that opposition is persistent and not offended if we ignore it, while continued guidance in all things is dependent upon our obedience.

In order for agency to operate properly, we must be enticed proportionately by good and evil. Before the world was created, God established that there would be a decreed level of evil influence, or opposition in our lives. This balance between good and evil is maintained by divine decree. When we receive an increase of spiritual blessings, we receive a proportionate increase in opposition.

Brigham Young made this observation on the proportionate application of opposition to the early missionary effort in a general epistle to the Church in 1856:

> It is the testimony of all the Elders that, while signal success attends their labours in all of these lands, being attended by the Spirit and power of the Lord in all of their ministrations, the opposition also increases in equal proportion. (Clark, *Messages of the First Presidency*, 2:196)

It is this ever-widening gap between good and evil which finally exalts. We become increasingly more obedient to God, and subsequently, magnificently powerful. At the same time, the opposition becomes equally intense. When we, through the grace of Christ, finally overcome, the victory is won at great cost, against overwhelming odds, and the victor's crown received with humility, and worn with elegance and grace. Were it not so, the victory would be shallow, and lack eternal significance.

The trials and trauma of life are essential to our growth. We acquire most of our strength of character through the things we suffer. Even for Christ, the Great Exemplar, the path was through tremendous opposition.

> Though he were a Son, yet learned he obedience by the things which he suffered. (Heb. 5:8)

One important difference between He and us, is that He learned his lessons only once. He did not suffer because He was disobedient, He simply learned obedience. We, on the other hand, must be taught again and again. We learn the same lessons over and over, wading through much affliction because of our pride and disobedience. Instead of having our trials propel us heavenward, as they did our Lord, we suffer and struggle to learn each lesson, and must experience the pain again and again to finally comprehend. This type of progress is excruciatingly slow and extremely costly, much more so than necessary. It is also very common.

There are two primary reasons why we may experience opposition sufficient to bring suffering. The first is because of transgressions, and the need to keep repeating the lessons to teach us obedience. This type of suffering is protracted, and much of the time unproductive.

The second type is because of our need to learn some important lesson in life. This type of suffering need not be prolonged. It propels us heavenward as fast as we can learn the associated lessons, develop obedience, and move on. This type of opposition works to our profound advantage, and promotes rapid growth.

Life thus takes on a reverse roller coaster aspect of ups and downs—reverse, because the trend is heavenward, rather than toward lower climbs. While on a spiritual high, we are built up, nourished, strengthened, and prepared; then opposition arises according to divine law to test, strengthen, and hone. In the learning stages of spiritual maturation this process is inescapable. It can be minimized by taking the Holy Spirit to be our guide, and thus learning the lessons of righteousness with less pain, or by abandoning the path of light and slinking away on some comfortable, forbidden path.

After one has taken the Holy Spirit to be their guide, and experienced the rebirth, they will have received every tool they need to minimize this dramatic spiritual cycling. Opposition is always equal and opposite to every spiritual blessing. In other words, when we receive a blessing, shortly thereafter the evil one will be allowed equal opportunity and equal power to oppose the blessing. In practical terms, what happens is that we experience a burst of spiritual growth, and shortly thereafter, we experience the divinely-decreed opposition. We experience a powerful onslaught of doubt, temptation, lies, and trials, and without the spiritual refinements typical of those spiritually reborn, we sink spiritually, until we are in such pain that we cry out for help.

This principle of equal opposition is much more profound than most people allow. It is this fact which has been the downfall of all the notable failures from Cain to King Saul to Judas to Sidney Rigdon. It is difficult to imagine Satan being allowed equal and opposite power to a heavenly manifestation such as a glorious appearance of Jesus Christ; yet Sidney Rigdon was with Joseph during several manifestations, and still fell away, not from doubt, but from pride. It does not matter how glorious our spiritual manifestations and views, the dark one has power to instill doubt even in that which we have beheld with our own eyes.

This truth is important because it allows us to recognize the source of this doubt, which God ordains we must experience. We may berate ourselves as being horribly weak if we were to receive a tremendous blessing, then doubt thereafter that its source was heavenly. We may even reason (with Satan's help) that if this truly had been of God, nothing could make us doubt. The important understanding here is the source of the doubt. Whether or not the recipient succumbs and grovels in the doubt, or rises above it, depends on the spiritual maturity and obedient nature of each person. Even in times of powerful deception, the Holy Spirit guides, and truth is as close as a whisper. No person need yield to a lie if they have their hand upon the rod of iron.

After the rebirth, we will have become so attuned to the Holy Spirit, and having obtained the full armor of the Holy Ghost, we will humbly submit ourselves to the Lord's guidance without being forced into humility through pain and sorrow. The temptation and lies still burst forth like a vile volcano, but we will be prepared by the Lord to resist them. Thus, the spiritual ups and downs cease to be so dramatic. The opposition is powerful, and does cause us to labor diligently to rise above it, but with the voice of revelation speaking sweetly in our hearts, we need not succumb to, nor be defeated by it.

With the greater blessings comes the greater opposition. Those walking the straight and narrow path beyond the rebirth are literally walking through spiritual stone, and the power required is tremendous. But, let this not strike fear into the heart, for those walking this path walk with joyful steps, and marvel as they watch the solid rock of opposition crumble before them and explode into dust at the touch of God's hand. These are the happiest people on earth, and they think not upon the raging battle before them, but upon their Savior's love, and His constant goodness and loving care. Their lives are filled with miracles, and they would not trade all the riches of the earth for a single day in the warmth of His approbation.

Opposition should not deter someone from plotting a course of spiritual growth because the blessings we receive while righteously overcoming trials are immensely compensating for the trials of opposition.

Prior to the rebirth it is the struggling back to previous heights which gives us the humility to rely upon the Lord, and thus the strength and spiritual growth to rise even higher than before. The process keeps repeating, with spiritual strength accumulating and opposition becoming more, until we finally enjoy the blessed rebirth of the spirit, and are thereby prepared for further and greater progress.

It would be unrighteous of us to assume that anyone struggling in life is suffering from the effect of sin. It is exactly this type of self-righteous judgment we are warned against. Let us not be like Job's friends, who accused him of gross sin because of his trials.

The Honeymoon Period

Many have experienced an aspect of spiritual growth which I have termed the "honeymoon period" for want of a better term.

It is important to understand because it is easy to discount our spiritual blessings without a realization of this principle. The following chart represents spiritual growth. It vastly oversimplifies what is actually a much more complex series of ups and downs, but it is adequate to illustrate what we are discussing.

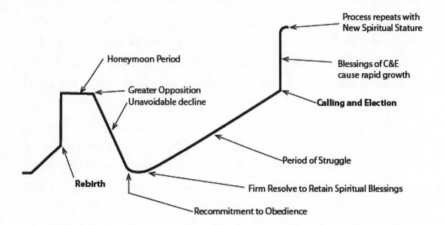

You will notice that there is a period of struggle and slow upward growth toward the rebirth. When this period is conducted under the direction of the Holy Spirit, there follows a spiritual event—in our chart, the rebirth. After the spiritual event, there is a sudden rise in spiritual power. With the rebirth the blessings include losing the desire for sin, reception of the Holy Ghost, and other blessings. Immediately after this growth there is a "honeymoon period" wherein we are left nearly without opposition to enjoy the blessings flowing from the event. During this time we receive charity, singleness of heart, total dedication, meekness, humility, and many other attendant refinements brought on by the Holy Ghost.

Some weeks or months following this period, the adversary is allowed to return with greater opposition than we were previously accustomed to. This brings on a spiritual decline which is unavoidable. This decline has nothing to do with our desires. During this time most people struggle valiantly to maintain their spiritual high. Without exception they find it impossible, not because they are weak or the spiritual event was not real, but because it is the ordained process of growth. We keep all the spiritual refinements—the faith, humility, patience, childlike obedience, and many others which we have discussed throughout this book. However, they are no longer unopposed, as it was during the honeymoon period. Now, we must struggle to exercise our gifts, and fight to keep spiritually attuned. Again, as it was before the rebirth, we must do what is right, *because it is right*, not because we are aglow with a hundred megawatts of spiritual power.

The spiritual decline lasts until we recommit ourselves to the same level of obedience we found so easy during the honeymoon period. A diamond-hard resolve to regain the former blessings begins the journey upward again. This is not a climb toward former blessings as one may be tempted to think, but a journey beyond for greater things.

You will notice that the next spiritual event occurs when we reach our former spiritual level in spite of everything the evil one has raged against us.

In fact, the period of struggle and growth which follows any major spiritual event lasts exactly as long as it takes us to dedicate ourselves to, and actually achieve, perfect obedience at that new level in spite of the opposition. It seems odd that we must keep relearning to be flawlessly obedient, but each spiritual level requires a new level of obedience, one which at first is easy because of the spiritual gifts acquired, and later difficult because of the increased opposition. When the new level of obedience becomes perfected within us, again in spite of increased opposition, then another spiritual manifestation unfolds itself, and the process begins anew.

It is this struggling in the furnace of our trials, while possessing all the spiritual gifts, which actually makes it possible to accomplish tremendous growth, which ultimately prepares us for the next great blessing awaiting us. There is a profound difference between going through trials clothed with the full armor of God, and going through them spiritually stark naked. Those who walk this course go with steady, sure steps, and even through tears of pain, they inwardly rejoice in their glorious blessings.

Were we allowed to remain unopposed after the honeymoon period, it would be nearly impossible to continue to test and prove us. During the honeymoon we have such great faith, charity, and eternal perspective that it would take a horrible calamity equivalent to Job's trials, to even begin to test our strength. Accordingly, the Lord mercifully allows us to come back to earth, as it were, to continue our trials.

The reason this concept is important is that few people who experience this understand why they have fallen from their former spiritual height. Some (with Satan's help) decide that the event was not real after all, or they conclude they must have committed some sin which has harmed them, or many other lies the dark one is able to conjure up.

Of course, it is possible to lose focus and indulge in sin, and thereby disqualify ourselves of former blessings. In this case the process would be much different than represented by our chart. Still, even when there is no sin involved, it is easy to become discouraged. This might happen if we did not understand why we had, figuratively, been lowered back to mortality through no fault of our own. While this may sound odd, it is nevertheless the case that those within the honeymoon period do not feel as much mortal weakness. They feel completely enveloped in God's love, and invincible to opposition. Their courage feels absolute, and their determination to serve God, flawless. They feel as if the heavens are about to burst open and they are about to be surrounded by Heavenly visitors. It is no wonder it is such a shock to be expelled from their private paradise for reasons they do not understand.

Repentance

The next principle we might expect to encounter as we prepare for the rebirth of the Spirit is repentance.

Repentance is only possible because of the Atonement of Christ, and is therefore subject to His divine approval. Repentance must be done His way to be acceptable, thus allowing the penitent to take part in the Atonement.

Most of us have been taught the five Rs of repentance:

Recognize, Remorse, Resolve, Recompense, and Reconcile. These are all recognizable steps along the way of true repentance. But creating a formula for repentance implies that by applying that formula, we might overcome sin, perfect ourselves, and thus be whole and sinless. It implies that the natural man has power to perfect and purify himself of his own strength, when, in fact he does not. It implies that he must overcome sin by this assumed strength prior to soliciting divine acceptance.

The truth of the matter is we are not able to rid ourselves of our sins except through the Atonement of Christ. No amount of self-discipline or formulized acts will actually cause our sins to be remitted.

The natural man is an enemy to God, and will be forever and ever, until he yields to the enticings of the Holy Spirit (Mosiah 3:19). It is yielding to the Holy Spirit which brings us the blessings of obedience and qualifies us for the blessings of the Atonement. It is the Holy Spirit which effects all the perfections of soul, attitude, and attribute, which purifies us. The natural man is powerless to achieve perfection in any other way. Another glance at the repentance process, as guided by the Holy Spirit, might yield a process similar to this:

1. Recognize that you have sinned through the light of Christ, the workings of your conscience. Recognize your fallen and unworthy status, and allow godly sorrow to instill remorse for your sins.

2. Resolve that you must purge this sin and many others from your life, knowing that you can only truly be clean when you receive a remission of all your sins. Be fully aware that this is a sweet and healing process, and that you need divine guidance to accomplish it.

3. Relinquish the direction of your life to the Lord. Obey the still small voice, knowing that it is the voice of the Lord, and He loves you and will guide you through this difficult period in your life. Fearlessly obey the voice of the Lord. Do *everything* you are prompted to do by the Spirit. Confess your sins to your bishop if prompted to do so.

4. Recompense those you have offended, and make amends as directed by the Lord and by Church authorities.

5. Reconcile your life to the Lord by yielding to the promptings of the Holy Spirit and putting off the natural man, and by becoming a saint through the Atonement of Christ (Mosiah 3:19).

6. Rejoice in your life cleansed from, not only this one sin, but all sin, and your soul newly reborn.

To understand this path to repentance, it helps to imagine a person's sins to be like a tree growing in his driveway, each branch on the tree representing a diverse sin. When the tree is small it does not block the whole road, and is easy to get around. It is easy to ignore it and still live an apparently normal life. Until we learn the lessons of obedience the tree continues to grow larger, and blocks more and more of the driveway, until passage becomes first difficult, then impossible. It becomes too painful to ignore, and our souls cry out for relief.

Following our revised six R's of repentance will give us divine guidance and great spiritual strength. In time, the Lord will purify our souls, and following the rebirth, we will no longer desire sin, and the tree will have been killed and removed.

On the other hand, by going through any other process, we will only be able to combat a single sin, and figuratively attempt to pluck a branch from the tree. While this is a worthy accomplishment, the problem is the tree remains alive and healthy. While we have been wresting this branch from the tree, it has been sprouting others.

Which of us has not found ourselves in this exact situation? We labor diligently to stop smoking, only to find that withdrawal from tobacco promotes swearing. We discipline ourselves to stop swearing, and lose control of some other aspect of our lives. The problem is that a natural man or woman has the capacity to entertain and develop multiple sins at the same time. We will never truly overcome sin until Jesus Christ changes our nature; until we no longer desire sin and He kills the tree once and for all.

Eventually, each person will find his or her life blocked by just such an obstacle of sin. Generally, people attempt to climb up the trunk and break branches from the tree with as much energy as they possess. While their enthusiasm is applaudable to be sure, unless this process humbles them to the point that they submit to the enticings of the Holy Spirit, and thus begin to experience its soul-mending influence, they fail to fully repent.

The problem remains—the tree continues to live and sprout new branches, or grow back a branch just broken off. This is because as long as the basic nature of the person remains unchanged, the tree of sin remains alive, and plucking off leaves and branches changes very little.

Trying to repent by cutting off branches will not kill the tree. It is a task worthy of a spiritual giant, which no one with such a life blockage of sin would be. A true spiritual giant understands a sweeter and divinely ordained means of repentance.

The only way to clear the path is to kill the tree, which implies abandoning it by obedience to the Holy Spirit. We must call the Master Forester to cut down the trunk, clear away the fallen timber, and rip the roots from the ground. Then, and only then, will the tree die. In our analogy, killing the tree represents a permanent change in the nature of the sinner, which can only be accomplished through by becoming a saint through the Atonement of Jesus Christ.

Consider the analogy of a person running from sin with all their strength, while looking back over their shoulder to make sure they are not getting too far ahead—just in case they might need to indulge a little! As long as we are in that type of race, we will expend all our energy running, rather than truly repenting and changing our lives.

So how does one repent if not by examining each errant behavior and working on it until it is eliminated, then moving on? As correct as this process sounds, it does not take advantage of the purifying, and empowering gifts of the Atonement. It attempts to forcibly strip sin from our nature using the willpower we possess. It assumes we must conquer each sin of our own power, then we are worthy of the Atonement. It ignores the fact that our capacity to sin always exceeds our capacity to obey, simply because we are natural men and women. Natural man cannot adequately change by his own power because, even after he has exhausted all his strength, he is still a natural man. Besides, it is not necessary. There is a better way—the way the Lord has ordained it.

Repentance is the act of turning away from sin, and is finally complete when we are no longer natural, but spiritual, in nature. When we transcend the natural man through the rebirth, the desire for sin simply goes away. Repentance is complete when we no longer even desire sin, when it becomes repulsive and repugnant. The natural man is not at all like that, but the spiritual man is in every way.

Don't let this concept become license to throw up your hands, embrace your sins, and wait for the change to occur. It is an invitation to throw aside your sins totally, rather than one at a time. It is an invitation to yield to the enticings of the Holy Spirit and to be reborn into a new creature who is spiritual, and who no longer desires sin. It is an invitation to come unto Christ and become clean every whit.

*The way to Perfection
is not through the
Disciplining and Reshaping of the Soul by the will of Man,
But
Through the Discipline of Obedience
and reshaping of the Soul
by God.*

In fact, this is an invitation to increased effort, to increased diligence and obedience. It is an invitation to experience life-giving success; to finally conquer your errant behavior and restore your soul. You have never had a greater invitation, because it comes from the Lord, and His grace is sufficient for all who yield unto him.

The result of true repentance is not just an absence of immoral actions, but a purity of spirit which can only be attained through guidance by the Holy Spirit, and sanctification through the Atonement of Christ.

Allowing time to elapse is not repentance. Payment must be made for *all* sins committed any time during your life. The justice of God demands it. Because something happened thirty years ago does not mean it has been forgiven. Every sin must be dealt with as the Spirit directs in order for us to be forgiven and the Atonement applied in our behalf. Unresolved sin is a blight upon the soul. It cankers and sickens the inner man. It limits our contact with the divine and damns our progression.

Payment is made whether the sinner is repentant or not. The most exacting and demanding payment for sin is to ignore it and let our souls pay the price through suffering. Rest assured the price will be paid. It may be paid in earthly suffering, sometimes it is paid in the hereafter—or both. Unwilling payment for sin does not exalt, and does not constitute repentance. Even after the price has been paid in this way, we may not actually be forgiven, because we have not repented, we have not changed our obedience and come unto Christ. We have just paid the price which justice demands. It may be that all we need to do is allow the Holy Spirit to guide us through the steps of repentance. It may well be that we overcame that weakness long ago, yet by a failure to repent, have not yet obtained the sweet relief of forgiveness.

Repentance is a change of heart, not just a change of actions. The actions change forever after the heart changes. There are two powerful virtues of the Atonement that assist us in repentance.

One is that through obedience and ordinances we can be forgiven of our sins. The other, less understood, blessing is that as we yield our will to Christ, He empowers us to change. He takes away our desire for the very transgressions that we wish to repent of. All who pay the price of obedience will experience this powerful change. After the divinely wrought changes you will be truly repentant, and worthy of the remission of sins promised by the ordinance of baptism.

BAPTISM

The next step on our preparatory journey to the rebirth of the Spirit is Baptism.

Baptism is the initiatory ordinance into the Church of Jesus Christ and the gateway into the celestial kingdom.

A person may enter any other kingdom without baptism, but the celestial kingdom is reserved for only those who began their journey home with baptism. Baptism must be performed by one who has proper priesthood authority. That authority is only found within Christ's true church.

After a person has listened to and obeyed their conscience, which is the light of Christ in their soul, they will be led through the steps of faith and true, soul-purifying repentance. They will be given the opportunity to be baptized. If they accept this ordinance with pure intent, they will have taken their first step upon that straight and narrow path which leads unto eternal life.

> And he commandeth all men that they must repent, and be baptized in his name, having perfect faith in the Holy One of Israel, or they cannot be saved in the kingdom of God. (2 Nephi 9:23)

Baptism is a covenant between the participant and the Lord. The individual promises:

1. To come into the fold of God; that is, to join His church and kingdom on earth.
2. To be called His people and take upon them the name of Christ.
3. To bear one another's burdens, that they may be light.
4. To mourn with those that mourn.
5. To comfort those that stand in need of comfort.
6. To stand as witnesses of God at all times, and in all places that ye may be in, even until death.
7. To serve God and keep His commandments.

The Lord for His part covenants that He will:

1. Pour out the Holy Spirit more abundantly upon them, until they eventually receive the baptism of fire and the Holy Ghost.
2. Redeem them and number them with those of the first resurrection, and give them eternal life (see Mosiah 18:7–10).

> Wherefore, my beloved brethren, I know that if ye shall follow the Son, with full purpose of heart, acting no hypocrisy and no deception before God, but with real intent, repenting of your sins, witnessing unto the Father that ye are willing to take upon you the name of Christ by baptism—yea, by following

your Lord and Savior down into the water, according to his word, behold, then shall ye receive the Holy Ghost; yea then cometh the baptism of fire and of the Holy Ghost; and then can ye speak with the tongue of angels, and shout praises unto the Holy One of Israel. (2 Nephi 31:13)

One of the great blessings which occurs because of baptism was noted in item 1 above. When a worthy person is baptized, the Lord pours out the Holy Spirit more abundantly upon them. We receive a greater endowment of that gift which we already enjoy—the light of Christ, that still small voice which quietly directed us this far begins to speak more profoundly to our souls. It will begin to lead us in ways not possible prior to baptism. This is not the same blessing as the actual receipt of the Holy Ghost. This gift is preparatory to the later constant companionship of that member of the Godhead.

THE STRAIGHT GATE

One enters upon the straight and narrow path through the waters of baptism.

> For the gate by which ye should enter is repentance and baptism by water. (2 Nephi 31:17)

Due to the fact that one enters the path through baptism, only those who are baptized by correct authority are on the path. This is not to detract from the fact that the Lord leads all humble people toward Him through their conscience, the light of Christ. It only defines the point at which a person has ceased wandering the multitudes of other paths which lead elsewhere, and has embarked upon a course which holds the promise of eternal life.

There is an additional reason why this is so:

> For behold, again I say unto you that if ye will enter in by the way, and receive the Holy Ghost, it will show unto you all things what ye should do. (2 Nephi 32:5)

Once on the path, the only way to walk its straight and narrow course is through following the direction of the Holy Ghost. This requires the gift of the Holy Ghost, which only members of Christ's true church have the privilege to receive.

While the straight and narrow path encompasses every gospel truth and ordinance, it defines more than this. It defines not only how we should live the gospel and how to prepare for its saving ordinances, but what we must do with all other aspects of our journey home to our Father in Heaven. This includes every aspect of life which has eternal significance: who we should marry, where we should live, where to work, when to repent, how to repent, when to pray, how to pray, what to ask for in prayer, how many children to have, how to teach them, how to endure each trial, how to fast, when to fast, what to fast for, how to exercise the priesthood, what words to use in priesthood blessings, the will of God in every part of our lives which affects our exaltation. It includes revealed truths and doctrines of universal worth, as well as some that are specific to us, and of little value to anyone else.

The journey is fraught with danger, and at times completely obscured by the mists of satanic darkness. The straight and narrow path is often so cleverly disguised by the adversary—lies masquerading as truth, deception in living color, sin advertised and sold as delightful—that one cannot distinguish the path through natural eyes. We must have the divine guidance of the Holy Spirit to succeed.

In Nephi's dream, the straight and narrow path led to the tree of life, which represented the love of God, and the joyous blessings of the rebirth. In actuality, that same path extends beyond the rebirth to all future spiritual blessings. This path is in fact, eternal and endless.

The path not only defines the shortest distance from where we are presently, to the rebirth and beyond, it defines additional performance, service, and obedience required of us. We are here not only to overcome the obstacles and return home, but to grow significantly, and accomplish a great deal of good in the process. It is impossible that anyone could do all this without divine assistance and constant guidance.

REMISSION OF SINS

The act of baptism does not guarantee a remission of sins. Baptism is an ordinance preparatory to the remission of sins. A willingness to be baptized does not necessarily show a willingness to obey every commandment, forsake every sin, and yield entirely to the promptings of the Holy Spirit.

It helps to understand when sins are actually remitted, or when they are blotted from the books, so that the Lord remembers them no more.

> Now this is the commandment: Repent, all ye ends of the earth, and come unto me and be baptized in my name, that ye may be sanctified by the reception of the Holy Ghost, that ye may stand spotless before me at the last day. (3 Nephi 27:20)

Notice the order presented: repentance, baptism, and sanctification through receipt of the Holy Ghost, and then, after all that, becoming spotless, which is, of course, to have your sins remitted .

> Yea blessed are they who shall believe in your words, and come down into the depths of humility and be baptized, for they shall be visited with fire and with the Holy Ghost, and shall receive a remission of their sins. (3 Nephi 12:2)

Again, the same order: faith, repentance, baptism, visitation of fire and the Holy Ghost, and finally, a remission of sins. We should be careful to not confuse the *gift* of the Holy Ghost with the *actual reception* of that member of the Godhead as a constant companion.

Sins are fully remitted and washed away when the individual is visited with fire and with the Holy Ghost. In most cases this event occurs sometime after baptism, usually many years later when their repentance is complete. When a spiritually mature individual of powerful spiritual stature is baptized, the baptism of fire and the Holy Ghost may immediately follow, making these two events essentially one.

It is my opinion that this is the exception rather than the rule. Most of us participate in the ordinance prior to spiritual maturity, and then enjoy the baptism of fire when our obedience calls forth this great blessing. Until the Rebirth occurs there is an intermediate step provided. This step is only of value before we traverse the straight and narrow path to the rebirth, and its attendant remission of sins. This step is, the Lord is willing to forgive us of individual sins as we forsake them. There is a difference between forgiveness of a sin, and the remission of all our sins. Forgiveness is conditional upon the fact that we never commit them again, whereas remission is permanent.

> Go your ways and sin no more; but unto that soul who sinneth shall the former sins return, saith the Lord your God. (D&C 82:7)

With forgiveness, as long as we do not repeat the sin, we are blessed and counted worthy on that subject. We may still have many other sins to repent of. In order for sins to be totally remitted, that is, blotted out and forgotten, we must experience the mighty change, which is to be born again. This latter, total remission of sins is what the verses in Third Nephi quoted above are referring to.

Repentance is a process, just like exaltation is a process. We may be forgiven by eliminating errant behavior throughout our lives. When we finally traverse the path to the tree of life by following the whisperings of the Holy Spirit, then we are fully repentant and become born again. Then, and only then, are we fully forgiven, and washed white in the blood of the Lamb.

The Lord is willing to forgive *a* sin. But He does not apply the Atonement and wash away *a* sin. The Atonement is so glorious and powerful that its application washes all sins from the sinner—every one of them. He is willing to remit sins, but will only do so when we experience the mighty change which occurs when we receive the Holy Ghost to be our constant companion. This visitation is also called the "baptism of fire and the Holy Ghost."

Elder McConkie explained it this way:

> Question: When do we receive the actual remission of our sins? When are we changed from our carnal and fallen state to a state of righteousness? When do we become clean and pure and spotless so as to be able to dwell with Gods and angels? What is the baptism of fire and the Holy Ghost?
>
> Answer: Sins are remitted not in waters of baptism as we say in speaking figuratively, but when we receive the Holy Ghost. It is the Holy Spirit of God that erases carnality and brings us into a state of righteousness. We become clean when we actually receive the fellowship and companionship of the Holy Ghost. It is then that sin and dross and evil are burned out of our souls as though by fire. The baptism of the Holy Ghost is the baptism of fire. (McConkie, *New Witness for the Articles of Faith*, 290)

The blessed reception of that glorious member of the Godhead is profound upon the soul. It is proceeded by the candidate literally being immersed in spiritual fire, which consumes the dross and burns away the unclean and impure, thus making that person worthy of that holy companion, and consequently also worthy of a remission of their sins. This will be discussed further in the section on "The Mighty Change."

Certainly, we must constantly strive to overcome each sinful act, and to do better each day. It would be spiritual suicide to throw up your hands and quit struggling to improve because Christ finally remits sins somewhere far down the road from where you think you are. It would be equally suicidal to not understand how to truly repent in order to receive the promised remission of sins. Lacking that truth would cause us to blunder through our lives, only to find out too late that we still have payment to make.

Let us then not cease to struggle against sin—but to change the focus of our attack. Instead of trying to repent by attacking individual actions alone, let us amplify our efforts by first yielding to the promptings of the Holy Spirit. More than just guidance in how to overcome individual actions, his presence changes our nature so that we acquire the strength, power, and an obedient spirit sufficient to overcome them all. His companionship eventually causes the very desire for sin to be purged from the soul.

The way to achieve a remission of your sins is to stop whatever you are doing and listen. Go to a quiet place and pray with all the energy of your soul for the Lord to direct you. Ask what your next step should be, then be quiet and listen. Listen hard, and pray hard for the Lord to improve your spiritual hearing. If you listen carefully, you will hear the Lord prompting you to do something. It will be a still, small voice, but it will be good, uplifting, and probably contrary to what you were planning to do. You will hear the message coming as if from your conscience, for that will be exactly from where it is coming. When you have learned to listen, you will have your hand upon the rod of iron. When you learn to obey, you will have wrapped your fingers around it, and you will have taken the first step in removing all sin from your life.

This grasping of the rod of iron, which is personal revelation, has everything to do with abandoning your sins, but may not initially address any specific sin. What this means is, the Holy Spirit may lead you through some preparatory work before actually directing you through repentance. It may, in fact, begin with a prompting to say your prayers, or read the scriptures, or go to church, or to actually stub out a cigarette, or go talk to the Bishop. But, whatever it is that the Lord wants you to do, to obey will be the most important decision you will ever make—for upon that decision hinges the rest of eternity. That is, until the next prompting comes, and then that one will be the most important, and so on, as you walk by faith with your fingers wrapped firmly around the rod of iron of personal revelation.

THE GIFT OF THE HOLY GHOST

In our preparations for the rebirth, we must receive the gift of the Holy Ghost. The priesthood ordinance of conferring the gift of the Holy Ghost prepares the way for the constant companionship of that member of the Godhead. The gift of the Holy Ghost confers upon a person the right to receive this blessing when the person has proven worthy. Receiving the gift of the Holy Ghost also allows a person increasingly greater access to the Holy Spirit, as he learns to obey its promptings. This increase in guidance by the Holy Spirit makes it possible to eventually receive the constant companionship of the Holy Ghost through the rebirth.

It is important to keep the distinction clear between the Holy Spirit, and the gift of the Holy Ghost. The Holy Spirit is the light of Christ administered by the Holy Ghost. The actual reception of the Holy Ghost as a constant companion is received after the rebirth, and adds a powerful dimension of revelation and other greater spiritual gifts which the Holy Spirit does not bestow.

After receiving the gift of the Holy Ghost, the Holy Spirit continues to guide and direct us as the still small voice. If we pay diligent heed to its direction we will find our spiritual power growing very quickly. The promptings increase in clarity, content, and importance. Our spiritual hearing improves as we obey its voice, and it becomes easier and easier to recognize the promptings. The greater our obedience, the greater the promptings become, until we begin to realize the presence and revelations of the Holy Ghost. It is at this stage that we begin to hear spoken words, sentences—even conversations with the source of all truth. We ask, seek, knock and receive. It is a magnificent experience, and it can be a permanent change in the lives of the obedient.

Receiving incremental installments of inspiration is not realizing the fulfillment of the gift of the Holy Ghost. The gift is only fully realized when we receive the Holy Ghost for a *constant* companion, and thus are born again, changed from a natural man to a spiritual man.

> The gift of the Holy Ghost is the *right* to have the constant companionship of the Spirit; the actual *enjoyment* of the gift, the *actual receipt of the companionship* of the Spirit, is based on personal righteousness; it does not come unless and until the person is worthy to receive it. The Spirit will not dwell in an unclean tabernacle . . . Those who actually enjoy the gift or presentation of the Holy Ghost are the ones who are born again, who have become new creatures of the Holy Ghost. (McConkie, *Mormon Doctrine*, 313; italics in original)

Understanding and becoming obedient to the Holy Spirit is essential to our spiritual growth. Being born again is essential to realizing the fulfillment of the gift of the Holy Ghost.

OBEDIENCE

The key to spiritual growth is obedience to the voice of the Holy Spirit. This message needs to be blazoned in the sky in letters a thousand feet tall. We consistently underestimate how great a role obedience plays in our spiritual progression. Spiritually, nothing is possible without it, and everything—absolutely everything—is possible with it. Until each person learns this single lesson they will falter, fumble, and fail spiritually. Until this lesson is burned into one's soul they will forever be on the spiritual outside looking in. They will look at those they admire, the prophets and apostles, the pure in heart, and those that glow with the fire of the Spirit—and admire them and wonder how they did it.

When those so blessed do reveal how it is accomplished, the inquirer often turns away in disbelief, desiring a more profound answer, some marvelous precept of great power, some pearl of great wisdom, some unfathomable mystery which by simply hearing they might also attain greatness. This truth rings forth for all who wish to be the Elect of God. Open your hearts and hear—*they learned how to obey.* Believe it or not, this is the great mystery for which you are seeking. Obey! Obey! Obey! The exalted are eternally obedient.

What is it you must obey? It is every word which proceeds forth from the mouth of God. It is the voice of the Holy Spirit, the voice of Jesus Christ. Everyone who hearkens to the voice of the Spirit comes unto God, even the Father.

> And I now give unto you a commandment to beware concerning yourselves, to give diligent heed to the words of eternal life. For you shall live by every word that proceedeth from the mouth of God. For the word of the Lord is truth, and whatsoever is truth is light, and whatsoever is light is Spirit, even the Spirit of Jesus Christ. And the Spirit giveth light to every man that cometh into the world; and the Spirit enlighteneth every man through the world, that hearkeneth

to the voice of the Spirit. And every one that hearkeneth to the voice of the Spirit cometh unto God, even the Father. (D&C 84:43–47)

Notice that I didn't say the commandments? This is not because the commandments are to be ignored. Obedience to the commandments by sheer determination and willpower has its reward, but it can be overwhelming. When you set your life in obedience to the voice of God, you will naturally, joyfully, almost without notice, be obeying all the commandments—every single one of them. And, as the above quotation teaches us, we will come unto the Father.

How many commandments are there? If you include instructions to grow a garden, repair your fences, and paint your barn, then add all the written commandments—there are thousands. You won't live long enough to obey them all. There are just too many barns that need painting in your life. So how do you ever become totally obedient when you can't possibly get to every barn and fence? It is simple, really. Listen to the voice of the Lord and He will direct you. When you are totally obedient to the will of God, you are totally obedient—even if a barn or fence remains unpainted. The reason you are totally obedient, even when a few things remain undone, is because you have an obedient spirit. If and when He sends you out to paint the barn you will obey. If He never sends you to paint the barn, you will also obey. You simply are obedient. In the end, the Lord will not judge us according to our barns; He will judge us according to our heart. When our heart is flawlessly obedient, we are judged as being flawlessly obedient, even if some obvious things never get done.

There is certain frustration awaiting anyone who attempts to perfect themselves without the aid of the Holy Spirit and empowerment of the Atonement. It is not uncommon for someone to make a list of everything they feel they should be doing in their lives, and then select a few to begin working on. As wholesome as this sounds, it will only create feelings of impotence and frustration. Read all the scriptures and nowhere is there an account of someone achieving spiritual power by making lists of needed improvements and then working the list! They all did it by obedience to the voice of the Lord. You must also, *there is no other way.* Why is it more desirable to be obedient to a list than to the voice of God? Why would we try to accomplish a divine task without divine assistance?

The Lord knows the exact course our lives should take, which sin should be eliminated first, which weakness should be addressed first, and which blessings we will need to accomplish these things. There is no need for us to create a list He already possesses. Ours could never be as inspired as His, or as gentle and caring. If we yield ourselves to His direction He will show us what to do first, and give us the power to do it. He will direct us, step by step, all along the way home.

Additionally, as we obey Him, He will change and purify our hearts. As our hearts become single to His glory, we will find the changes we thought most impossible will just quietly, sweetly occur. The patience which previously eluded us, the gentleness we never knew, the love and brotherly kindness we thought unattainable, the powerful prayers and faith we yearned for, yet never attained—all these and many more precious gifts will simply distill upon our souls.

Paul the Apostle described it this way:

> But the fruit of the Spirit is love, joy, peace, longsuffering, gentleness, goodness, faith, meekness, temperance. (Galatians 5:22–23)

What sweet solace there is in this, what peace, and hope! Not only is it gloriously possible for us to become perfect in Christ and radiate a portion of His love and perfections, it is all a gift. Note well, it is not a free gift, but it is a gift, and is given to those who love to obey Him. Again the way to perfection is not through the disciplining and reshaping of the soul by the will of man, but through the discipline of obedience, and reshaping of the soul by God. Since there is no other way, anything else we attempt in its place cannot succeed—and is not of God!

Again, to what are we to be obedient? It is the voice of the Lord in our hearts and minds. Consider Enos's testimony:

> And while I was thus struggling in the spirit, behold, the voice of the Lord came into my mind again . . . And after I, Enos, had heard these words, my faith began to be unshaken in the Lord (Enos 1:10–11)

Even the prophets and apostles receive revelation this way. The reason they became prophets was partly because they learned to obey these promptings. Consider Nephi's words on this subject. He was discussing how Isaiah, one of the greatest of the Old Testament prophets, received the revelations he recorded in the book that bears his name:

> Behold they were manifest unto the prophet by the voice of the Spirit; for by the Spirit are all things made known unto the prophets (1 Nephi 22:2)

Such powerful truths, revelations, and knowledge are available to everyone who is willing to be led by the voice of the Spirit. Things are made known to the prophets this way, and things are, or at least can be, made known unto you in exactly the same way.

If you want to have revelation in your life, learn to hear and obey the voice of the Lord. This is the way God has ordained it. There is no other way. There is no other method. There is no other voice which leads unto eternal life.

It is impossible to grow spiritually beyond the level of our obedience. The Lord will bless us and grant us line upon line, right up to the line on which we choke. For example, if we refuse to respond to a prompting to drive within the speed limit, then our spiritual acuity is indeed stunted. If we stumble on something larger, like refusing a church assignment when prompted to accept, we stunt our growth at this level by our unwillingness to obey. We damn ourselves from further growth until the Lord again calls and finally finds us willing to obey His voice.

The most damaging effect of these minor transgressions and failures to yield to the enticings of the Holy Spirit, is it disqualifies us from further revelation until we are ready to be obedient. It doesn't matter how desperate our need becomes, if we are disqualified, the heavens are sealed until we humble ourselves and are again obedient.

The process of spiritual growth need not be like chewing rocks. Since the only thing that limits us is our ability to obey, then a sincere commitment to obedience will cause one's growth to become meteoric, until the next level of discomfort is reached and we again find some new command we are not (yet) willing to obey. This spiritual growth can be so fast that it is breathtaking. We can at times attain spiritual power so fast that we may actually beg the Lord to give us a chance to assimilate all we have learned before He rockets us higher. Consider the lives of those whom the scriptures testify achieved spiritual greatness. For most of them it was but a short trip from catching fish to becoming fishers of men, a short trip from childhood to visionary, to ship builder, to prophet, a short trip from a lad of fourteen, to one familiar with the face of the Lord.

Obedience is always the correct response.

A friend of mine coined this phrase in a sacrament meeting talk she gave. It so succinctly summarizes the gospel of exaltation that it needs to be engraved on the cornerstone of every building in Zion. It is so simple that the spiritually immature may scoff, yet those who have pierced the heavens know of its absolute truth and power. The Master calls, and those who flawlessly obey, the Master exalts.

Every spiritual giant started life as a natural man. The course from natural man to spiritual man need only be as long and torturous as it takes for us to learn obedience. For those whose flaws preclude absolute obedience, exaltation is an absolute impossibility.

PERSONAL REVELATION

In order to continue to prepare to be born again, we must become fluent in the language of the Holy Spirit and personal revelation.

Personal revelation defines the straight and narrow path upon which we are to journey home. There is no other path or course of life by which we can reach exaltation. No one will accidentally wander through life and find themselves exalted in the end.

There are many forms of revelation: the still small voice, burning in the bosom when truth is presented, bursts of understanding, dreams, visions, personal visitations, patriarchal blessings, flashes of insight, prophetic words in priesthood blessings—and many others. All these means are employed from time to time, but most often it is the still small voice which communicates the will of God. All revelation comes through our mind and heart unless, due to special reasons known only to the Lord, he chooses to open a vision, or send a messenger. As discussed earlier, even the prophets of God receive revelation this way.

> Yea, behold, I will tell you in your mind and in your heart, by the Holy Ghost, which shall come upon you and which shall dwell in your heart. Now, behold, this is the spirit of revelation; behold, this is the spirit by which Moses brought the children of Israel through the Red Sea on dry ground. (D&C 8:2–3)

Paint this picture in your mind. Moses is standing on the bank of the Red Sea surrounded by thousands of terrified people, crying and begging him to save their lives, and threatening to betray him. The most powerful army of that time is bearing down on them to slaughter them all. As Moses stands there the Holy Ghost whispers:

"Lift up thy rod and smite the waters, and they will divide." Without hesitation, he steps forward and strikes the waters with his staff and they part before him as he watches in calm gratitude.

Imagine Joseph Smith languishing in Liberty Jail, kneeling amid the cold and filth, praying with all the power of his soul. He begs the Lord, and pleads, "God, where art thou? and where is the pavilion that covereth Thy hiding place?" (D&C 121:1). And, thus begins one of the most powerful revelations we have. How did that prayer get on paper? And, how did the response of the Lord get written down? How did a searching prayer become scripture? It happened as most revelation happens. The Lord simply prompted. "Arise, and write." Joseph obeyed, and as the words tumbled from his own heart he wrote them down, and as the Lord spoke comfort to his soul and poured forth profound revelation, Joseph wrote it down. There were no angels visible. The Lord didn't appear to Joseph—just a quiet voice in his mind and a burning in his heart. Joseph's life was filled with this type of revelation. He translated the Book of Mormon and made penned revelation this way. The major part of the Doctrine and Covenants came this way. He preached, prophesied, and lived his life after this manner.

TRIALS AND OPPOSITION

Our journey to the rebirth will not be unopposed. It is occasionally said: "The Lord could have merely assigned us to our respective rewards because He knows how we will come out. But we needed to come to this life to prove ourselves to ourselves, not to Him." While this statement sounds true, it is incomplete, and barely scratches the surface of the purpose of this life. Only a small part of what we are doing in this life is proving ourselves. The largest part is developing the attributes of godliness, or in other words, growing to become like Christ.

The Lord could not have taken us from our premortal state, clothed us in a body, and exalted us even if He knew we would eventually be worthy of such a gift.. The reason is we were not at all like Him. We were immature, inexperienced, untried, unrefined, and unworthy. We understood nothing of faith (for we dwelled in the presence of God). We knew nothing of pain, physical suffering, birth, death, disease, hunger, thirst, fatigue, torture, torment, tyranny, temptation, or a thousand other things. These refinements and experiences can come only through mortal trials and opposition

Why must we experience the vicissitudes of life? There are at least two reasons: First, in future worlds as gods ourselves, we will be guiding our own children through similar events on their way to godhood, and we must call upon our own experiences to give us compassion, wisdom, and judgment. Even Christ had to "descend below all things" so that He would know how to be the light of the world.

Second, most growth is attained at great expense. The process of life and opposition molds and shapes the soul. Pain and suffering of life builds character and turns our hearts to God for guidance. The guidance of the Spirit refines, purifies, and perfects. In this life, we are born into spiritual darkness with only the light of Christ to cause us to seek greater light.

Due to our status as natural men and women, we generally lead our lives in a self-gratifying manner until we find ourselves on the left hand of God, wandering down some forbidden path, trembling with fear and stumbling in darkness. The pain we experience can become so exquisite that we fall to the ground and cry like infants, begging God to deliver us from the darkness and agony into which we have wandered. God lets us suffer just long enough that we develop a determination to seek the light again. He then grants us direction, a whisper of hope, a glimpse of His love, and we begin to claw our way back into the light.

It is the fight to return to the light that strengthens spiritual muscles and sets righteous resolve in immutable stone. The scars on our soul remind us of what we left behind, and how glorious the deliverance has been. The lifted burdens teach us the value of the Atonement and the immense love of God. The blessed relief gives us the compassion to turn and warn our neighbors. It is the trials of this vale of tears that ultimately make us worthy to return home.

Faith, Hope, and Charity

Moroni, the last, great prophet in the Book of Mormon, devotes the entire chapter of Ether 12, and part of Moroni 7, to teaching us about faith, hope, and charity and how to attain them. Moroni, like Nephi of old, understood the tremendous joy and necessity of obtaining these gifts.

Nephi's vision of the tree of life teaches us how to partake of the joyous fruits of charity by walking the straight path to the tree of life, which represents the love of God, or charity.

Moroni is speaking of that same process, a divinely ordained sequence of events leading up to the tree of life, or as Moroni described it, faith, hope, and charity.

Faith

We previously discussed faith (see "Faith in Christ"), and already understand faith is a gift given because of personal righteousness. It is a gift of the Spirit that infuses the soul of the obedient. The greater our association with the Holy Spirit, the greater is our faith. Therefore, the more obedient we become to the promptings of the Holy Spirit, the greater will be our contact with the divine, and our faith will grow proportionately. The key then to developing faith is the same process as developing personal revelation, and that is obedience to the promptings of the Holy Spirit. All of us begin life small and fearful and wonder if we can remain faithfully on the path.

Homecoming by John M. Pontius

With eyes uplifted I was born,
With gifted faith and by fear torn,
To paths of life with sorrow strewn,
In solid stone of conflict hewn.

And from my youthful vantage thought
The road seemed awfully steep and hot,
And wondered if I'd one day breach
The path, or distant summit reach.

I ran at first with youthful fire.
And despite desire, I soon did tire,
And stopped at crossroads halfway there
To gaze down new roads broad and fair.

Where others met me on their way
To find the road where riches lay.
They beckoned me to join them there.
Their mocking laughter filled the air.

The Spirit stirred within my heart.
The lofty goal my soul did chart.
The path was steep and bones did lay
Where weary souls had gone astray.

O'er rock and cliff and crag I climbed,
For years, 'til life's last bell had chimed.
Reborn by grace a worthy soul
I'd gained much more than journey's goal.

His face I knew, His voice I'd heard,
He'd granted me the surer word.
Much brighter view, the veil now gone.
Lost memories sweet rush on and on.

"Come to my arms," I heard Him say.

"Thou faithful son come here to stay."
With loved ones near, no need to roam.
 I knew this place—I had come home.

Hope

The greater our faith becomes, the greater our endowment of hope. Hope is also a gift of the Spirit. Faith precedes hope, which comes as a natural result of faith.

Moroni begins his powerful teaching on hope by reminding us of the promise of God by quoting the prophet Ether.

> Wherefore, whoso believeth in God might with surety hope for a better world, yea, even a place at the right hand of God, which hope cometh of faith, maketh an anchor to the souls of men, which would make them sure and steadfast, always abounding in good works, being led to glorify God. (Ether 12:4)

Moroni is telling us that anyone who has faith in God "might with surety" hope for exaltation. The term "might" means it is possible, or at some point will occur. The term "with surety" means this knowledge is revealed. A non-revealed feeling of hope would be the byproduct of logic. We know we are keeping the commandments, and generally feel good about ourselves. In this light, we hope we are acceptable unto God, and hope for a place in the kingdom of God.

A surety of hope, or revealed hope, would occur when the Holy Ghost communicates to us that we *are* acceptable, that the course of our life *is* pleasing to God. Thereafter, we would have *hope*, a revealed assurance of acceptability that exceeds normal hope in that it is an actual knowledge.

Hence, the prophet Joseph Smith says that to acquire faith sufficient to exalt them, men must gain the actual knowledge that the course of life which they are pursuing is according to the will of God.

An actual knowledge to any person that the course of life which he pursues is according to the will of God is essentially necessary to enable him to have that confidence in God, without which no person can obtain eternal life. It was this that enabled the ancient saints to endure all their afflictions and persecutions . . . knowing (not believing merely) that they had a more enduring substance." (Smith, *Lectures on Faith*, 57)

When one receives this sublime assurance that the course of life one is pursuing is pleasing to God, the additional gift of hope has been instilled in the soul. Hope, like faith, is a gift of God. Like faith, it will evaporate without the constant influence of the Holy Spirit. *Hope is an assurance born of revealed knowledge that you are worthy, acceptable, and on the straight and narrow path.* It is not a promise of eternal life, nor is it a remission of sins. It is an assurance that you are on the path to those goals.

How does this blessed revelation come? The same way Moses knew how to divide the Red Sea. "Behold I will tell you in your mind and in your heart" (D&C 8:2). Moroni says hope will make the recipient "sure and steadfast, always abounding in good works, being led to glorify God" (Ether 12:4).

Humility

Humility is one of the attribute changes the Holy Ghost effects within us when we experience the mighty change. It is also a gift of the Spirit, and a source of great power.

A great insight on humility is recorded by the prophet Helaman concerning the true members of the church in his day. They were undergoing persecution by those who considered themselves good members, but who resented their humility and obedience. He records:

Nevertheless they did fast and pray oft, and did wax

stronger and stronger in their humility, and firmer and firmer in their faith of Christ, unto the filling their souls with joy and consolation, yea even to the purifying and the sanctification of their hearts, which sanctification cometh because of their yielding their hearts unto God. (Helaman 3:35)

Does it strike you as a contradiction in terms to say "stronger and stronger in humility?" How can humility be strength? It is because yielding to the promptings of the Holy Spirit is an act of humility that brings spiritual strength. It is subordinating our will to Christ's. It is cheerfully using our agency, our freedom, to abandon our will to His. More specifically, His will becomes ours in that the desires of our hearts are to do as He would do. As we recognize and obey the promptings of the Holy Spirit we experience the powerful, life-changing events that follow in rapid succession. Our views become clearer and clearer until the mists of darkness that periodically shroud the straight and narrow path no longer have the power to blind us. The world and its enticements lose their appeal. We yearn for the joy of His presence. And we become stronger and stronger in our humility and obedience to His voice.

Yielding to the promptings of the Holy Spirit brings great joy and consolation into the soul, and eventually effects the sanctification and purification of the rebirth. Such promises, such sublime possibilities, are held out to those who learn to hear and obey. And as Helaman testifies, it all comes because of our yielding our hearts unto God.

There comes a time when it requires very little faith to obey a prompting because we have experienced how obeying promptings always, always works miracles in our lives and in the lives of others. We begin to hunger and thirst after more light and knowledge, begging the Lord to use us, to direct and lead us to the next assignment. Our spiritual hearing improves until we hear, understand, and obey every word that proceeds forth from the mouth of God. Thereafter, we begin to receive greater direction, answers to prayers, new and vital understandings about scripture, visions, dreams, prophecies, and power in the priesthood. Different people have different spiritual gifts and manifest different blessings. Whatever these gifts may be, they are astoundingly beautiful. Virtue garnishes our thoughts unceasingly. Our confidence waxes strong in the presence of God, and the doctrine of the priesthood distills upon our souls as the dews from Heaven. We become, in fact, "stronger and stronger in [our] humility, firmer and firmer in the faith of Christ, unto the filling [of our] souls with joy and consolation."

From Nephi's vision of the tree of life we learn and understand that the greatest joy and consolation the human soul can receive is charity, the pure love of Christ (see "The Tree," above).

CONFIDENCE IN PRAYER

Hope gives the recipient confidence in prayer, power in living, and an overwhelming sense of the goodness of God, which would naturally lead one to glorify God.

So many of the prayers we utter begin with a string of apologies and petitions for forgiveness. While this is generally appropriate, consider a prayer where your first perception is one of acceptance. Imagine how your heart would soar as you address your Father in Heaven. Imagine the humility and gratitude you would feel toward Him from whom you had received acknowledgment of your acceptability before God. You would feel welcome there.

> Paul the apostle described it thus: "Let us therefore come boldly unto the throne of grace, that we may obtain mercy, and find grace to help in time of need." (Hebrews 4:16)

As one who possess hope, and knows of a surety of your worthiness, your prayers will take on an aspect of confidence you have never felt before. You will quickly find that the same still small voice with which you have become familiar now directs your prayers. Such divine direction instills powerful faith that your petition has been heard and answered. You will feel joy and acceptance in the presence of God, and your prayers will lengthen and deepen in meaning and sincerity. Your daytime thoughts will naturally gravitate unto prayer. As you drift off to sleep at night, you will feel your soul soaring in prayer, and you will have the sleep of angels.

WEAKNESS BECOMES STRENGTH

Moroni then draws his teaching together with these potent words of the Savior:

> And if men come unto me I will show unto them their weakness. I give unto men weakness that they may be humble; and my grace is sufficient for all men that humble themselves before me; for if they humble themselves before me, and have faith in me, then will I make weak things become strong unto them. (Ether 12:27)

How many thousands of us have struggled with our weaknesses and found the hope we needed in this verse, yet knew not how to claim its promise. To claim these promises, we must learn the message of the tree of life. Every blessing comes by clinging fast to the rod of iron. Humility is nothing more than a willingness to subordinate our will to His. When He calls, we answer. When He sends, we go. When He commands, we obey. Humility, true Christlike humility, is foreign to the natural man. Yet, as our Savior refines and purifies us, we are gifted with this in abundance. If we humble ourselves before Him, then His grace is sufficient for us. He will lovingly bless us with what we lack. We won't be perfect, but what we are will be enough.

GRACE

And what is this grace of which the scriptures testify, and because of which the Savior of mankind will give us power over our weaknesses? Nephi put it this way:

> For we labor diligently to write, to persuade our children, and also our brethren, to believe in Christ, and to be reconciled to God; for we know that it is by grace that we are saved, after all we can do. (2 Nephi 25:23)

Consider this verse:

> And we know that justification through the grace of our Lord and Savior Jesus Christ is just and true; And we know also, that sanctification through the grace of the Lord and Savior Jesus Christ is just and true, to all those who love and serve God with all their mights, minds, and strength. (D&C 20:30–31)

Elder McConkie adds this:

> All things that exist are manifestations of the grace of God. The creation of the earth, life itself, the atonement of Christ, the plan of salvation, kingdoms of immortal glory hereafter, and the supreme gift of eternal life—all these things come by the grace of Him whose we are. (McConkie, *Mormon Doctrine*, 338–39)

Grace is all these things, and more. *Grace is when the Savior gives us that which we have not earned, but that for which we have qualified.* Indeed, we cannot earn eternal life, or any other blessing. Were it not for the Atonement of the Savior paying for our sins, we could not qualify for any blessing.

Earning implies fair payment. "You work for an hour, and I'll pay you an hour's wages." If we had to accomplish what Christ has done for us, it would cost more than we could possibly pay. The price is simply too high for mortal man. We are incapable of self-generating perfection, and therefore cannot earn needed blessings. We can, however, qualify for them through obedience long before we approach anywhere near perfection.

Except for Jesus Christ himself, all who have lived fall short of the glory of God (Rom. 3:23). Even when we are as perfect as mortals may become, we are still imperfect by God's standards, and were we to receive fair payment, we would receive far less than exaltation. Without the Atonement and the grace of Jesus Christ, once we are guilty of sin, any obedience is swallowed up by our guilt. Without His grace the law demands payment we cannot make. Since only the totally pure enter His rest, without His grace, all would be excluded.

Nephi expressed it this way:

> And by the law no flesh is justified; or, by the law men are cut off. . . . They perish from that which is good, and become miserable forever. (2 Nephi 2:5)

King Benjamin exclaimed:

> I say unto you, my brethren, that if you should render all thanks and praise which your whole soul has power to possess, to that God who has created you, and has kept and preserved you, and has caused that ye should rejoice . . . I say unto you that if ye should serve him who has created you from the beginning, and is preserving you from day to day, by lending you breath, that ye may live and move and do according to your own will, and even supporting you from one moment to another—I say, if ye should serve him with all your whole souls yet ye would be unprofitable servants . . . He doth require that ye should do as he hath commanded you; for which if ye do, he doth immediately bless you; and therefore he hath paid you. And ye are still indebted unto him, and are, and will be, forever and ever; therefore, of what have ye to boast? And now I ask, can ye say aught of your-selves? I answer you, Nay. Ye cannot say that ye are even as much as the dust of the earth; yet ye were created of the dust of the earth; but behold, it belongeth to him who created you. (Mosiah 2:20–25)

Truly, a mortal cannot earn eternal life. If this were possible, there would be no need for a Savior, a plan of exaltation, a true church, or even a mortal experience. The fact that it cannot be earned is what made it necessary for a Redeemer. Christ paid the price for our sins with His Atonement, and conditioned upon our obedience, applies that payment for us. This act of love-inspired intercession in our behalf is called grace. Again, grace is when the Savior gives us that which we have not earned, but for which we have qualified by obedience to His voice and laws.

Let us read Moroni's affirmation again with our new understanding:

> And if men come unto me I will show unto them their weakness. I give unto men weakness that they may be humble; and my grace is sufficient for all men that humble themselves before me; for if they humble themselves before me, and have faith in me, then will I make weak things become strong unto them. Behold, I will show unto the Gentiles their weakness, and I will show unto them that faith, hope and charity bringeth [them] unto me [Jesus Christ]—the fountain of all righteousness. (Ether 12:27–28)

He wants us to "behold" and learn these precious truths. Faith comes as a gift of God because of obedience. Faith grows into hope, a revealed knowledge that the course of life we are pursuing is pleasing to God; which knowledge will become an anchor to our souls, making us sure and steadfast, always abounding in good works.

This great hope is a gift of God and flows naturally from faith. And as hope flows naturally from faith, so the rebirth and charity, that which is most precious and joyous to the soul, flows naturally from hope. Even so, the promise of exaltation flows forth from the rebirth, and as surely as the day follows the night, the promise of kneeling in the presence of our dear Savior and bathing His feet with our tears follows that glorious election.

Carefully consider Moroni's words.

And again, my beloved brethren, I would speak unto you concerning hope. How is it that ye can attain unto faith, save ye shall have hope? And what is it that ye shall hope for? Behold I say unto you that ye shall have hope through the atonement of Christ and the power of his resurrection, to be raised unto life eternal, and this because of your faith in him according to the promise. Wherefore, if a man have faith he must needs have hope; for without faith there cannot be any hope . . . and if a man be meek and lowly in heart, and confesses by the power of the Holy Ghost that Jesus is the Christ, he must needs have charity; . . . Wherefore, my beloved brethren, if ye have not charity, ye are nothing, for charity never faileth. Wherefore, cleave unto charity, which is the greatest of all, for all things must fail—But charity is the pure love of Christ, and it endureth forever; and whoso is found possessed of it at the last day, it shall be well with him. Wherefore my beloved brethren, pray unto the father with all the energy of heart, that ye may be filled with this love, which he hath bestowed upon all who are true followers of his Son, Jesus Christ; that ye may become the sons of God; that when he shall appear [to each of us, individually] we shall be like him, for we shall see him as he is; that we may have this hope; that we may be purified even as he is pure. Amen. (Moroni 7:40–48)

TAKE MY YOKE UPON YOU

The path to perfection is only as difficult as each person chooses to make it. If we keep letting go of the rod of iron and wandering off, then fighting our way back, it will become a task of exceeding difficulty and pain. We will battle every fault, every weakness, and every imperfection we possess, until we are bruised, bloodied, and defeated. Then, once the pain is sufficiently intense, once the anguish is seemingly permanent, once it has cost more than we could ever have realized and we have been beaten into submission by the travails of life and buffetings of Satan, then perhaps we will humbly submit ourselves to the Lord.

"Lord, I can't do this any longer. It hurts too much. I have lost so much, and gained so little. I have paid a heavy price for my rebelliousness. I cry night and day. My heart cries out in constant pain, I stumble and fall, I feel filthy and alone. But, please, please hear my plea. I will do whatever Thou wilt direct me to do. Just please forgive me, and lead me in the path of righteousness, and give me the strength to stay there, for I know the pain of the forbidden paths and yearn for the joy and rest of the righteous."

If this is your prayer, then you are ready to feast on the Savior's own words:

> Come unto me, all ye that labor and are heavy laden, and I will give you rest. Take my yoke upon you, and learn of me; for I am meek and lowly of heart: and ye shall find rest unto your souls. For my yoke is easy and my burden is light. (Matthew 11:28–30)

What a beautiful promise this is. What hope and peace is offered here. The Savior is the one commissioned to defeat Satan and the world. We can't do His work for Him. All we need do is conquer ourselves by yielding to His will. He will bear our burdens and give us rest if we just cast our burdens upon Him and take upon us His yoke.

How does one cast one's burdens upon the Lord? The answer is twofold. First, repent. When the humbled soul is ready, repentance is a fantastic relief. Second, yield yourself to His guidance through the Holy Spirit, which first manifests itself as your conscience. Depend on Him for solutions, wait upon Him for direction, and obey with all the courage and energy of your soul. Spend less energy and emotion trying to figure things out, and put that effort into developing faith and obedience. Your investment in the Lord will pay rich dividends. He is the "kindly light" that that leads us on.

Lead Kindly Light

> Lead, kindly Light, amid th' encircling gloom;
> Lead thou me on!
> The night is dark, and I am far from home;
> Lead thou me on!
> Keep thou my feet; I do no ask to see
> The distant scene—
> One step enough for me.
>
> I was not ever thus, nor pray'd that thou
> Shouldst lead me on.
> I loved to choose and see my path, but now,
> Lead thou me on!
> I loved the garish day, and, spite of fears,
> Pride ruled my will.
> Remember not past years.
>
> So long thy power hath blessed me, sure it still
> Will lead me on.
> O'er moor and fen, o'er crag and torrent, till
> The night is gone.
> And with the morn those angel faces smile,
> Which I have loved long since,
> And lost a while!
> (John Henry Newman, *Hymns*, no. 97)

Do you believe that Jesus Christ knows what is best for you and will truly bear your burdens for you? If you believe this, yet still are trying to do it all yourself, you either don't value His offer, think yourself unworthy of such help, or you don't trust Him to live up to His promises. Whatever the reason that keeps you from accepting His guidance is the very same reason that will keep you out of the celestial kingdom. Christ's way is the only way. Any other way we attempt is doomed for failure. Trust Him. He will not forsake you nor leave you stumbling, frightened, and alone.

How can we take upon ourselves Christ's yoke? We do it by learning the lesson of the tree of life and taking hold of the rod of iron. His yoke is nothing more than what He asks us to do—His revealed will to us individually. This is the rod of iron. This is the yoke He asks us to bear in His name. Compared to the yoke of worldly sorrow, confusion, pain, and doubt that we presently carry, His yoke is exceedingly light and easy to be borne. When we insist on carrying our own yoke, we do not know where it will take us, and we will sorrow the whole trip. When we accept His yoke, we know precisely where it takes us, and we walk the path with joyful steps and a peaceful heart.

If we do this, He will bear our burdens, not in the sense that they will disappear or even lessen in intensity. Indeed, the adversary may be stimulated to greater efforts against us when he sees our obedience. But still the promises are profoundly true. The Lord will direct us through every obstacle of life, and give us strength unimagined before. He will be our guide, comfort, and stay. He will give us work to do which will be of eternal consequence, and in our obedience we will "wax stronger and stronger in [our] humility, and firmer and firmer in the faith of Christ, unto the filling [of our] soul with joy and consolation." (Helaman 3:35).

And what is this consolation that the Lord will give us? It is the great comfort of knowing the prize is worth infinitely more than the price. It is the blessed relief that fills the souls of the righteous, those who know their suffering and travail has obtained for them a promise of eternal reward. It is the peace of knowing we are being lovingly led through the furnace of our afflictions by the kindly light of His Holy Spirit. It is the supreme joy of knowing our place in His Kingdom is sure.

Charity

We have previously discussed charity (see "The Tree," above). It is the love that fills the Savior's heart and caused Him to give his life for us. When we are blessed to have this divine attribute infused into our souls, it is the most joyful and desirable of all things. It purifies and quickens the soul, making the recipient courageous, yet loving and gentle.

Charity comes into our hearts when we are worthy of it. Charity is experienced in fleeting amounts as one draws nearer to the time of the rebirth, and given as a grand enhancement to the soul when one is born again. Thereafter, charity fills the soul as long as worthiness remains. In due time, when one is blessed to have one's calling and election made sure, a greater endowment of charity is given. Such is also true when one is ushered into the presence of the Lord.

While charity is primarily a blessing of divine love, and fills the soul with joy, it has the unexpected effect of making the recipient fearless. This glorious courage causes the recipient to take rapid and boldly obedient strides forward.

This aspect of the divine gift of charity strikes each individual differently, causing some to accept callings they never would have otherwise, or perhaps to become a fearless missionary. It may cause the recipient to abandon timidity and previously unconquerable fear, or to accept trials and persecution with saintly patience. However it manifests itself, it is the most comforting of all feelings. This blessing is so sweet that the Holy Ghost claims one of his titles because of it—the Comforter. Charity casts glaring light into the dark, scary corners of our world.

Moroni, who knew and wrote so much about this perfect and powerful love, makes this single reference to the fearlessness it engenders.

> Behold, I speak with boldness, having authority from God; and I fear not what man can do; for perfect love casteth out all fear. (Moroni 8: 16)

Charity also causes one to see the world through spiritual eyes, and, in a limited way, to enjoy the Savior's perspective of our world. Suddenly, most of what was of great importance appears as children's toys of little significance. Much of what previously enticed and excited us falls behind a velvet curtain of righteous desire, and the enormity of the goodness of God opens to our view, as if it were a glorious sunrise of surpassing beauty, in expanse as broad as eternity. We walk away from our previous lives enthralled by the glory of the path before us, and the purity of the love we feel firing our souls. Blessed with a glimpse into eternity, we can see nothing but the straight and narrow path, and our feet fall joyfully within its confines, making that straight and narrow path as broad as the highway upon which rides the chariot of God. Purified, our souls seek and find the throne of God in mighty prayer and worship so pure it joins the angels of heaven in singing His praise.

In divinely inspired prayer, we receive even as we ask, and rejoice in miracles newly born. In knocking as one true and faithful in all things and seeking further light and knowledge, in the due time of the Lord, the gates of heaven open before us to reveal to our view the glories of His perfection, and our souls expand with that joy which surpasses the understanding of man.

CHAPTER FOUR

Rebirth of the Spirit

REBIRTH OF THE SPIRIT

In the previous chapter, we explored how to prepare for the rebirth. When we take these steps with real intent, a powerful change occurs in our lives.

Being born again, being changed from the carnal and fallen state of a natural man into the righteous state of a spiritual man, is the first hallmark of spiritual greatness. The scriptures refer to it by many names because it works many vast and glorious changes upon the soul. It is referred to as being "filled with hope and perfect love," because charity is the blessed love that permeates the soul of the recipient. (Moroni 8:26) It is referred to as being "born again," because we receive gifts of the Spirit that change us from a natural being to a spiritual man or woman. (Mosiah 3:19) It is called being "sanctified by the reception of the Holy Ghost" because it is at that point our sins are forgiven (3 Nephi 27:20)

It is referred to as having your soul "filled with joy" because that is what happens. (Mosiah 4:3) It is called "being filled with the Holy Ghost" because you feel the glow of his presence constantly thereafter. (Alma 36:24) It is called the "baptism of fire and the Holy Ghost," because the Holy Ghost baptizes the person in spiritual fire, which purifies and cleanses. (2 Nephi 31:13) It is called "receiving a remission of sins," because it is at this point that one realizes a total remission of their sins. (Moses 6:59) It is called "becoming the sons and daughters of God," because this spiritual rebirth brings one into the spiritual family of Jesus Christ (Mosiah 5:7, 25–29).

The Lord named this mighty event with divine wisdom. Being born again is a mighty change (Alma 5:12–14). It is much, much more than a spiritual mile marker along the path. It is qualifying to have the Holy Ghost become your constant companion and work a change within your soul that defies the power of language to describe. The change is so profound it creates a new person who has no more desire to do evil, but to do good continually (Mosiah 5:2). A new child is thereby born, a spiritual infant—pure, clean, loving, and obedient. The old person of sin is simply burned away by the purifying influence of the Holy Ghost, and all that is left is this new creature of Christ. (Romans 6:6) Gone is much of the pettiness, the selfishness, the powerful motivations to please and titillate the flesh. We are gifted with a willingness to submit to all things which the Lord sees fit to allow us to experience. We become as a child, submissive, meek, humble, patient and full of love. (Mosiah 3:19) These impure attributes are largely removed at the rebirth.

However, this is not a state of perfection, it is a state of sanctification that burns the dross from the soul and leaves purity in its wake. Because of the power of this event, the nature of the person is changed so he or she no longer desires sin. We remain mortal, and subject to mortal temptations, except that most of our impure motives have been burned away, and without the inclination to sin, former temptations lose their power. This state of purity remains as long as the person endures faithfully thereafter (see "The Honeymoon Period," above). Abandoning the path of light would plunge him back into spiritual darkness, and the urgings of the flesh would return again with renewed power. While the person thus reborn finds himself purified, perfection (such as can be attained in this life) still lies in the future. But the rebirth change is the first major step toward the ultimate goal of perfection.

This powerful cleansing does not create a vacuum. In the place of impurity comes the warm and purifying glow of charity, a flood of faith, and a perspective on life that is eternal in orientation. Born anew is a spiritual infant of faith, dignity, and righteousness.

This powerful change is so startlingly real, so magnificently potent, so wonderfully life-enriching, it is called "the mighty change" in the scriptures.

Even though it is a powerful change, few people realize they have been born again until later in life when the Lord causes them to reflect upon the past. The Lord has not revealed why this is His plan. Perhaps, it is to keep us humbly striving forward rather than stopping to feel pride in our achievements, or becoming lax along the way.

The question then begs to be answered—"Have I been born again?" There are two great witnesses that may be called to answer this question. The first is the essence and fabric of your soul. If your life is filled with charity; if you have no more desire to sin; if your love of God approaches adoration; if your soul yearns for and rejoices in prayer; if the scriptures speak joy to your soul; if the Holy Ghost is your constant companion; if your primary motivation is no longer to accumulate wealth, power, position, worldly acclaim, or honor, but to serve God—if all these things are true without exception, then you have been born again and did not know it.

The second great witness is the very source of truth that becomes the constant companion of those reborn. Inquire of God if you have been born again, and, if you have the courage and spiritual acuity to hear the answer, He will reveal the truth to you through the Holy Ghost. If you have so ordered your life that you can ask such a question and receive the answer, you have either received the rebirth, or it will not be far distant.

The greater question may be—"Have I retained the blessings of the rebirth?" (see the whole of Alma 5, particularly verses 26–27). If you felt these refinements at one time, but no longer do, then you have fallen back, and must again earn the blessings of the rebirth. It makes no difference if you once experienced the rebirth if you have slipped from that blessing and do not presently possess the attendant refinements. Even if you once experienced it, the straight and narrow path again lies before you, and the rod of iron will guide you just as surely toward your goal the second time.

The Lord told Nicodemus:

> Except a man be born again, he cannot see the kingdom of God. (John 3:3)

Alma taught:

> Now I say unto you that ye must repent and be born again; for the Spirit saith if ye are not born again ye cannot inherit the kingdom of heaven. (Alma 7:14)

> And the Lord said unto me: Marvel not that all mankind, yea, men and women, all nations, kindreds, tongues and people, must be born again; yea, born of God, changed from their carnal and fallen state, to a state of righteousness, being redeemed of God, becoming his sons and daughters; And thus they become new creatures; and unless they do this, they can in nowise inherit the kingdom of God. (Mosiah 27:25–26)

These verses should end all debate on the subject of the necessity of being born again. Being born again is not optional.

For persons who never knew the gospel truths in this life, it is undoubtedly possible to accomplish these things in the next. In the case of those who know the gospel plan, who have read the scriptures, who should understand and be living by what those scriptures teach, who have been given the gift of the Holy Ghost—"awful is the state" of such people who procrastinate the day of their repentance.

> But wo unto him that has the law given, yea, that has all the commandments of God, like unto us, and that transgresseth them, and that wasteth the days of his probation, for awful is his state! (2 Nephi 9:27)

This is the day of our probation. We are emphatically told that now is the time for us to perform our labors.

> For behold, this life is the time for men to prepare to meet God; yea, behold the day of this life is the day for men to perform their labors. (Alma 34:32)

We were granted this life as a time to perform our labors and qualify for an eternal reward. Those of us who have the truth must not delay the rebirth until the next life. Let us, therefore, not waste the days of our probation.

How can we heed the warning and make ourselves worthy of the rebirth? There should be no mystery to it. We simply allow the Holy Spirit to guide us into total obedience, which calls forth profound blessings.

It is worth noting again that being born again and faithfully enduring to the end in that state of righteousness, are the minimum requirements to enter the celestial kingdom. Once a person earns this blessing, they will be afforded the opportunity to continue their progression after this life. That is, they will be able to complete their labors, if they so desire, and qualify for a place in the highest degree of the celestial kingdom.

Occasionally, people are blessed to experience the rebirth with a full understanding of what is happening to them. This has happened to individuals and to groups of people. The exact number is not recorded, but apparently thousands of King Benjamin's people received the rebirth simultaneously, and very dramatically.

King Benjamin, the ancient Nephite prophet/king, lived his life serving God and his people. As he was nearing the end of his life, he was instructed by an angel of the Lord to deliver a powerful sermon to his people to instruct them in how to experience this mighty change. His words were so powerful that everyone who heard them was filled with the Holy Ghost and experienced the mighty change.

After King Benjamin had concluded his powerful address, the people were so touched

> They all cried with one voice, saying: Yea, we believe all the words which thou hast spoken unto us; and also, we know of their surety and truth, because of the Spirit of the Lord Omnipotent, which has wrought a mighty change in us, or in our hearts, that we have no more disposition to do evil, but to do good continually. (Mosiah 5:2)

Again, the necessary attitude changes, the walking away from sin, and the constant motivation to do good are all spiritual refinements accomplished not by the individual but by Christ through the Holy Spirit. The price we must pay to experience these spiritual refinements is total obedience to the voice of God.

It is no wonder that some would-be Saints walk away from the battle doubting they can do it. The fact of the matter is that by themselves, they cannot. Unaided by the Holy Spirit, neither can anyone else. The divine truth is that God has ordained a way for all to accomplish these things, a way that is within the abilities of us all. If we are willing to obey the Holy Spirit, Christ will change us so we become pure and holy, worthy of the rebirth and all other blessings. If you do not understand this simple, lifesaving truth—that Jesus Christ through the Holy Spirit makes the changes in our hearts as we become obedient—it could seem hopeless when you view the magnitude of your imperfections.

Think again upon the tree of sin in the driveway. It is contrary to the economy of God's plan to try to conquer each individual shortcoming by our own genius and willpower. He promises that if we will yield to the enticings of the Holy Spirit, He will work a mighty change in us, which will remove our disposition to do evil, and thus the tree will die, and the master gardener will rip it from our soul, roots and all.

This mighty change was so significant that King Benjamin's people were:

> Willing to enter into a covenant with our God to do his will, and to be obedient to his commandments in all things that he shall command us, all the remainder of our days. (Mosiah 5:5)

Remember, these were church members. This was a renewal or reaffirmation of their baptismal covenant. *Such is required of all people before they receive the rebirth.* It is made during mighty prayer and is the result of a rock-solid resolve. This covenant is more than sincere, it is a prophetic statement of fact. (Meaning the Holy Spirit has prepared you, and now is prompting you to make this covenant. The statement thus becomes prophetic.) You will obey! Your soul is set upon a course from which you will not depart. For all the remainder of your days, and on into eternity, you will obey. Imagine King Benjamin's joy as he raised his arms and pronounced this great benediction upon the people.

> And now, because of the covenant which ye have made ye shall be called the children of Christ, his sons, and his daughters; for behold, this day he hath spiritually begotten you; for ye say that your hearts are changed through faith on his name; therefore, ye are born of him and have become his sons and his daughters. (Mosiah 5:7)

BECOMING SONS AND DAUGHTERS OF CHRIST

There is powerful imagery in these words that must be understood. Being born again is a literal term. We are talking about a birth process parallel to the mortal experience of birth. Due to their renewed covenant to obey Christ's every command, King Benjamin's people were spiritually begotten, spiritually conceived, the seeds of eternal life planted by Jesus Christ through the Holy Spirit. They understood that these commands would consist of every word which proceeds forth from the mouth of God (D&C 84:44), which is the word of God in its every form—written or revealed. They covenanted to obey them all. Because of this, the Lord worked a mighty change in their hearts. They were born again and thus became His sons and His daughters.

This rebirth imagery is so profound that many times in the scriptures the term "become as a little child," refers to the rebirth process. Remember, anyone who is born again experiences the mighty change and is purified and literally changed to have the desirable attributes of a child. They become humble, meek, and submissive—all these and more.

Those reborn are spiritually adopted by Jesus. They have qualified for a place in the great celestial family of Christ. However, this qualification is conditional upon faithfully enduring to the end, and is a precursor to having one's calling and election made sure.

This process of becoming the spiritual offspring of Christ is so important that one cannot be exalted without it. Christ is the spiritual father of the righteous. He has provided a way through the Atonement that we may become like Him, and once again be worthy to enter into the presence of the Father. When we finally qualify for a place in the kingdom, we become Christ's spiritual offspring, His sons and His daughters. Having been adopted into His spiritual family, we take upon ourselves His name, just as an adopted earthly child takes upon himself the name of his new parents.

Baptism is the ordinance that begins the rebirth process. When the baptismal covenant is sealed by the Holy Spirit of promise and becomes fully effective, we will be cleansed from all our sins. When the gift of the Holy Ghost is sealed by the Holy Spirit of promise, then we will have been born again.

King Benjamin continues his great discourse by telling his people that because they have taken upon themselves the name of Christ, they have become His sons and daughters. Having entered the spiritual family of Christ, He becomes their head. In other words, He is the head of the family in which they are saved. As such, they have a spiritual birthright, which is a place of honor in their Father's Kingdom.

> And under this head [meaning their spiritual father, Christ] ye are made free, and there is no other head whereby ye can be made free. There is no other name given whereby salvation cometh; therefore, I would that ye should take upon you the name of Christ, all ye that have entered into the covenant with God that ye should be obedient unto the end of your lives. (Mosiah 5:8)

We partake of the Sacrament, and thereby renew our covenants that we "are willing to take upon [ourselves] the name of Christ."

Consider the words of Moses:

> That by reason of transgression cometh the fall, which fall bringeth death, and inasmuch as ye were born into the world by water, and blood, and spirit, which I have made, and so became of dust a living soul, even so ye must be born again into the kingdom of heaven, of water, and of the Spirit, and be cleansed by blood, even the blood of mine Only Begotten. (Moses 6:59)

We enter this world as natural men through the natural birth process, which consists of the water and blood of our mothers, and our own spirit. Likewise, we must be born again as spiritual beings in a similar, though spiritual, process: through the waters of baptism, the guidance and purification of the Holy Ghost, and the blood of the Savior.

ENDURING TO THE END

After this powerful rebirth of the Spirit we must faithfully endure to the end. This might seem odd in that we will have experienced the mighty change and will have no more desire to do evil. Why warn us to endure to the end? Wouldn't it be second nature to us, after so many blessings?

Being reborn is not to receive the guarantee of eternal life, or to have your calling and election made sure. As discussed above, the rebirth can be experienced multiple times until we can dedicate ourselves to that degree of obedience that qualifies us for the greater gifts.

It is not uncommon for people to experience the rebirth more than one time. This generally happens because they go through a period of dedication in their lives, such as serving a mission, and qualify for the rebirth and receive the blessings all without realizing what they accomplished or how they did it. Shortly after the rebirth, Satan resumes with increased power, and without this vital knowledge, many people fail to maintain their obedience and consequently fall from the blessings.

Part of the purpose of this book is to highlight the path with sufficient plainness that we may walk it with a full understanding of what we are doing. Once the blessings are bestowed, we will know both what we have done and how we did it. We will also know how to maintain the blessing through continued obedience.

Note well this warning: The rebirth is generally more difficult to accomplish the second (or third) time. Sinning against the greater light has greater consequences.

Here is another warning as well: To endure righteously is to press forward. To be born again is not an end point, nor is it a place to relax or stop. It is a new door, a new beginning, a new world of spiritual opportunity. The command is to be born again and endure to the end in that state of spiritual attunement. To endure means to continue with the level of obedience and valiance that brought you unto this blessed state. Enduring to the end in a state of spiritual stagnation will not qualify anyone for eternal life.

Merely continuing as an active member of the church who has not received the rebirth may not be the type of enduring to the end which exalts. Every living person endures to the end of their life. They endure whatever life presents, then they die. There is no exaltation in this. We are commanded to become sanctified and then maintain that sanctified state unto the end of our lives. This is the enduring to the end which exalts. It is a false "All is well in Zion" doctrine that causes one to believe that enduring to the end of a life filled with mediocre obedience and dormant faith will exalt. This false notion is part of the grand deception that keeps so many virgins blissfully unwise and unfit for the Kingdom.

> I know that if ye shall follow the Son, with full purpose of heart . . . repenting of your sins, witnessing unto the Father that ye are willing to take upon you the name of Christ, by baptism . . . then [after all these things] shall ye receive the Holy Ghost; yea, then cometh the baptism of fire and of the Holy Ghost; and then [after the baptism of fire] can ye speak with the tongue of angels, and shout praises unto the Holy One of Israel [which is pure praise and worship] . . . Wherefore, ye must press forward, with a steadfastness in Christ, having a perfect brightness of hope [which is revealed knowledge of worthiness], and a love of God and of all men [which is charity], Wherefore if ye shall press forward feasting upon the words of Christ [which is personal revelation], and endure to the end [in this state of righteousness], behold, saith the Father: Ye shall have eternal life [which is to have your calling and election made sure]. (2 Nephi 31:13, 20)

This scripture plainly manifests the necessary order of the spiritual events that bring us these greater blessings. This order is the same for every person in every age. There are intermediary steps, but the process never varies, nor is there any other way.

1. Faith
2. Repentance
3. Baptism
4. Gift of the Holy Ghost
5. Baptism of fire (which is to be born again)
6. Then we can speak with the tongue of angels
7. Calling and election made sure
8. Endure to the end

> And now, behold, my beloved brethren, this is the way; and there is *none other way* nor name given under heaven whereby man can be saved in the kingdom of God. And now, behold, this is the doctrine of Christ, and the only and true doctrine of the Father, and of the Son, and of the Holy Ghost, which is one God, without end. Amen. (2 Nephi 31:21, emphasis added)

After having obtained the Baptism of Fire, we must press forward, enduring to the end. If we do this the time will come when the Father proclaims: "Ye shall have eternal life," which literally constitutes having your calling and election made sure. If a person were to die sometime between having been born again and the blessed assurance of exaltation, if that person were enduring faithfully, the person would still qualify for eternal life. If we are blessed to continue living long enough after being born again, and we endure faithfully, the time will come when we will have our calling and election made sure.

The Rebirth—Process or Event

Much energy has been spent in debating whether the rebirth is a process or an event. The intensity of the debate overstates the significance of the question. If we accept that the rebirth is absolutely necessary, and submit ourselves to the promptings of the Holy Spirit, we will be born again regardless of the form it takes.

From the scriptures we see that the rebirth can be either a process that culminates in an event, or one lacking an event. When a person finds the courage to make absolute obedience the maxim of their lives, the rebirth lies just a short time away. To do it without this level of obedience takes years of struggle and effort.

Those who spread the process out over a lifetime, learning their lessons slowly but effectively, may not realize the rebirth event in their lives, yet still enjoy the blessings and refinements attendant to the rebirth.

It appears there are several acceptable ways to walk the straight and narrow path unto the rebirth. The ideal way is straight and narrow, entered upon knowingly, traveled with real intent, and completed with a real and unmistakable event. This makes the traveler a spiritual warrior and worker of great righteousness. The resultant knowledge makes the person "sure and steadfast, always abounding in good works, being led to glorify God" (Ether 12:4). It additionally opens the doors to further blessings, including having a calling and election made sure. It makes the traveler powerful in faith and effective in his or her priesthood power.

The other method is likewise real, and the blessings and refinements are equally operative in the lives of those who walk it. It is much longer, and spans most, if not all, of the lifetime of those who travel it. The trials experienced are longer in duration, yet often less intense. The spiritual blessings are the same, but spread out over many years of time, thus making them less recognizable, and consequently, less rejoiced over.

That which is lost, however, is of great worth. Lost is the surety of purpose and powerful service of the other method. Lost is the opportunity to knowingly teach and involve others (including spouse and children) in the rebirth process. Lost is the powerful faith and potent priesthood power. Lost is the visibly open door to calling and election and further spiritual blessings. Yet, it is a way fully acceptable to the Lord, and one upon which the majority of His children walk. Those who successfully traverse it will enter the celestial kingdom.

Those who proceed beyond the rebirth will enter a higher reward within the celestial kingdom, and will have a proportionately greater degree of joy in this life and in the hereafter. It is not known when, or even if, the two parties will ever become equal in power. It may be that those with the greater obedience will forever enjoy the greater reward. The Lord rewards men according to their obedience and righteous desires. If their obedience continues in an accelerated pattern throughout eternity, then there may never be a equalizing of rewards received.

The process is unmistakable in either case. It is the process of learning to live by personal revelation. Throughout our lives, throughout all of humankind, the Holy Spirit labors to teach the supreme principle of obedience to the voice of the Lord.

This learning process takes the form of promptings which, if obeyed, bless and guide our lives. If disobeyed, the resultant pain should be recognized as the consequence of ignoring the promptings. Most people comment many times, "I knew that was going to happen," before it finally occurs to them why they actually knew it. Gaining a knowledge that the reason we know these things is because the Lord reveals them to us is a powerful step in the process of spiritual maturation.

The more powerful process takes exactly the length of time it requires for us to develop absolute obedience to His voice. Those who discount the need for personal revelation are not involved in either process. Those who are pressing diligently onward, and who are looking forward to the precious fruits of the tree of life, are those who have the rod of iron in a firm grip and refuse to release it. The process is punctuated by bursts of revelation that warm the soul, light the way, and foreshadow the power of the rebirth itself.

As discussed earlier, few people recognize the rebirth for what it is and continue on their way, basking in the presence of the Holy Ghost, thinking it no more than a wonderfully uplifting prayer or a joyful spiritual experience, which has lifted their spirit and somehow left them different. This, and the availability of the slower process, undoubtedly contributes to the idea that the rebirth is a process lacking an actual event.

The natural birth process begins with conception, gestation, and growth to a certain stage of maturity. Thereafter is a period of intense labor and pain which ends in a blessed birth which brings forth a pure and innocent child.

The spiritual birth process parallels this. It begins with an inception, and goes through a long gestation and growth. There follows a period of intense labor and pain, then finally a blessed event, and a pure and innocent child is born—again.

Image of God in Your Countenance

Alma gave a similarly stirring discourse to his people as King Benjamin did with his subjects. Alma pointedly asks:

> And now behold, I ask of you, my brethren of the church, have ye spiritually been born of God? Have ye received his image in your countenances? Have ye experienced this mighty change in your hearts? (Alma 5:14)

Alma was challenging his brethren to reexamine their spiritual lives. Speaking to those who had become complacent in their obedience, he asks if they have been born again and received His image in their countenance, which accompanies the mighty change of heart.

The companionship of the Holy Ghost purifies and begins to infuse the recipient with the attributes of godliness. In time, these changes are so significant that we begin to become like unto God. That is, we receive and exhibit a small portion of the perfections of God. This changing, purifying process, is so profound that when we are finally allowed into the presence of God, we will actually be like unto Him. This process is referred to as "receiving the image of God in your countenance." The outward evidence of having the image of God in your countenance is a glow of purity and spiritual greatness.

This spiritual glow is not limited to those who have been reborn. All people who are on the straight and narrow path will have a Christlike glow about them. It is most apparent in the face and eyes. It is a gift of the Spirit to be able to perceive this light in others. It is the glow of spiritual fire which lights the faces of the righteous. You can see it in the faces of all the General Authorities. You can see it in the faces of all who are spiritually mature: bishops, patriarchs, stake presidents, and many, many of your sisters and brothers.

This light in the countenance of the righteous is not visible to all. It cannot be photographed, nor is it measurable. It is visible to nonmembers who are growing spiritually, and is often the way they recognize the missionaries as true messengers, for they see the missionaries glow as they teach the gospel. This light that shines in the faces of the righteous is an indicator that they either have, or are in the process of receiving, the image of God in their countenance.

> And if your eye be single to my glory, your whole bodies shall be filled with light, and there shall be no darkness in you; and that body which is filled with light comprehendeth all things. (D&C 88:67)

When a person conforms to the voice of the Lord, darkness is swept away as the Holy Ghost fills the person with light. The more light these people enjoy, the greater their comprehension of truth, until the single purpose of their lives is to obediently serve Him from whom they have received so much.

Does it seem incomprehensible that you could change significantly enough that your motivations and the intent of your heart become single to the glory of God? If so, you still do not comprehend how powerful the changes are that the Holy Ghost makes in the soul at the rebirth. The natural man never will be single to the glory of God. The spiritual man is that way by nature. And when your eye is finally single to His glory, you will be filled with His light. When you have become purified and cleansed by the Holy Ghost, you will also have the image of God in your countenance, and once filled with such light, you may (in time) comprehend all things.

Sing the Song of Redeeming Love

Alma further questions his brethren of the church:

> If ye have experienced a change of heart, and if ye have felt to sing the song of redeeming love, I would ask, can ye feel so now? (Alma 5:26)

What is this song? For some it takes the form of a prayer that occurs for the first time somewhat before or after you experience this mighty change of heart, which is the spiritual rebirth. Having had your soul filled with the joy of pure charity and a bright awareness of the remission of your sins, you feel such a profound sense of love that you soon seek the Lord in prayer. As you kneel in humble silence, the Holy Spirit burns within until you are consumed with spiritual fire. You raise your voice as the Spirit gives utterance. Your words soon become an outpouring of worship and praise so pure it transcends speech, eclipses poetry, and is more beautiful than music.

It is the song of the angels and the incense of precious odors that ascends up before the throne of God day and night. It is the "song of redeeming love," and is sung only by those divinely inspired to sing it. It is soul-filling, and is pure, sustained revelation. It is a two-way exchange of love of the highest magnitude, and while seeming to be only moments long, may last many hours. It refines the soul as nothing else can and leaves the participant fulfilled, fed, and overjoyed. This is when you finally understand the phrase, "My cup runneth over." Ever after your prayers yearn for this celestial height, and your spoken words of praise, while pure and heartfelt, seem pallid by comparison. While we may partake of this outpouring of worship many times, it is like all other revelations and comes according to the will and timetable of God. It must be earnestly sought after to be enjoyed.

Nephi outlines the process of being born again and receiving this gift of praise. He calls it "speaking with the tongue of angels." He describes it this way:

> I know that if ye shall follow the Son, with full purpose of heart . . . repenting of your sins, witnessing unto the Father that ye are willing to take upon you the name of Christ, by baptism . . . behold, then shall ye receive the Holy Ghost; yea, then cometh the baptism of fire and of the Holy Ghost; and then can ye speak with the tongue of angels, and shout praises unto the Holy One of Israel. (2 Nephi 31:13)

Nephi sensed that his brethren were a bit confused about speaking with the tongue of angels. It is possible that the only way to understand it fully is to experience it. Therefore, he offered this additional explanation:

> Why do ye ponder these things in your hearts? Do ye not remember that I said unto you that after ye had received the Holy Ghost ye could speak with the tongue of angels? . . . feast upon the words of Christ; for behold the words of Christ will tell you all things what ye should do. (2 Nephi 32:1–3)

He is telling us to make ourselves worthy to receive the Holy Ghost, and then we will be able to speak with the tongue of angels. He wants us to feast upon the words of Christ, which is the same as yielding to the promptings of the Holy Spirit, and it will show us everything we should do to acquire this great gift.

When we finally are blessed to speak with the tongue of angels and sing the song of redeeming love, these blessings will be fruit plucked from the tree of life, which is most desirable above all things, yea and the most joyous to the soul!

Justification

Justification is a process that begins at baptism and continues throughout life. When an ordinance is justified, the Holy Ghost places his stamp of approval upon that act, and the promised blessings are bestowed. Justification of baptism thus becomes a remission of sins. Justification of the gift of the Holy Ghost becomes the constant companionship thereof. Any and all acts of the priesthood must be justified before the associated blessings and rewards are given.

While we speak of an act being justified, it is, rather, the person who is being justified in having participated in that act. Justification is the process, which culminates in a person being justified. When a person has been fully and completely justified, he will have had his calling and election made sure. That is, he will have become justified in all ordinances, covenants, contracts, bonds, and performances into which he has entered.

Justification is defined by Elder Bruce R. McConkie in this way:

> What then is the law of justification? It is simply this: "All covenants, contracts, bonds, obligations, oaths, vows, performances, connections, associations, or expectations" (D&C 132:7), in which men must abide to be saved and exalted, must be entered into and performed in righteousness so that the Holy Spirit can justify the candidate for salvation in what has been done . . . *An act that is justified by the Spirit is one that is*

sealed by the Holy Spirit of Promise, or in other words, ratified and approved by the Holy Ghost. This law of justification is the provision the Lord has placed in the gospel to assure that no unrighteous performance will be binding on earth and in heaven, and that no person will add to his position or glory in the hereafter by gaining unearned blessings. (McConkie, *Mormon Doctrine*, 408; italics in original)

Justification also has the indispensable effect of allowing imperfect people to participate in the ordinances of God when they think they are ready, and then to receive the promised blessings when they finally are. Baptism, for example, might be finally justified, and the candidate's sins remitted, many years after the ordinance was performed. Even the realization of the promises given in the temple are delayed until worthiness calls forth justification by the Holy Spirit of promise, and the blessings are bestowed.

SANCTIFICATION

The process of sanctification begins at baptism and continues until the person is fully sanctified. There are increasingly greater stages of sanctification. Sanctification parallels justification. As one is justified, or in other words, as the promised blessings of priesthood ordinances are realized, one is also sanctified. One who has experienced the rebirth of the Spirit has been sanctified by the Spirit and has become pure and saintly. It is also true that increasingly greater degrees of sanctification await those who press forward and have their calling and election made sure. A full measure of sanctification occurs when we finally become perfect in Christ, and are allowed to enter His presence.

There are several stages along the path at which time the participant is said to have been sanctified. Such is true of the rebirth, having one's calling and election made sure, and others. Even though these holy events bring with them greater degrees of sanctification, sanctification itself is more of a process than an event.

> *Sanctification* is a state of saintliness. (McConkie, *Mormon Doctrine*, 675; italics in original)

> And we know also, that sanctification through the grace of our Lord and Savior Jesus Christ is just and true to all those who love and serve God with all their mights, minds, and strength. (D&C 20:31)

Sanctification is a state of spotlessness that occurs when the Holy Ghost so touches a person's soul that the dross and unrefined are burned out of it. It is a state of purity and acceptability before God. We finally qualify for this blessing when we have so ordered our lives that we love and serve Him with all our might, minds, and strength.

> Now this is the commandment: Repent, all ye ends of the earth, and come unto me and be baptized in my name, that ye may be sanctified by the reception of the Holy Ghost, that ye may stand spotless before me at the last day. (3 Nephi 27:20)

> Now they, after being sanctified by the Holy Ghost, having their garments made white, being pure and spotless before God, could not look upon sin save it were with abhorrence; and there were many, exceedingly great many, who were made pure and entered into the rest of the Lord their God. (Alma 13:12)

When people are sanctified, they become pure and spotless, washed clean by the atoning blood of Christ, having their garments made white. They become purified by fire and the Holy Ghost. Sanctification eventually makes a person worthy to stand in the presence of God.

Even after enjoying a degree of sanctification through the rebirth, or through having our callings and elections made sure, we will be mortal still and subject to temptation and opposition of all types. We will have become pure, cleansed, and holy—not perfect. Whether a person long endures in this state of sanctification depends on his or her capacity to continue to obey.

This truth may distill a little hopelessness into some who read it. Either because they fear they may never measure up sufficiently to become pure and spotless or they fear that once sanctified they may fall therefrom and condemn themselves. Others may ascribe these perfections and promises to the prophets and assume they are not for the average member.

It is not the Holy Ghost telling them they cannot succeed, nor whispering that these blessings are reserved for a select few. The idea that all would-be saints must become pure and spotless and look upon sin with abhorrence need not make us feel hopeless. Most people know they are neither pure nor spotless, and may actually look upon sin as enticing and desirable—but forbidden. *Except for Jesus Christ, every person who has ever been sanctified previously felt impure and unworthy.* The difference is that the sanctified learned to be obedient to the promptings of the Holy Spirit (and consequently, the commandments), and thus were led and changed until they became worthy of sanctification.

Be not dismayed by the apparent enormity of the task at hand. All these wonderful changes and purity of purpose begin to happen as a natural consequence of obedience to the Lord as revealed to us by the Holy Spirit. We can either attempt to climb this mountain by ourselves—in which case it is an impossible task—or we can yield to the enticings of the Holy Spirit and let the Savior carry us up the mountain in the arms of His love.

Constant Companionship of the Holy Ghost

The laying on of hands for the gift of the Holy Ghost is in anticipation of the time when we qualify for the constant companionship of that member of the Godhead. Being born again, receiving a remission of all sins, and receiving the constant companionship of the Holy Ghost, occur simultaneously.

> The second birth begins when men are baptized in water by a legal administrator; it is completed when they actually receive the companionship of the Holy Ghost, becoming new creatures by the cleansing power of that member of the Godhead. (McConkie, *Mormon Doctrine*, 101)

Although we have discussed it many times so far, this concept bears repeating because it seems difficult for many to understand. The changes and perfections of the soul that are required of man to bring him "unto the measure of the stature of the fulness of Christ" (Ephesians 4:13)—to make us like He is—all come as a result of the refining influence of the Holy Ghost.

None of the attributes of God can be successfully imitated, nor can they be assumed by an act of will on the part of man. We cannot self-generate charity, for example. It must be infused into our souls by the Spirit of God. We can discipline ourselves to display all of the charity or faith we have, but unless it has be gifted to us by Jesus Christ, the counterfeit would melt away and be exposed in the heat of adversity. We cannot, by any act of will, create faith. A person cannot grit his teeth and summon up faith by flexing spiritual muscles. Faith is a gift, and comes as a response to righteous obedience—and in no other way.

When a person has been born again, he has qualified for the constant companionship of the Holy Ghost. This great gift infuses the recipient's life with great blessings of faith, charity and much more. It opens the door to the ministering of angels. It punctuates one's life with revelations, bursts of understanding, and views of the workings of God. The doctrine of the priesthood begins to distill upon the soul. One finds new purpose and joy in living that exceeds human understanding.

The term "constant" should not be construed to mean permanent, for blessings after the rebirth are contingent upon obedience and righteousness, just as they were prior to the rebirth. People thus reborn may transgress the laws of God and place themselves in situations that do not invite the presence of the divine. In this case, they would cease to experience the presence of the Holy Ghost until they had repented.

There is a principle to be discovered here that brings further joy into the lives of the righteous. This principle becomes operative after the rebirth, which causes a person's eyes to become single to the glory of God, and the total intent of his or her heart to be obedient. The moment such a person experiences the withdrawal of the Holy Ghost, he or she can instantly repent, receive immediate confirmation of forgiveness, and continue on with his or her life of righteousness. Needless to say, this process only operates in the case of minor transgressions committed out of weakness or ignorance, rather than rebelliousness.

The constant companionship of the Holy Ghost is so profound that it literally propels those who receive it into a different world. Their thoughts become the mirror of their righteous desires. Their worldly possessions become a temporary collection of "things," which are at the Lord's disposal. Their eyes focus upon the heavens, and the world, with all its boisterous and hollow pleasures, fades into the background. They begin to view this life as temporary, and everything in it of worth only to the extent that it promotes eternal goals. Their former goals, ambitions, hobbies, and delights lose their allure. They look upon their former entertainments as kindergarten toys of little value. They feel themselves being compelled to express their love and joy in service to their fellow man. They glory in their blessings, and bask in their Savior's love.

Those thus reborn soon find that they may only discuss their blessings when prompted by the Holy Ghost. The reason is not that they are secret; it is that these things are so sacred that telling them to the wrong people may create feelings of resentment and envy, and may prejudice them against sacred things. So we remain humbly silent, year after year. Speaking when moved.

I do not believe this will always be the case. The time must come when we as a people are all recipients of these sacred things. Then we will be prepared to build Zion and welcome the Lord back to cleanse the earth. As we draw nearer to that day, we will certainly rejoice from the rooftops in what our Savior has done within the deep and sacred recesses of our souls.

Having the constant companionship of the Holy Ghost is not to have constant revelation. Revelation, instruction, visions, insights, and doctrine are given only as the Lord sees fit, and as we are prepared to receive them. The most notable effect of the constant companionship of the Holy Ghost is a feeling of worthiness, peace, and acceptance from God. Some people experience it as an enduring devotional or spiritual feeling, or motivation to unending prayer. The scriptures speak often of praying constantly in our hearts. They are making reference to this joyful by-product of the rebirth. Even as one enjoys the constant companionship of the Holy Ghost, the still small voice of the Holy Spirit continues to guide in all matters of right and wrong, good and evil, truth and falsehood.

The Holy Ghost speaks in his true character as a powerful revelator only when the truths communicated exceed the more limited role of the Holy Spirit.

This constant companionship of the Holy Ghost has the effect of continuing to exalt and purify. Any contact with that member of the Godhead uplifts and refines. Constant companionship exalts. If one persists in obedience and endures trials faithfully, one will in time be privileged to hear the Father's voice pronounce upon him or her the promise of exaltation.

Working Out Your Own Salvation

The concept of "working out our own salvation," used in the context of "perfecting ourselves," is an incorrect understanding of the doctrine of Christ. The idea that we, through our own efforts, may perfect ourselves and thus "earn" eternal life is a dangerously erroneous teaching. It is simply impossible and incorrect to believe that mankind can "perfect ourselves" by any amount of good works.

Such doctrine ascribes to the natural man powers he does not have. It tricks the unwary into years of frustration and unavoidable failure. It negates the need for personal revelation and sidesteps being born again. It scoffs at absolute obedience and never approaches having a calling and election made sure. Such doctrine constitutes an almost perfect delusion, making purity and exaltation a mere, unattainable mirage. It launches the unenlightened on an all-absorbing journey, leading them away from exaltation on a path that holds no promise. It robs them of the benefits of the Holy Spirit and the simple truths of the straight and narrow path.

If we could exalt ourselves, we would be living on a par with Jesus Christ, and his Atonement would be unnecessary. Satan is the only one who would teach that the Atonement is not necessary. The dark beauty of this delusion is that those caught within it still believe in the necessity of the Atonement. They just think they must become perfected through their own labors and works *before* the Atonement is applied.

> For we labor diligently to write, to persuade our children, and also our brethren, to believe in Christ, and to be reconciled to God; for we know that it is by grace that we are saved, after all we can do. (2 Nephi 25:23)

The word "after" doesn't mean that we must do everything of our own power; obey every commandment, do every good deed, and eliminate every flaw from our soul and *then* grace is applied. It means that every act of good is empowered by grace. We are reconciled to God by grace. We know good from evil by grace. We receive promptings, revelation, ordinances, and forgiveness by grace. And even empowered by grace every step of the way, we are saved by grace "after all that we can do". The message of this verse isn't that all of this happens in a timeframe *after* "all we can do." It means that we are saved by grace *beyond* "all that we can do."

What a demonically ingenious lie this is to believe in salvation by works. The evil one doesn't attempt to persuade us to not believe in the Atonement, but places it beyond our reach by tricking us into believing that we must become "perfect" before we have access to the Atonement, which is, in fact, impossible. We simply are not capable of becoming perfect through our own labors and works.

Why not do it the Lord's way? Just yield to the enticings of the Holy Spirit, and let Him effect the changes. We only begin to become perfected when our lives are infused with the Holy Ghost and that divine member of the Godhead burns away the imperfections of our souls with fire, thus making us pure, clean, and sanctified by grace beyond anything we can do by ourselves.

Rather than working our way into the Celestial Kingdom, we must become "perfect in Christ."

> *Yea, come unto Christ, and be perfected in him*, and deny yourselves of all ungodliness; and if ye shall deny yourselves of all ungodliness, and love God with all your might, mind and strength, then is his grace sufficient for you, that by his grace ye may be perfect in Christ. (Moroni 10:32; emphasis added)

Our part of the formula is that we lay our will upon the altar and choose to deny ourselves of all ungodliness, which means simply that when we are presented with a choice between right and wrong, kindness or meanness, service or selfishness, good or bad that we listen to the voice of our Savior, and choose to obey.

Each time we obey, then is the grace of Christ sufficient for us—in other words, Christ takes over from there. He empowers us to succeed with our decision to act in obedience—regardless of the magnitude of our weaknesses blocking the way. It also means that the cumulative effect of His grace will change us, bring about the rebirth, make our callings and elections sure, and offer us all other blessings we seek. It means that there is no other path. There isn't a different set of rules for the greater blessings. In everything we seek—His grace is sufficient.

This process of grace will sweetly bring us to the point that we are keeping all of the commandments. We will pay tithing, attend church, repent, serve with valiance, love one another, exercise great faith, possess true priesthood power, do missionary work with zeal, and obey all other commandments written or revealed. Imagine a church filled with such saintly people. Why, we would have to think of a special name for them, something like "The Church of Jesus Christ of Latter-day Saints," or why not just call them "Zion, the pure in heart"?

ZION

The ultimate attainment for any dispensation of the Lord's people is to establish a Zion society. There have been several notable successes. The City of Enoch was one of these. The people were so righteous that Christ walked with them, and the glory of God illuminated the city day and night. God later took the whole city up to dwell with Him until we are ready to join them in preparing the world for the triumphal return of Christ.

After Christ visited the Americas following his Resurrection, the people established Zion and lived almost two hundred years in that blessed state.

Enoch called the people to repentance and gathered the righteous into the City of Enoch. The wicked stood far off and feared Zion's power and glory. Nephi's Zion was successful because all had stood in the presence of the Savior at His appearing after his Resurrection.

Joseph Smith's Zion failed because the people were spiritually unprepared to obey the laws that would have sanctified them and empowered them to build Zion. In their defense, they were all new converts, and most were not yet able to live the higher laws that govern Zion.

The next time Zion is established will be just before the Second Coming, and will be done Enoch's way. Only those who are worthy of Zion will be admitted. Righteousness will prevail because wicked people will be excluded. Zion will not welcome people simply because they are Christians, or even Latter-day Saints. Only the pure in heart, the spiritually sanctified, and the elect of God will enter Zion and escape the calamities of the time. The Savior will dwell in Zion, and only such people as are worthy to walk and talk with the Savior will be able to dwell there.

You simply cannot understand what Zion is without yearning for it and begging the Lord to let it be established once again. But in a larger sense, it is not up to the Lord. It is up to us. When there is a body of the pure in heart, Zion will again be established.

It is possible, even necessary, that Zion societies exist in our day of as few as one person. We become a Zion individual when we become pure in heart, sanctified, and prepared to live in the presence of the Lord. Qualifying for this great blessing is a process that begins at the rebirth. When the Lord issues the call to fully establish Zion for the last great time, all who have taken upon themselves the qualifications of Zion will be gathered into a great and glorious whole. Then and only then, will Zion exist as a city, and eventually fill the whole earth.

DOCTRINE OF THE PRIESTHOOD

Those who have been born again have the pleasure of being taught by the Holy Ghost, who has become their constant companion. The Lord inspired Joseph Smith to record this powerful lesson on receiving the doctrine of the priesthood. His words are directed to people of a high spiritual caliber.

> Let thy bowels also be full of charity towards all men and the household of faith. (D&C 121:45)

This pinpoints the degree of spiritual progression of those to whom the following promise is being made. He is addressing those who have come along the straight and narrow path and partaken of the fruit of the tree of life, and thus had their souls infused with charity. In other words, this promise is given to all those who have experienced the rebirth. He then commands:

> And let virtue garnish thy thoughts unceasingly. (D&C 121:45)

While being born again places the happy recipients into a state of saintliness, it does not make them super-mortal. They remain subject to temptation (which in fact increases), and they find themselves in a state of blessedness that is maintained by diligence and valiant effort. It is entirely possible to transgress without falling from such a height. The key word here is "transgress." Transgression implies making a mistake out of weakness or ignorance, not willful, defiant disobedience. For one reborn, the withdrawal of the Spirit after such a transgression is immediate and painful. The thought of offending the Lord and causing the Spirit to withdraw is so adverse to the purity of their souls that repentance can be instantaneous.

Lessons are quickly learned, determination is set, and application of the atoning blood of Christ is immediately realized. It is the most perfect of all ways to live, and keeps the humble followers of Christ always within the warmth of His embrace.

Being born again is a state of purity, not perfection.

Purity implies virtue, a remission of sins coupled with valiant obedience. It does not mean the recipients are perfect, either in attitude, attributes, performance, or control of their minds.

The only thing that has been perfected is their intent—the flesh remains weak. The temptations rage on, and they continue to rely on the mercies of the Atonement for a remission of their sins past, present, and future.

Therefore, the admonition to continue to allow virtue to garnish their thoughts unceasingly is an important one. After having successfully accomplished this:

> Then shall [your] confidence wax strong in the presence of God. (D&C 121:45)

This confidence is such as most have never before experienced. It is a divine approbation, a loving welcome and invitation to linger and worship, to bask in His love, and to ask as prompted by the Holy Ghost. The prayers of the righteous are powerful, and they are always answered. Why? Because they approach God with great faith and confidence, and they only ask for those things which the Holy Ghost instructs, which things are in total harmony with the will of God.

> And if ye are purified and cleansed from all sin, ye shall ask whatsoever ye will in the name of Jesus and it shall be done. But know this, it shall be given you what ye shall ask. (D&C 50:29–30)

Who is purified and cleansed from sin? They are those who have been born again and beyond. When we are in mighty, confident prayer and are instructed to ask, we rejoice even as we ask, because we know the answer, the promised blessing has already been granted, indeed has been given. This is confidence in prayer. It is what the scriptures call "mighty prayer" and "praying in the Spirit."

> Likewise the Spirit also helpeth our infirmities: for we know not what we should pray for as we ought: but the Spirit itself maketh intercession for us with groanings [strivings] which cannot be uttered. (Rom. 8:26)

> And it shall come to pass that he that asketh in Spirit shall receive in Spirit. He that asketh in the Spirit asketh according to the will of God; wherefore it is done even as he asketh. (D&C 46:28, 30)

Thus having arrived at the blessed point where we may ask according to the will of God, we have completed the preparatory steps to being able to have the doctrine of the priesthood revealed to us.

> Let thy bowels also be full of charity towards all men, and to the household of faith, and let virtue garnish thy thoughts unceasingly; then shall thy confidence wax strong in the presence of God; and the doctrine of the priesthood shall distill upon thy soul as the dews from heaven. (D&C 121:45)

And, what is the doctrine of the priesthood? It is nothing less than being taught the exalting mysteries of godliness. When we are ready to receive and apply the doctrine of the priesthood, it will come upon our righteous, prayerful request and will open our view to greater things. These are the truths and principles that can only be obtained by personal revelation, those things that bring joy and life eternal.

> If thou shalt ask, thou shalt receive revelation upon revelation, knowledge upon knowledge, that thou mayest know the mysteries and peaceable things—that which bringeth joy, that which bringeth life eternal. (D&C 42:61)

When we are prepared to ask, they will distill upon our souls as the dews from Heaven.

THE MYSTERIES OF GOD

The mysteries of God are eternal, saving principles that must be sought after and obtained by all seekers of righteousness. They are mysteries because they cannot be taught to one another, but must be received by each spiritual pilgrim directly from the Lord.

The mysteries of God are both great and small. As members of His true church, we have already obtained many mysteries that we do not recognize as such, simply because they are commonly held by the members of His church. But still, they were mysteries prior to our obtaining them through personal revelation.

One of these "mysteries" is a testimony of the restored gospel. This does not immediately strike us as a mystery because it is so essential to our faith, yet it is a mystery. It is obtained by every faithful person individually through the Holy Spirit, and as a result of each person's own spiritual quest. It is knowledge that can come no other way than through personal revelation, and that is withheld from all who do not seek it. To these it is a mystery, and one of considerable opacity.

Every missionary who has taught the gospel knows the process whereby a testimony comes, and knows that their investigators cannot obtain their testimonies any other way. One of the greatest frustrations of missionary work is seeing people come so close to obtaining their own revealed testimonies, only to turn aside because of some small objection which they cannot intellectually reconcile. All missionaries learn by repeated experience that no combination of words can communicate a testimony to another. You can speak with power, authority, testimony, and with inspired beauty, and still, until the listeners themselves seek it, they will not receive their own testimonies. When you consider that of the thousands who are taught, only a small few embrace the gospel, it is easier to see a testimony as a mystery of godliness.

All parts of our spiritual understanding were once mysteries, and now stand revealed before us. All we wish to obtain, and actually must in order to be exalted, remains a mystery of godliness until the Holy Spirit reveals the eternal truth directly to our souls.

Consider the words of Paul:

> But we speak the wisdom of God in a mystery, even the
> hidden wisdom, which God ordained before the world unto
> our glory: Which none of the princes of this world knew: for
> had they known it, they would not have crucified the Lord of
> glory. But as it is written, Eye hath not seen, nor ear heard,
> neither have entered into the heart of man, the things which
> God hath prepared for them that love him. But God hath
> revealed them unto us by his Spirit: for the Spirit searcheth all
> things, yea, the deep things of God. For what man knoweth
> the things of a man, save the spirit of man which is in him?
> even so the things of God knoweth no man, but the Spirit of
> God. Now we have received, not the spirit of the world, but the
> spirit which is of God; that we might know the things that are
> freely given to us of God. Which things also we speak, not in
> the words which man's wisdom teacheth, but which the Holy
> Ghost teacheth; comparing spiritual things with spiritual. But
> the natural man receiveth not the things of the Spirit of God:
> for they are foolishness unto him: neither can he know them,
> because they are spiritually discerned. (1 Corinthians 2:7–14;
> see also Ephesians 3:1–12)

The natural man cannot know the mysteries of God because
they are spiritually discerned, but for those who have the Spirit
of God, we may receive of them freely. All these glorious, saving
truths are being made manifest unto his saints as quickly as they
can receive and obey them.

> Even the mystery which hath been hid from ages and from
> generations, but now is made manifest to his saints. (Colos-
> sians 1:26)

The gospel encompasses all truth from the sublimely simple,
to that which is too profound for mortal man to comprehend
without divine aid. It is useless to speculate about what these
greater mysteries might be until they are revealed to each of us
in their proper time. Until then, the Lord has ordained a certain

level of these essential truths that may be taught openly among the Saints. Apparently this level has varied with different dispensations of the gospel, and with time within dispensations, according to the heed and diligence the people have given to truths revealed. With disobedience comes a lesser bestowal of truth. With the greater obedience comes the greater "portion of the word."

> It is given unto many to know the mysteries of God; nevertheless they are laid under a strict command that they shall not impart only according to the portion of his word which he doth grant unto the children of men, according to the heed and diligence which they give unto him. And therefore, he that will harden his heart, the same receiveth the lesser portion of the word; and he that will not harden his heart, to him is given the greater portion of the word, until it is given unto him to know the mysteries of God until he know them in full. (Alma 12:9–10)

Even while shutting the door in the faces of those who collectively doubt, He opens it wider for those who individually qualify. It has always been the case that the mass of humanity has rejected the greater light, while the righteous few have sought after it with great diligence. To all such, the following promise is given.

> But great and marvelous are the works of the Lord, and the mysteries of his kingdom which he showed unto us, which surpass all understanding in glory, and in might, and in dominion; Which he commanded us we should not write while we were yet in the Spirit, and are not lawful for man to utter; Neither is man capable to make them known, for they are only to be seen and understood by the power of the Holy Spirit, which God bestows on those who love him, and purify themselves before him; To whom he grants this privilege of seeing and knowing for themselves; That through the power and manifestation of the Spirit, while in the flesh, they may be able to bear his presence in the world of glory. (D&C 76: 114–18)

As the above verse proclaims in gloriously beautiful words, one of the greatest mysteries we may obtain in this life literally invites us into the presence of our Savior. Within the gospel of Jesus Christ, we are blessed to have glorious things revealed to us as a church. My paternal grandfather used to say, "I don't understand all I know about it." This certainly applies to our understanding about the restored gospel. If we understood, and truly lived, all we know about the gospel, we would be Zion indeed, and spiritual blessings similar to those surrounding the dedication of the Kirtland Temple would be commonplace. Those portions of our knowledge that remain misunderstood are a large portion of the mysteries we must obtain in this life in order to be exalted.

An example of such a mystery is the sacrament and what role it plays in our lives. Like you, I partake of the sacrament routinely, yet it has taken me many years to comprehend what impact it has upon me, and I probably still do not fully grasp its meaning. For me, at least, the sacrament is a glorious mystery I prayerfully seek to understand every Sunday. Such mysteries abound in our lives.

There is another body of mysteries that are not commonly known. The scriptures seem to refer to these as the "hidden" mysteries (see D&C 76:5–10; 1 Corinthians 2:7; D&C 77:6; and D&C 101:33).

> It is almost superfluous to suggest that those who seek the truth and desire understanding will, by instinct, reserve judgment on issues they may not understand . . . until the mystery of godliness, on whatever point is involved, has been set forth in full. . . . We shall study many things about the Son of the Highest, some of them plain and easy and simple; others, deep, hidden, and mysterious. (McConkie, *Promised Messiah*, 5–6)

> It is with the writings of Jareditish Moriancumer even as it is with most of the Nephite teachings of Jesus. They are reserved for the faithful, they can be understood only by the power of the Spirit, and they have not been revealed as yet to

us. Though the milk of the word, as found in the translated portion of the Book of Mormon, has been given to prepare us for the meat of the word, as found in the sealed portion of that holy book, it is clear that our faith is not yet great enough to enable us to receive the hidden mysteries of the kingdom. (McConkie, *Mortal Messiah*, 4:370)

Why are they hidden? It is because they are meaningless in any other context than profound personal righteousness. Prior to that time, they would not only be misunderstood, but would demand obedience on a scale impossible for the aspiring, yet underdeveloped soul to render. In other words, they would tend to condemn rather than bless. Hence, in His divine mercy, He withholds, or keeps hidden, the greater truths of His gospel. Still, these truths are readily available to all who so order their lives that they progress from truth to truth within the gospel path.

There is a divinely ordained and powerful process whereby these truths are revealed to all who qualify. That process is an extension of the path upon which we already walk, and about which we understand the most basic of all truths, that of obedience. When the time comes that we may approach these glorious and profound blessings, they will come to us through obedience to those laws upon which they are predicated (D&C 130:20–21). As we approach that time, those laws, those truths, those doctrines of righteousness "shall distil upon thy soul as the dews from heaven" (D&C 121:45).

In fact, the higher functions of the Melchizedek Priesthood are to reveal the mysteries of God, to cause the heavens to open to the ministration of heavenly beings, and to invite us into the presence of the Father and the Son.

The power and authority of the higher, or Melchizedek Priesthood, is to hold the keys of all the spiritual blessings of the church—to have the privilege of receiving the mysteries of the kingdom of heaven, to have the heavens opened unto them, to commune with the general assembly and church of the Firstborn, and to enjoy the communion and presence of God the Father, and Jesus the mediator of the new covenant. (D&C 107:18–19)

We are even told that it is understanding (and acting upon) the mysteries of God that brings a person great joy, even eternal life.

> If thou shalt ask, thou shalt receive revelation upon revelation, knowledge upon knowledge, that thou mayest know the mysteries and peaceable things—that which bringeth joy, that which bringeth life eternal. (D&C 42:61)

Obtaining, by revelation, the mysteries of God, will reveal the wonders of eternity and things to come. This process will bring great wisdom and understanding, and put down the foolish wisdom of man. All this He does by enlightening the faithful with His Spirit.

> For thus saith the Lord—I, the Lord, am merciful and gracious unto those who fear me, and delight to honor those who serve me in righteousness and in truth unto the end. Great shall be their reward and eternal shall be their glory. And to them will I reveal all mysteries, yea, all the hidden mysteries of my kingdom from days of old, and for ages to come . . . Yea, even the wonders of eternity shall they know, and things to come will I show them, even the things of many generations. And their wisdom shall be great, and their understanding reach to heaven; and before them the wisdom of the wise shall perish, and the understanding of the prudent shall come to naught. For by my Spirit will I enlighten them. (D&C 76:5–10)

Finally, this great promise:

> For whoso is faithful unto the obtaining these two priesthoods of which I have spoken, and the magnifying their calling, are sanctified by the Spirit unto the renewing of their bodies. They become the sons of Moses and of Aaron and the seed of Abraham, and the church and kingdom, and the elect of God. (D&C 84:33–34)

Consider these words carefully, for they are profound, and each has eternal meaning. Being "faithful unto the obtaining" is much more than merely having the ordinances pronounced in our behalf. It implies righteous reception of true priesthood power. "Magnifying their calling" implies valiance in performance, obedience to the will of God, and enlarging their office in the eyes of those they serve. Being sanctified implies sanctification by the Holy Ghost, which is a state of purification and saintliness, of being born again, a topic we have discussed. "Renewing of their bodies" implies a newness, a change brought about in a physical way that makes them "the sons of Moses and Aaron and the seed of Abraham." Becoming the seed of Abraham invokes the covenant of God to Abraham that his seed would be those who would gain eternal life in every generation after him. This promise makes us worthy participants in that great covenant. And becoming "the church and kingdom, and elect of God" is nothing less than having your calling and election made sure, the earthly promise of exaltation.

Great and glorious are all the words and works of God.

THE COUNSELS OF GOD

For although a man may have many revelations, and have power to do many mighty works, yet if he boasts in his own strength, and sets at naught the counsels of God, and follows after the dictates of his own will and carnal desires, he must fall and incur the vengeance of a just God upon him. (D&C 3:4)

The Lord wants us to understand that our performance in this life cannot be measured according to how many revelations or mighty works we may do. It is a fascinating idea that one could do mighty work, and have many revelations, all the while setting at naught His counsels and following the dictates of our own will.

How does one set at naught the counsels of God? We must constantly choose between the source of all truth, and the source of all evil. On the side of truth, we obey the direction of God, which comes through the whisperings of the Holy Spirit. On the other end of the spectrum, we obey the dictates of our own will and the carnal desires that are championed by the evil one.

It is instructive that the above verse does not pit the counsels of God against the counsels of the evil one. The contest between good and evil is not taking place somewhere in the vastness of space, it is occurring within the hearts and minds of mankind. What actually takes place is that the Holy Spirit whispers truth, which appeals to the spirit within us, and the evil ones whisper lies, which appeal to the natural, or physical, part of us. Thereafter we make decisions depending upon which is of greater importance to us—our spiritual recognition of truth and our desires to walk in the paths of righteousness, or the will of the flesh and our inherited lust for the world and its rewards. To choose the will of the flesh is to set at naught the counsels of God.

The plan of exaltation is exquisitely perfect. It distills to this simple explanation. The Lord stripped us of all knowledge of our premortal nobility, then placed us in a world filled with equal proportions of good and evil. He surrounds us with the light of Christ, which acts as a constant reminder and motivation to feed the spirit and do good. The evil one surrounds us with the darkness of temptation, which acts as a constant reminder and motivation to titillate the flesh and choose evil.

> And now, my sons, I would that ye should look to the great Mediator, and hearken unto his great commandments; and be faithful unto his words, and *choose eternal life, according to the will of his Holy Spirit; And not choose eternal death, according to the will of the flesh* and the evil which is therein, which giveth the spirit of the devil power to captivate, to bring you down to hell, that he may reign over you in his own kingdom. (2 Nephi 2:28–29; emphasis added)

To be faithful unto His word is to be faithful unto His voice, which comes via the still small voice of the Holy Spirit. To turn aside the voice of His counsels, through our disobedience, is to trample Him under our feet.

> For the things which some men esteem to be of great worth, both to the body and soul, others set at naught and trample under their feet. Yea, even the very God of Israel do men trample under their feet; I say, trample under their feet but I would speak in other words—they set him at naught, and hearken not to the voice of his counsels. (1 Nephi 19:7)

To hearken unto the voice of the Lord, and hold fast to it, is to set at naught the counsels of the evil one, and his snares, to frustrate and foil his dark schemes. It is to see through the mists of darkness, uncertainty, lies, and confusion of this world and walk in the full light of His gospel plan.

> And I said unto them that it was the word of God; and whoso would hearken unto the word of God, and would hold fast unto it, they would never perish; neither could the temptations and the fiery darts of the adversary overpower them unto blindness, to lead them away to destruction. (1 Nephi 15:24)

Having thus instructed Joseph Smith (in D&C 3:4, quoted above) in the purpose of the counsels of God, and the absolute necessity of obeying them in order to fulfill His calling as the prophet of the church, He gives this well-deserved chastisement:

> Behold, you have been entrusted with these things, but how strict were your commandments; and remember also the promises which were made to you, if you did not transgress them. And behold, how oft you have transgressed the commandments and the laws of God, and have gone on in the persuasions of men. (D&C 3:5–6)

There is a certain amount of comfort in knowledge that even the greatest of God's servants succeed in spite of their failings. What makes them great is that they learn from their mistakes, reorder their obedience, and continue on with greater disciple-ship. What differentiates us from them is our inability to order our lives to obedience. We have a tendency to return to our spiri-tual wallows and lay back down in the mud. In a word, their greatest asset is an obedient heart, not a supernatural ability to circumvent either adversity or transgression.

> For, behold, you should not have feared man more than God. Although men set at naught the counsels of God, and despise his words. (D&C 3:7)

It is my great hope that all who have read thus far find power-ful significance in the above verse. If the meaning is not mani-festly transparent to you, either I have failed you, or you have not read with understanding. The counsels of God are His words, His voice unto us. It is His Holy Spirit, through which he coun-sels with us day and night. To ignore or disobey His words, is to despise His voice, and consequently to despise He who is the Savior and shepherd of our souls. In Joseph's case, his disobedi-ence sprang from a fear of men: their demands upon him and a fear of their anger if he disappointed them. He had an obedient heart, he just (temporarily) feared man more than God.

Equipped just as we presently are, we can recognize the voice of the Master and be diligently faithful. We should understand with perfect clarity that "the works, and the designs, and the purposes of God cannot be frustrated, neither can they come to naught." We must never forget that every choice we make to obey or disobey is a choice between the celestial kingdom and a dif-ferent reward. If we choose to be flawlessly obedient, we will be supported in all our trials, and He will be with us in every time of trouble.

> The works, and the designs, and the purposes of God cannot be frustrated, neither can they come to naught. For God doth not walk in crooked paths, neither doth he turn to the right hand nor to the left, neither doth he vary from that

which he hath said, therefore his paths are straight, and his course is one eternal round. Remember, remember that it is not the work of God that is frustrated, but the work of men. (D&C 3:1–3)

CELESTIAL LAW

Our Heavenly Father, through His son Jesus Christ, governs all parts of His kingdom with law. No part of it is devoid of law, nor is there any part that escapes His just dominion. Every blessing we receive from Him is by obedience to an associated law. These laws were formulated and put into effect before the earth was created.

> There is a law, irrevocably decreed in heaven before the foundations of this world, upon which all blessings are predicated—And when we obtain any blessing from God, it is by obedience to that law upon which it is predicated. (D&C 130:20–21)

In order to qualify for the celestial kingdom each supplicant must abide the law associated with that kingdom and live it fully. This law is immutable, and will apply to all people of all ages. Abraham will enter the celestial kingdom by obedience to this law, and so will we. It is foolish to think that God will require less of us because we live in a different dispensation of time. The requirements were irrevocably decreed before the world was created, and all men must abide by them to be exalted.

> Therefore, they must needs be chastened and tried even as Abraham, who was commanded to offer up his only son. For all those who will not endure chastening, but deny me, cannot be sanctified. (D&C 101:4–5)

> And unto every kingdom is given a law; and unto every law there are certain bounds also and conditions. All beings who abide not in those conditions are not justified. (D&C 88:38–39)

> For he who is not able to abide the law of a celestial king-
> dom cannot abide a celestial glory. (D&C 88:22)

What is the law of the celestial kingdom? This law will be
more fully defined later (see "The Law of the Celestial Kingdom," below). Living this law is so important that even the attendant glory of the resurrection depends upon our living it. The
scriptures are very plain about the truth that everyone will be
resurrected with differing degrees of perfection. Only the very
righteous will receive the full glory of the resurrection. We must
understand that all glory will be rewarded on the basis of worthiness. This includes the level or degree of glory with which the
body is quickened in the resurrection.

> For notwithstanding they die, they also shall rise again,
> a spiritual body. They who are of a celestial spirit shall receive
> the same body which was a natural body; even ye shall receive
> your bodies, and your glory shall be that glory by which your
> bodies are quickened. Ye who are quickened by a portion of the
> celestial glory shall then receive the same, even a fullness. And
> they who are quickened by a portion of the terrestrial glory
> shall then receive of the same, even a fullness. And also they
> who are quickened by a portion of the telestial glory shall then
> receive of the same, even a fullness. (D&C 88:27–31)

In other words, the level of glory which we achieved while
living (as evidenced by the law we live in this life), is the same
glory we will have after the resurrection—except that it will be
expanded to become a fulness. If we are living a celestial law in this
life, we have an earthly portion of celestial glory. That is, we have
the Holy Ghost as our constant companion, (in time) the assurance
of eternal life, great spiritual refinements, power in the priesthood,
and eventually the company of Deity. When the resurrection takes
place, we will be quickened with a celestial glory on a heavenly
scale. And being resurrected with such glory, we will be like unto
God, and entry into His kingdom will be sweet, natural, and glorious. Paul was speaking of the resurrection when he attested:

There are also celestial bodies and bodies terrestrial. . . .
There is one glory of the sun, and another glory of the moon,
and another glory of the stars: . . . So also is the resurrection
of the dead. It is sown in corruption; it is raised in incorrup-
tion . . . It is sown a natural body; it is raised a spiritual body.
(1 Corinthians 15:40–44)

For each person, the time will come when the "die will be
cast," and the opportunity to change the outcome forever lost.
All blessings, including the degree of perfection manifest in the
resurrection, will be based upon personal righteousness and the
law we choose to live in this life.

The Trial of Your Faith

We, as spiritual pilgrims, are on a course designed to test and
try us. The need for concentrated, soul-stretching growth makes
this life, of necessity, challenging and painful. In the course of the
journey home, we will be tested to the limits of our ability. This
is a wholesome and God-ordained part of the plan. The object of
this life, among other things, is to learn obedience, and in the process develop the attributes of godliness. Absolute obedience, as we
have already discussed, is that which makes it possible for us to
qualify for exaltation. Don't be dismayed by the apparent enormity
of the task. Even if it seems beyond your ability, it is well within
your reach as you are guided by the Holy Spirit and enabled by the
Atonement. And when you have received the Holy Ghost within
your soul, the course is joyful no matter how challenging it may
seem. Heavenly Father wants all of us to return to Him and has
tailored the plan so all who will obey Him and yield to the enticings of the Holy Spirit will be strengthened sufficient to the task.

I will prove you in all things, whether you will abide in
my covenant, even unto death, that you may be found worthy.
(D&C 98:14)

Therefore, they must needs be chastened and tried, even as Abraham, who was commanded to offer up his only son. For all those who will not endure chastening, but deny me, cannot be sanctified. (D&C 101:4–5)

You will experience many challenges throughout your sojourn here on earth, and you will experience many trials of your faith. However, *the* trial of your faith generally occurs only once. It is a test of such gravity that it appears to be a contradiction or paradox. (A paradox is something that appears impossible, but is in fact true.) During the test, the still small voice of the Holy Spirit will be your guide.

It requires great faith to follow the still small voice, especially in times of great trial, sorrow, suffering, and confusion. This is the reason the Lord showed Lehi the mist of darkness that obscured the rod of iron. When these trials arise, we can't see where to go. We can't penetrate the darkness with reason and logic. Only holding onto the iron rod of the word of God will direct us through these times.

The purpose of the test is twofold. It demonstrates our willingness to obey Him at all costs, even unto death. Secondarily, it sets our faith in the guiding voice of the Christ in immutable stone. It makes of willing soldiers, powerful generals clothed in the full armor of God. It tempers the metal of the soul as nothing else can, and is absolutely essential to our spiritual development. As Doctrine and Covenants 101:4–5 above indicates, if we truly desire exaltation, we *will* be tried, even as Abraham.

We can learn about the "trial of your faith" from Abraham's experience. In Abraham's case, he knew that human sacrifice was vile and abhorred by God. He himself had been bound to a sacrificial altar and was miraculously delivered through divine intervention (see Abraham 1:11–15).

The Lord had promised him many blessings, the greatest of which were all to be fulfilled through his beloved son, Isaac. He knew that if he sacrificed Isaac, the promised blessings could not be fulfilled, yet the Lord commanded him to offer up his only son, his beloved son, and source of his eternal promise, as a sacrifice. This obvious contradiction, this paradox as it were, was not lost on him. He must have struggled tremendously, yet while he struggled, he prepared his journey to the mount to sacrifice his son. He did not know how the Lord would reconcile the obvious contradictions. But such was his faith that he was willing to obey, believing that, if necessary, God would raise his son Isaac from the dead. (Hebrews 11:17–19)

Such obedience and faithfulness is also expected of us if we desire the ultimate celestial reward. The test *will* come. It will come when we are prepared and when we have become capable of such obedience—not before. It will be the most difficult, soul-wrenching experience of our lives, but it will not overwhelm us because we will be prepared with the power of great faith and the voice of the Spirit in our hearts.

It is impossible to know what form this test might take, or to even recognize when it begins. You will not know if you are being tried as Abraham was, or if this is just another trial. The only way you might know that what you just experienced was "the trial of your faith," is that it will occur after the rebirth, it will in some way involve a paradox, and you will shortly thereafter find your calling and election made sure.

It may seem inscrutable, almost as if these great blessings are hidden behind an impenetrable stone wall. While it is true that great blessings require great sacrifice, they are not outside our reach. They are reserved for the very obedient, but they are not in any way impossible. Is the promised reward worth the price to achieve it? How do you think Abraham, who already sits upon his throne, would answer that question?

Moroni, speaking of being allowed to see the Lord said:

> Wherefore, dispute not because ye see not, for ye receive
> no witness until after the trial of your faith. (Ether 12:6)

Joseph Smith outlined the course this way:

> After a person has faith in Christ, repents of his sins, and is baptized for the remission of his sins and receives the Holy Ghost, . . . which is the first Comforter, then let him continue to humble himself before God, hungering and thirsting after righteousness, and living by every word of God, and the Lord will soon say unto him, Son, thou shalt be exalted. *When the Lord has thoroughly proved him, and finds that the man is determined to serve Him at all hazards*, then the man will find his calling and his election made sure. (Smith, *Teachings*, 150; emphasis added)

The process is identical no matter the prophet describing it:

- Faith
- Repentance
- Baptism
- Reception of the Holy Ghost (which is to be born again)
- Living by every word of God (obedience)
- The trial of your faith
- Having your calling and election made sure

What is of great interest here is the added information about the trial. We are to be thoroughly proven. That means not only numerous trials, but one of significant consequence. Then, when we manifest that we are determined to serve Him at all hazards, which means even when it is dangerous, humiliating, terrifying, life threatening, and very bitter, He will seal upon us the promise of eternal life.

So why would anyone walk into a course of life that was going to so dramatically try them? The reason is that if we hope and expect to obtain eternal life, this is the price we must pay. The only way to avoid it is to step off the path, bow our heads in defeat, and accept a terrestrial reward.

Because Abraham is the great example of the type of trial required of the righteous, Satan may hiss this lie to those contemplating this great trial: "One of your children will die! Are you willing to sacrifice one of your children?" The lie is clever, insidious, and intended to attempt to frighten away the would-be faithful. It is often successful, at least for a time. Many people contemplating this epic trial at one time or another struggle with this fear. For some, this fear stalls their progress for many years, perhaps even permanently. Yet know this, *it is a lie.* Study the scriptures and the lives of those you know to be righteous. Few, if any of them, lost their children as part of their trial. Even Abraham, the exemplar, did not. Isaac lived to a ripe old age. Satan is the father of lies, and this is just another one of his loathsome offspring.

The test *isn't* what we are asked to sacrifice, it is *that* we are willing to sacrifice.

THE LAW OF CONSECRATION

The early Saints attempted many times to live the law of consecration as a church and community. Both in the East, and in the Salt Lake Valley, notable "experiments" with this law were attempted. Some of them were fairly successful, and operated in a modified form for years. Eventually, they were all disbanded, usually because of the desire of those participating to seek their own fortunes, rather than comingle success with the community. While these attempts were genuine, they were not actual manifestations of the law of consecration, but were experiments upon the concept of community economy in various ways. While the full application of the law of consecration will ultimately include principles of community economy, it has much more to do with personal commitment and righteousness.

The law of consecration continues to this day to be required of the elect, but in a different way than was attempted among the early church members. In those days, the Saints were required to dedicate and actually transfer their material possessions by legal means, to the church.

There were no rigid requirements of spiritual acuity prior to entering into this order. It is easy to understand that without the spiritual purity and refinements that make material possessions of little worth and that fill the soul with love for one's fellowman, giving up our material "things" could be very difficult.

It seems apparent the main reason the former-day Saints failed to build Zion was because they were not ready to live the law of consecration. In other words they were not spiritually prepared.

In our day, the dedication required of us is spiritual, rather than material. It is true that we dedicate all our material possessions to the Lord for the building of Zion, but the actual fact of yielding those possessions to the Lord is done as directed by the Spirit of the Lord, rather than by deed or other legal means. It is done according to the will of the Lord, communicated by revelation to each individual.

Consecration is the highest degree of personal commitment and dedication to which the mortal soul can ascend. It is only possible after purification of the heart by the Holy Ghost, attendant to and following the rebirth of the Spirit.

In due time, the law of consecration will be fully implemented in Zion. When it is, it will be largely spiritual, and far less importantly, material. When this happy day comes in our latter-day Zion, it will succeed because of the prior purification and sanctification of the hearts of the people. Once the people are pure before the Lord, then the implementation of the material aspects of this order will no longer be "experiments" but will be lived according to the perfect order revealed by the Lord at that time. In those glorious days to come, we will be perfect before the Lord, and that perfection will make us one in all things, and there shall be no poor among us, either spiritual or material.

And the Lord called his people zion, because they were of one heart and one mind, and dwelt in righteousness; and there was no poor among them. (Moses 7:18)

After the rebirth, worldly things lose their allure. As a person basks in the presence of the Holy Ghost after the rebirth, this inclination to sacrifice all earthly possessions strengthens and matures. When it is fully implemented, the desire to accumulate worldly things is gone, thus making a covenant to consecrate them all very natural and entered into with thanksgiving.

It is apparent that the greater blessings require greater degrees of devotion to the Lord. The way we make this devotion manifest is through promises made and kept before the Lord. Such promises are common in the lives of the faithful. In the sacramental prayers, we promise to always remember Him and keep His commandments. When any such promise is made in the proper manner, under the influence of the Holy Ghost, and with real intent, the Father promises in return to bless us in a specific way. Such a two-way promise is a covenant. There are lesser and greater covenants. Lesser ones bring lesser, though vital, blessings and are available to all who desire to make them. Greater covenants bring greater, even astoundingly beautiful, blessings and are available to those who qualify themselves to make them.

This may seem odd that some covenants, and their associated blessings, are withheld from us until we qualify to participate in them. Yet all the covenants one may make in this life are exclusionary, meaning that one must qualify to participate in them. Even baptism, the first and most basic of all covenants, is based upon worthiness. Another manifestation of this is that only faithful members may enter into the temples and participate in the ordinances and covenants found therein.

Even beyond those wonderful temple ordinances, there are covenants of which we generally know but little, and for which each person must personally qualify. That which qualifies us for the greatest of these are the covenants which lead to consecration.

The Lord has a perfect and powerful means whereby He makes known unto His faithful children how they may qualify for and enter into these lofty covenants. One need not know, actually *must* not know, what that process is until it is revealed to him or her step-by-step by the Holy Ghost.

The concept of consecration cannot be understood by those with carnal minds. It is foolishness to them. Until the mighty change occurs, we see things from the natural world looking out. From that vantage, spiritual things seem remote, unnecessary, and somewhat unattractive. After the change, we see things from the spiritual world looking out, and worldly things seem remote, unnecessary, and unattractive. To the elect, the things of this world are only meaningful to sustain life and to benefit the Lord's work.

Do not be misled or falsely persuaded to believe this is an unhappy or unfulfilling way to live. Those who live this law are the happiest people on earth. They know they will be exalted, for such has been revealed to them. They know worldly possessions are temporary and worthless, and therefore have no motivation to struggle after them. Their minds and hearts are centered on promised glories and rewards that astound the human mind. Worldly possessions are as dust that has little eternal value.

To the elect, this world is a stage whereon they are playing a role, reading from a script written by the Lord. The props on the stage belong to the Lord, and even though He has written the script to allow them to call certain things "mine," they in fact still belong to Him, and when the play is over they will walk off the stage with the same amount of "things" they walked on with—nothing. So, for the spiritually mature, there is no point in accumulating excess stage props unless the script calls for it. To abandon the script and start rounding up "things" would be to lose our leading role in the play, and since we could not be trusted to adhere to the script, we would become uninvolved, even unaware, of the play that is still being performed all around us.

All covenants are preparatory to some blessing that follows as soon as we fulfill our promises to the Lord. The covenant of consecration is preparatory to profound blessings that await the truly faithful. When you are ready and have tasted the sweet fruits of the rebirth, and your soul is set upon a course that cannot be altered; after you have been tested and found valiant, unswerving, and true; then, and only then, during mighty prayer, when the Holy Ghost directs, and the communication is vast, eternal and profound, will you humbly lay your offering upon the altar, and it will be accepted, and the glorious blessings will be bestowed.

CHAPTER FIVE

Beyond the Rebirth

As we noted earlier, being born again is the minimum require-ment for entering the celestial kingdom. But it is not the greatest accomplishment we can strive for in mortality. We believe in eternal progress, which means that we can progress forever. It also means that there is no limit to what we can accomplish here in mortality. Beyond the rebirth, we can seek and obtain having our calling and election made sure.

MAKING YOUR CALLING AND ELECTION SURE

Having your calling and election made sure is a tremendous milestone on the path to exaltation. While the scriptures refer to "calling and election," there is little information on how to accomplish it. The reason this is so is that each person must arrive

at this blessing through a course plotted for him or her personally by the Holy Spirit. What is required of each individual will
vary considerably. In addition to the gospel requirements that are
common to all paths, each person will have special and specific
tasks required of him or her.

Each of us who was capable of a celestial glory received our
"calling" in premortal life. In that world we were instructed in
our life's mission. We knew what we were to be and do in this
life to qualify for a celestial reward. It is unlikely that we knew
every detail of our future lives, but we knew enough to make an
informed covenant to fulfill our assigned work.

> Now the Lord had shown unto me, Abraham, the intelli-
> gences that were organized before the world was; and among
> all these there were many of the noble and great ones; And
> God saw these souls that they were good, and he stood in the
> midst of them, and he said: These I will make my rulers; for
> he stood among those that were spirits, and he saw that they
> were good; and he said unto me: Abraham, thou art one of
> them; thou wast chosen before thou wast born. (Abraham
> 3:22–23)

Each man who receives the priesthood in this life was also
ordained to that priesthood in the premortal world.

> And this is the manner after which they were ordained—
> being called and prepared from the foundation of the world
> according to the foreknowledge of God, on account of their
> exceeding faith and good works . . . are called with a holy call-
> ing, yea, with that holy calling which was prepared with, and
> according to, a preparatory redemption for such. (Alma 13:3)

In other words, because of the ability of God to see all things
in all periods of time—past, present, and future—He knew who
would make themselves worthy to receive and officiate in the
Priesthood. He therefore caused a preparatory redemption for
them, which made them worthy to receive that holy calling in the

world of spirits. All this was possible because of their exceeding faith and good works.

Thus, worthy men and women who were to become the elect, and whom He would make His leaders, priests, and prophets, were ordained to their callings. Worthy male spirits were also given the Priesthood. This constitutes the foreordination and "calling" of mankind.

> Actually, if the full blessings of salvation are to follow, the doctrine of election must operate twice. First, righteous spirits are elected or chosen to come to mortality as heirs of special blessings. Then, they must be called and elected again in this life, an occurrence which takes place when they join the true Church (D&C 53: 1). Finally, in order to reap eternal salvation, they must press forward in obedient devotion to the truth until they make their "calling and election sure" (2 Peter 1), that is, are "sealed up unto eternal life" (D&C 131:5). (McConkie, *Doctrinal New Testament Commentary*, 2:274–75)

> Like Peter, he teaches that the saints are called to "eternal life" (1 Tim. 6:12), called to "the promise of eternal inheritance" (Heb. 9:15), but he explains also that the Lord's calls are the result of foreordination and grow out of faithfulness in preexistence (2 Tim. 1:8–9). "God hath from the beginning," that is, from before the foundations of the world "chosen you (his saints) to salvation through sanctification of the Spirit and belief of the truth: Whereunto he called you by our gospel, to the obtaining of the glory of our Lord Jesus Christ" (2 Thessalonians 2:13–14). That is, the saints were foreordained in the councils of eternity to believe the truth, to be sanctified, and to save their souls; and then in this life they are called to that gospel whereby these eternal promises can be fulfilled. (McConkie, *Doctrinal New Testament Commentary*, 3:328–29)

When we speak of the promises given to "man" we mean "mankind." There is no greater or lesser promise given to men and women, but we stand equal in opportunity and glory before the Lord. It is unfortunate that in the cultures that have predated ours, womenkind have been viewed at times with unequal potential. This principle is enthroned in these words by Spencer W. Kimball.

> We had full equality as Father's spirit children. We have equality as recipients of God's perfected love for each of us. . . . Remember in the world before we came here, faithful women were given certain assignments, while faithful men were foreordained to certain priesthood tasks. While we do not now remember the particulars, this does not alter the glorious reality of what we once agreed to. (Women's Fireside, Salt Lake City, Utah, 15 Sept. 1979)

Elder James E. Talmage offers even further insight:

> [But in the light of the gospel] woman occupies a position all her own in the eternal economy of the Creator; and in that position she is as truly superior to man as is he to her in his appointed place. Woman shall yet come to her own, exercising her rights and her privileges as a sanctified investiture which none shall dare profane. (*Young Woman's Journal*, October 1914, 602.)

After we received this premortal calling, Heavenly Father covenanted with us that if we would be true and faithful to this calling that He would choose or "elect" us in the day of judgment to come and dwell with Him and receive all that He has. This choosing, this election as it were, was a conditional promise. One of the greatest of these conditions was that we fully avail ourselves of the restored gospel, wherein we make covenants which prepare us to become the elect of God. Finally, we must progress forward in great devotion until we make that conditional promise sure.

> And if by a long course of trial and obedience, while yet in this life, a man proves to the Lord that he has and will abide in the truth, the Lord accepts the exhibited devotion and issues his decree that the promised blessings shall be received. The calling, which up to that time was provisional, is then made

sure. The receipt of the promised blessings are no longer conditional; they are guaranteed. Announcement is made that every gospel blessing shall be inherited. (McConkie, *Doctrinal New Testament Commentary*, 3:330)

Joseph Smith exclaimed:

Oh! I beseech you to go forward, go forward and make your calling and your election sure. (Smith, *Teachings*, 366)

The term "making your calling and election sure" means that you have qualified for the promised election in advance of actually completing your work. When our lives are so set upon obedience and service that we shall never depart therefrom, when our souls are aglow with the constant companionship of the Holy Ghost, when our garments have been washed white in the blood of the Lamb, when we have been tested and found true and faithful in all things—then we will be blessed to know that our reward is eternally secure. In essence, the outcome of the judgment day is made known a millennium prior to its convening. This is done through the foreknowledge of God.

To have one's calling and election made sure is to be sealed up unto eternal life; it is to have the unconditional guarantee of exaltation in the highest heaven of the celestial world; it is to receive the assurance of godhood; *it is, in effect, to have the day of judgment advanced*, so that an inheritance of all the glory and honor of the Father's kingdom is assured prior to the day when the faithful actually enter into the divine presence to sit with Christ in his throne, even as he is "set down" with his "Father in his throne" (Rev. 3:21). (McConkie, *Doctrinal New Testament Commentary*, 3:31–32)

The question that immediately enters the mind is, "Well, couldn't God have told us at any time?" The answer seems obvious; He has always known that the elect would succeed, but reserves informing them of their yet-future achievement until their resolve is so firmly set that it cannot be altered.

I consider that He tells us as soon as the telling of it will not change the outcome of our lives. In all things, our agency must remain inviolate. Even revealed truth cannot give us unearned advantage or cause us to be more or less than we are capable of being.

It is important to note that those thus elected and sealed up are still mortal, and subject to temptation and transgression. They still have work to do, lessons to learn, trials to experience, and flaws to overcome. Perfection remains a goal still an eternity away, awaiting the attainment of the full glory promised those who truly become like God.

In many ways the elect are in a new and strange world. They understand much, but are often constrained from speaking. The Spirit stops them from plainly testifying and teaching of these things unless the hearers are prepared. This is not because they absolutely must not be taught; indeed, the opposite is true. The Holy Spirit strains to instill these truths in the soul of every spiritual seeker. The obstacle is that much of what they know cannot be taught because of its sacred nature, and because people are unprepared, even at times unwilling, to learn and obey the simple truths that would make them the elect of God. God, in His mercy, generally will not give knowledge that condemns, preferring to wait until the candidate is prepared to benefit from the revealed truths.

The Holy Spirit also constrains from communicating these things because of their gloriously sacred nature. It would be sacrilegious to inform someone of such a powerful blessing and then have that person ridicule it. Even feelings of doubt, envy, or jealousy on the part of the hearer places the glorious blessings in a "pearls before swine" setting. Thus the Spirit only gives sacred sanction when the heart of the hearer is pure and can rejoice with you in these glorious blessings.

The elect no doubt understand the workings of the Holy Spirit, and the glorious companionship of the Holy Ghost in intimate detail. They abhor sin and shrink at the coarseness and vileness of the world, yet find themselves still subject to temptation and personal failings. The paradox can be challenging. They cannot escape that which they detest because they remain to serve within it. They cannot order their flesh to cease to be what it is, nor can they stop temptations from infesting their minds.

The elect love their fellow man, yet are repulsed by mankind's depravity. They are often rebuffed and ridiculed by those they love. They speak the truth and are not heard. Even in the Church, the unenlightened doubt and debate. They testify, and that of which they bear witness is not comprehended. They prophesy and are threatened. It is a wonderful and paradoxical world in which they find themselves. For the first time they are inescapably in the world, but spiritually not a part of it.

It was probably this wonderful strangeness that prompted Nephi to exclaim these poignant words.

> Behold, my soul delighteth in the things of the Lord; and my heart pondereth continually upon the things which I have seen and heard. Nevertheless, notwithstanding the great goodness of the Lord, in showing me his great and marvelous works, my heart exclaimeth: O wretched man that I am! Yea, my heart sorroweth because of my flesh; my soul grieveth because of my iniquities.
>
> I am encompassed about because of the temptation and the sins which do so easily beset me. And when I desire to rejoice, my heart groaneth because of my sins; nevertheless, I know in whom I have trusted. My God hath been my support; he hath led me through mine afflictions in the wilderness; and he hath preserved me upon the waters of the great deep. He hath filled me with his love even unto the consuming of my flesh. He hath confounded mine enemies, unto the causing of them to quake before me.
>
> Behold, he hath heard my cry by day, and he hath given me knowledge by visions in the nighttime. And by day have I waxed bold in mighty prayer before him; yea, my voice have I

sent up on high; and angels came down and ministered unto me. And upon the wings of his Spirit hath my body been carried away upon exceedingly high mountains. And mine eyes have beheld great things, yea even too great for man; therefore I was bidden that I should not write them.

O then, if I have seen so great things, if the Lord in his condescension unto the children of men hath visited men in so much mercy, why should my heart weep and my soul linger in the valley of sorrow, and my flesh waste away, and my strength slacken, because of my afflictions? And why should I yield to sin, because of my flesh? . . . Awake, my soul! No longer droop in sin.

Rejoice, O my heart, and give place no more for the enemy of my soul . . . . Rejoice, O my heart, and cry unto the Lord, and say: O Lord, I will praise thee forever; yea, my soul will rejoice in thee, my God, and the rock of my salvation. (2 Nephi 4:16–30)

It appears Nephi was struck by the paradox of his situation. He had been in the presence of the Lord, seen visions of all the works of God from the beginning to the end of time, and still he struggled with temptation and urgings to sin.

Nephi's struggling was the result of the purity of his spirit and his inability to tolerate any sin at all. His sins were of the type that we might daily commit, perhaps without even noticing. Yet in one infused with the Spirit of God, who walks daily in the light of His love, even anger or impatience or temptation would seem abhorrent. Still he knew in whom he trusted. He knew his exaltation was secure, and he gloried in the Lord and praised Him in mighty prayer.

RIGHTEOUS PARENTS

Nephi's opening words in the Book of Mormon state that he had been born of goodly parents. In one half of the first verse he mentions that he was taught in the learning of his father, then writes about his father for several more chapters, recording Lehi's prophetic calling, his visions, dreams, and tremendous revelations.

It seems shortsighted to assume that Nephi's gratitude to his parents was entirely for his education, rather than the tremendous spiritual heritage of being the son of a prophet of God. The first event recorded in the Book of Mormon was Lehi's vision where he was privileged to look into heaven and see:

> God sitting upon his throne, surrounded with numberless concourses of angels in the attitude of singing and praising their God. (1 Nephi 1:8)

Nephi, living now in the Americas, was writing as an older, matured and powerful prophet himself. He understood the wonderful heritage his righteous parents had bequeathed him. It is no wonder he began the record of his life by recording his father's prophetic calling.

There is a powerful tie between one who has his calling and election made sure and his posterity. Nephi understood this fully, and in writing the account of his own ministry, could scarcely begin without paying proper tribute to his parents to whom he owed so much. Indeed his opening words still publish his gratitude and respect twenty-five hundred years later, for he understood clearly that his great blessings were in large part due to the promises made to his father, Lehi.

Joseph Smith, the Prophet of the Restoration, explained:

> The servants of God are sealed in their foreheads, which signifies sealing the blessing upon their heads, meaning the everlasting covenant, thereby making their calling and election sure. When a seal is put upon the father and mother, it secures their posterity, so that they cannot be lost, but will be saved by virtue of the covenant of their father and mother. (Smith, *Teachings*, 321)

Notice that the seal is placed upon the heads of the parents when they have their calling and election made sure, not when they are married in the temple. Elder McConkie adds this valuable insight when commenting upon the above quotation:

> "The servants of God are sealed in their foreheads, which signifies sealing the blessing upon their heads, meaning the everlasting covenant, thereby making their calling and election sure. When a seal is put upon the father and mother, it secures their posterity, so that they cannot be lost, but will be saved by virtue of the covenant of their father and mother." (*Teachings*, p. 321.) Thus *if both parents and children have their calling and election made sure, none so involved shall be lost*; all shall come forth to an inheritance of glory and exaltation in the kingdom of God. (McConkie, *Doctrinal New Testament Commentary*, 3:493)

Families are eternal in nature, which means their structure predates this world. In other words, they were organized before the world was created. The foreknowledge of God gave Him power to assign celestial children to celestial parents. Perhaps even then we did not realize the full import of those familial relationships, nor the powerful wisdom and purpose of those assignments.

When people make their callings and elections sure in this life, their children become participants in those same blessings. To say it differently, when those great promises are given to a parent, one of the great blessings associated therewith is the revealed knowledge that the parent's children are of like spiritual virtue, and similarly foreordained to make their calling and election sure. These are more than good kids, they are spirits *foreknown by the Lord*, to be the elect of God. The parent is unaware of this until the promises are given, of course. Nevertheless, it occurs.

My perception of the process is this: When the promises are given to the parent, the children are promised exaltation by virtue of the *children's* righteousness. The children's righteousness is both premortal and future, as is the parent's to a large degree. These children are celestial in their own right, and their eventual reward is secured by their own righteousness. What is secured by the parent's righteousness is the privilege of being a parent of these valiant spirits. In other words, the children and parent are sealed together by virtue of their combined righteousness. The children are exalted by virtue of their own righteousness.

It should be apparent that these children are not "predestined" to such greatness but may, through their own disobedience, fail to measure up to the promised blessings. Still, knowing that your exaltation extends to your children and grandchildren is of supreme comfort, and a source of great spiritual power.

Consider the account of Alma the Younger, son of the prophet Alma, who had been persecuting the church and fighting against God. Finally the Lord sent an angel to arrest Alma's decay and spoke these words to the wayward son:

> Behold, the Lord has heard the prayers of his people, and also the prayers of his servant, Alma, who is thy father; for he has prayed with much faith concerning thee that thou mightest be brought to the knowledge of the truth; therefore, for this purpose have I come to convince thee of the power and authority of God, that the prayers of his servants might be answered according to their faith . . . And now I say unto thee, Alma, go thy way, and seek to destroy the church no more, that their prayers may be answered, and this even if thou wilt of thyself be cast off. (Mosiah 27:14, 16)

This divine communiqué had an immediate and lasting effect upon Alma's son. He mended his ways and in due time became a prophet in his own right.

How many distraught parents do you suspect have begged the Lord to intervene in their children's lives but received no such miraculous relief from the Lord? Understanding that God is no respecter of persons, and is absolutely, eternally just and fair, why is it that Alma's son got what appears to be preferential treatment? The angel gives the answer in explaining why he had come: "That the prayers of his servants might be answered according to their faith."

Why did the elder Alma have the faith which was sufficient to open the heavens and call forth angels? It is my belief that the larger part of his extraordinary faith came because he had heard the Lord's own voice promising him eternal life, for himself *and* his posterity. Therefore, in spite of his son's evil behavior, he knew his son's true celestial nature.

God's sending forth an angel did not result in Alma the Younger receiving an unfair advantage, it resulted in Alma the Elder receiving blessings he had been promised, and Alma the Younger taking his premortally promised place. Alma the Elder had perfect faith that he could make this request because of the Lord's own words, and did so with tremendous faith and impact.

Laman and Lemuel, the sons of the prophet Lehi, were similarly unrighteous, and their father undoubtedly prayed as fervently, and with equal faith as did Alma the great high priest. The Lord sent angels to Laman and Lemuel as well, and gave them numerous, undeniable witnesses, all of which they eventually rejected. While the scriptures are silent on this subject, it appears that children thus sealed up by promises to their parents may willfully reject their own promise and position. It may be this principle that is echoed in the words of the angel to Alma the Younger: "Even if thou wilt of thyself be cast off." (Mosiah 27:16). Although the angel had come from the presence of God to call Alma's son to repentance, Alma the Younger could still choose to be cast off if he desired, but it would be in the face of the absolute knowledge that he was choosing evil rather than good. The most inviolate principle of this life is our God-given agency with which we choose our own reward. This agency remains fully operative in all of God's children, regardless of their parents' righteousness.

ETERNAL MARRIAGE

While exaltation is a personal achievement, it is not a personal reward. In order for any person to enter into the fullest measure of exaltation, he or she must be married to a spouse equally fit for exaltation. Without a companion a person is incomplete, and regardless of personal achievements, he or she is not yet able to inhabit the highest of all celestial rewards.

When a righteous soul walks a path of obedience, and yet is not blessed with a companion in this life, that faithful soul will be "given" a righteous companion at an appropriate later time. The key here is to walk a path of personal righteous and trust that the Lord will bring your eternal love into your life when it is time.

Sometime before the day of judgment we must all be sealed to a righteous companion.

> They must be sealed for time and for all eternity in a temple; then their union will last forever, and they cannot be separated because God has joined them together, as he taught the Pharisees. (Smith, *Doctrines of Salvation*, 2:43–44)

It will be a glorious occasion when humble, purified men, or women, present themselves before the Lord on the day of divine judgment, and are welcomed with loving embrace, found fully worthy to dwell forever with Him whose voice they had loved, and whom they had valiantly served throughout the days of their probation.

Consider what magnitudes of greater joy will fill our souls when after rejoicing in the arms of our beloved master, we finally turn and beckon to our eternal companions, who likewise come forth and receives the same loving welcome. Imagine the joy it will be to stand nearby as your spouse rushes into the arms of the Lord and finally falls at His feet in joyful adoration. Imagine what love, elation, worship, and praise will envelope your heart as he or she, found acceptable and perfect before the Judge of all mankind, turns with equal love to embrace you, his or her everlasting love and companion. Imagine the eternal thrill, the righteous pride it will engender, to watch as each righteous, perfected son and daughter enters the Savior's embrace and then lovingly rushes into your own arms. Consider what satisfaction, what peace, what eternal joy it will be to stand within the glow of His glory as generation after generation of your righteous offspring come forth to receive their exaltation at the hands of Him whose blood was spilt for us, and then come to take their place within your kingdom, their great spiritual forefathers.

Can we contemplate such a scene and not feel the glow of spiritual fire, the Spirit-born confirmation that such is our heritage, our birthright, our promised future. Can anyone imagine such a scene without a loving, glorified companion standing by his or her side? Would anyone even want such a life, without one of perfect love to share it with? What joy could we feel in gazing upon a celestial sunrise, if there were no loved one near to turn to and see even the beauty of celestial perfection pale in comparison to the love in his or her eyes.

It is the rare marriage where husband and wife are equal in their spiritual evolution. Most often one spouse is slightly, if not significantly, more advanced than the other. The question, therefore, frequently arises. "Can I achieve the rebirth, even have my calling and election made sure, even though my spouse is uninterested in spiritual things? What will happen if my loved one never chooses to grow spiritually and I do?"

The answer to the first question is a resounding *yes*!

Exaltation is a personal and individual quest. No person will be exalted because of a spouse's faithfulness, nor will any be held back because of another's disobedience. Regardless of your gender, or even your marital status for that matter, you may, and actually *must*, achieve all these things without regard to any other living person. Revelation is called "personal" because it flows to each person individually and guides and blesses the individual. In the same context, exaltation is a personal achievement.

Now to the second question, "What will happen to my spouse?" What will happen is that your spouse will suddenly be living with a person endowed with a personal and profound relationship with God. You will be in a position to call forth the power of God, and He will fling open the windows of heaven and pour out upon you, and your spouse, such blessings as neither of you ever thought possible. Your spouse will begin to find miracles happening in his or her life, such that his or her views and understanding will begin to expand at a breathtaking rate.

Ultimately what occurs will depend upon your spouse.

If your spouse yields to the enticings of the Holy Spirit, and accepts and embraces the miracles and joy he or she sees in your life and his or her own, your spouse too will begin to seek, and eventually find the same blessings you have found. In the eternal world your companion will rejoice that you found the courage and spiritual greatness to begin the journey for you both.

If your spouse rejects the marvelous new light in your life, then you may well be blessed with new and greater opposition to overcome. What will you do then? You will listen intently to the promptings of the Holy Spirit, the voice of the Lord in your soul, and you will rejoice as you continue and eventually complete your journey home. Will it be easy? No. But it will bring you eternal life and everlasting joy, and it will be eternally worth the price.

It is perhaps paradoxical that exaltation is a personal quest, yet we cannot be fully exalted without an equally righteous companion. I give this council to all who fear they are making the journey alone:

- Obey the Lord and trust Him with all your heart. Do what you must with love and kindness. Never coerce or manipulate.
- Allow your companion all his or her agency, even if he or she uses it unwisely.
- Encourage with kindness.

- Speak with power only when prompted.
- Trust your spouse. Believe in him or her and his or her process even if you do not understand or agree with it.
- Trust the Lord to do everything possible to bring that precious soul to exaltation—including keeping you as his or her righteous companion.
- Don't give up until the Lord does.
- Be faithful—Be fearless—Be patient.

It takes great faith to obey. Why is this so? It is because we cannot foresee the eventual outcome of our obedience. We can only believe, and eventually know, that every obedient choice calls forth glorious blessings and opens doors into the eternal realm. In time you will no longer fear to do what is right. You will no longer fear the outcome of your obedience. Why should you? A great truth will sweetly distill upon your soul, and this is that the Lord honors, upholds, and delights to bless those who obey Him. You will be guided, comforted, prospered, and filled with that joy which surpasses the understanding of man all the days of your life.

For one to be exalted in the highest degree of the celestial kingdom, one must be a participant in the new and everlasting covenant of marriage. The steps for those thus endowed are the same as for everyone else. In addition to temple marriage, they must have faith, repent, be baptized, receive hope and charity, be born again, and both have their callings and elections made sure. Then, and only then, will the additional promises of their eternal marriages be realized.

It is an incorrect belief that just participating in the temple endowment and temple marriage assures the participants the full blessings of eternal life. It must be understood that the endowment, like baptism and all other ordinances of the church, is first performed and then later ratified by the Holy Spirit of promise. Until this ratification occurs, the promises are withheld.

This error apparently stems from an incorrect interpretation of Doctrine and Covenants 132:19. Let us analyze this verse to see what it is teaching us:

> And again, verily I say unto you, if a man marry a wife by my word, which is my law, and by the new and everlasting covenant, and it is sealed unto them by the Holy Spirit of promise . . . and it shall be said unto them—Ye shall come forth in the first resurrection (D&C 132:19)

Having an ordinance sealed by the Holy Spirit of Promise makes that ordinance of effect in heaven and throughout eternity. To have one's marriage thus sealed is to have the guarantee that the marriage covenant will be in effect after this life. Temple marriage is only valid for those who enter the highest degree of the celestial kingdom. In other words, what this verse is teaching is that in order for the promises to be realized, each member of the couple must have his or her calling and election made sure. To hear these blessed words from the heavens, "Ye shall come forth in the first resurrection," is to have one's calling and election made sure. This is an experience separate from and in addition to the marriage ceremony. Note these words of Elder McConkie relative to this same verse:

> Then the revelation speaks of that obedience out of which eternal life grows, and still speaking both of celestial marriage and of making one's calling and election sure says: "Verily, verily, I say unto you, if a man marry a wife according to my word, and they are sealed by the Holy Spirit of Promise, according to mine appointment "that is, if they are both married and have their calling and election made sure. (McConkie, *Doctrinal New Testament Commentary*, 3:344)

> Then shall they be gods, because they have no end; therefore shall they be from everlasting to everlasting . . . . Except ye abide my law ye cannot attain to this glory. For strait is the gate, and narrow the way that leadeth unto the exaltation and the continuation of the lives. (D&C 132:20–22)

Please take comfort in the fact that having your calling and election made sure can take place after this life as we continue the righteous walk of this life beyond the grave.

The promise is so significant that qualifying for the promised blessing will make the recipients gods! They will receive from the Father all that He has, including His glorious power. Thereafter, His work and glory will be their work and glory. The gate is straight, and the way narrow. There is no room for deviation or false steps. Only those living by constant revelation will be able to walk its narrow confines. Those who do so will have their eyes upon the heavens, and the path will seem as broad as life itself. It only seems narrow and confining to those who watch their feet. Those who successfully negotiate the path will be led "unto exaltation and the continuation of the lives." Notice the plurality—lives. This is the promise of eternal offspring, the right to procreate, as God does. Only in the highest order of the celestial kingdom are we allowed this blessing.

> Verily, verily, I say unto you, except ye abide my law ye cannot attain to this glory. For strait is the gate and narrow the way that leadeth unto the exaltation and continuation of the lives, and few there be that find it, because ye receive me not in the world neither do ye know me. (D&C 132:21–22)

And, why are there so few who actually find it? Because they do not abide the laws associated with the blessings. In other words, they begin along the way, but they do not finish the course. They do not follow the straight and narrow path all the way to its glorious conclusion.

> But if ye receive me in the world, then shall ye know me, and shall receive your exaltation; that where I am ye shall be also. This is eternal *lives*—to know the only wise and true God, and Jesus Christ, whom he hath sent. I am he. Receive ye, therefore, my law. (D&C 132:23–24; emphasis added)

In order to obey this command we must understand what He means by "receive me in the world." He restates the same promise and gives us what he means in the following verse:

> But to as many as received me, gave I power to become my sons; and even so will I give unto as many as will receive me, power to become my sons. And verily, verily, I say unto you, he that receiveth my gospel receiveth me; and he that receiveth not my gospel receiveth not me. (D&C 39:4–5)

It is tempting to stop there and assume divine sonship for all who have accepted His gospel through faith, repentance, and baptism. But as we have often noted so far, the process extends beyond those initiatory steps. The Lord saw fit to instruct us also in what He means when He refers to His gospel in the very next verse.

> And this is my gospel—repentance and baptism by water, and then cometh the baptism of fire and the Holy Ghost, even the Comforter, which showeth all things, and teacheth the peaceable things of the kingdom. (D&C 39:6)

To receive Him in the world then implies the full gospel course, including the glorious rebirth of the Spirit, the baptism of fire and the Holy Ghost. As we have discussed earlier, the rebirth is the minimum requirement for entering the celestial kingdom. It makes the meaning of the former scripture much more clear, then, when He states:

> But if ye receive me in the world, then shall ye know me, and shall receive your exaltation; that where I am ye shall be also. This is eternal lives—to know thee the only wise and true God, and Jesus Christ, whom he hath sent. I am he. Receive ye, therefore, my law. (D&C 132:23–24)

The first and most important way in which we receive the Savior in this world is through the rebirth. Participating in this blessing makes us conditional sons and daughters of God; conditional, because our status may be lost through disobedience.

Like many gospel principles, there are multiple levels of understanding here, all of which are true. The second true form of receiving Him is when a person makes his or her calling and election sure. In this blessing, that person receives from Him the (nearly) unconditional promise of eternal life. Only shedding innocent blood, or the unpardonable sin, can take this promise from us.

A third way in which we may receive Him in this life is when we actually enter His presence, which we will discuss in greater detail later.

In the verse quoted above, He promises us great blessings if we will receive Him in this life. This is eternal lives. He is making reference to a family by using the plural form of lives. Receiving Him, with both partners having their callings and elections made sure, seals the family unit throughout eternity. Receive ye therefore my law. Or in simpler words, if you want eternal lives, receive and obey my law. And what is this law? It is the law of the celestial kingdom.

THE LAW OF THE CELESTIAL KINGDOM

To understand precisely what this law is, is to know the way back into His presence. To understand this law with clarity is to pierce the darkness of the world and catch a glorious glimpse of His everlasting plan of happiness for His children. For this reason, I consider that by opening this topic we have entered upon sacred ground.

The Master wants us to know the law both guarding and guiding the way to exaltation, and begins His greatest teaching on this subject with these words of glorious promise to Joseph Smith:

> Wherefore, I now send upon you another Comforter, even upon you my friends, that it may abide in your hearts, even the

Holy Spirit of promise; which other Comforter is the same that I promised unto my disciples, as it is recorded in the testimony of John. This Comforter is the promise which I give unto you of eternal life, even the glory of the celestial kingdom; which glory is that of the church of the Firstborn, even of God, the holiest of all, through Jesus Christ his Son. (D&C 88:3–5)

The Holy Spirit of promise is the Holy Ghost bestowing blessings promised by previous ordinances of the priesthood (see "Justification," above). When the Holy Spirit of promise is fully received, then all priesthood ordinances will become justified, and in full force. Thereafter, that person will have his or her calling and election made sure, and will have the promise of eternal life in a very literal and profound sense. As the above scripture states, all this is through Jesus Christ.

Having pronounced upon Joseph his exaltation, Christ thereafter proceeds to describe the entire process whereby Joseph had received these great blessings. What follows is of supreme importance to us. As with other truths of great worth, they are not stated plainly enough that all who read them understand what is being said. There is mercy in this, as those who do not understand are not condemned by unheeded truth, and those who are ready to know will be taught the precious truths by the Spirit of Truth. Speaking of Jesus Christ, the scripture continues:

He that ascended up on high, as also he descended below all things, in that he comprehended all things, that he might be in all and through all things, the light of truth; Which truth shineth. This is the light of Christ. (D&C 88:6–7)

A great deal of the suffering and agony Christ experienced on our behalf was to prepare Him for His mission as the source of all truth. This, as the scripture states, is the light of Christ. Or in other words, the light of Christ is the source of all truth. Stating the same thing another way, there is no source of truth other than Christ. What follows in the scripture is an enlightening discussion on what the light of Christ means to us. It is the power that gives and sustains life, keeps the stars and planets in their proper orbit, and gives order throughout all existence. Further, it is:

> The light which is in all things, which giveth life to all things, *which is the law by which all things are governed*, even the power of God who sitteth upon his throne, who is in the bosom of eternity, who is in the midst of all things. (D&C 88:13; emphasis added)

Consider the impact of these words. Not only is the light of Christ the source of all truth, and the origin of our conscience, but it is the law by which all things—including ourselves—are governed.

When any divine command is sent forth, whether it be something as complex as creation of a new world, or as sublime as a prompting, it is done through the light of Christ. When He commands the elements to form into a world, He speaks and is obeyed. Presumably, it sounds the same to the elements as it does to us. When He whispers, all creation obeys. All, that is, except mankind.

He voices His law, not in a voice of thunder, but in a still small voice. This is the "law of Christ," this is the "law of the celestial kingdom," this is the law that, if obeyed, will yield eternal life. This is the great and grand truth that shines so brightly most fail to comprehend, mostly because they seek elsewhere for that which they already possess; that which shines within us; that which begins us our conscience and matures through obedience; that which we often disregard, is the law by which we are governed. Those who hear and obey will be exalted, those who do not—will not. It is really just that simple.

> And they who are not sanctified through the law which I have given unto you, even the law of Christ, must inherit another kingdom, even that of a terrestrial kingdom, or a

telestiaI kingdom. For he who is not able to abide the law of the celestial kingdom cannot abide a celestial glory. (D&C 88:21–22)

We have discussed all through this book how sanctification comes as a result of obedience to the voice of Christ. What we are being taught now is that this is not only the source of all truth, but is also the law of the celestial kingdom.

Not only is the straight and narrow path the *only* way, it is literally the law against which we will be judged, and as a direct result of which we will be either welcomed into the celestial kingdom or asked to depart into another kingdom.

Notice the last sentence of the above verse. If we cannot abide the law, we cannot abide the glory. If we can't be obedient to the voice of revelation, we cannot attain the glory that such obedience would naturally bestow upon us. When we obey the celestial law, we are quickened by a portion of the celestial glory in this life. And if we are quickened by a portion of celestial glory in this life, when we are resurrected, we will receive a fulness of the same glory.

> They who are of a celestial spirit shall receive the same body which was a natural body; even ye shall receive your bodies, and your glory shall be that glory by which your bodies are quickened. Ye who are quickened by a portion of the celestial glory shall then receive of the same, even a fullness. (D&C 88:28–29)

The scripture further explains that when we choose to humble ourselves and be governed by the law of Christ, we will be preserved, perfected, and sanctified by the same. And when we rebel and seek to become a law unto ourselves, then the law cannot sanctify us, nor can anyone or anything else.

> And again, verily I say unto you, that which is governed by law is also preserved by law and perfected and sanctified by the same. That which breaketh a law and abideth not by law,

but seeketh to become a law unto itself, and willeth to abide in sin, and altogether abideth in sin, cannot be sanctified by law, neither by mercy, justice nor judgment. Therefore, they must remain filthy still. (D&C 88:34–35)

The course to eternal life may at times seem overwhelming. But know this, and do not despair: even though your goals and aspirations are the most lofty, and at times seem unreachable, the way to accomplish them is truly simple. Learn the lesson of the tree of life! Take hold of the rod of iron of personal revelation and obey the law of the celestial kingdom. God does not require us to perfect ourselves, or to develop godly attributes by our own labors. He will give us all those marvelous things. He will change us in a mighty way. He will exalt us, if we obey Him. Hear it again. He will exalt us. He will work the changes. He will purify us. He will cleanse us—if we will obey Him.

It sounds simple, and it is simple. However, simplicity does not mean it is easy. It is a lifelong task. It is designed to be so demanding that only the very, very obedient will accomplish it. Do not count yourself out. Of the billions who have lived, you are among the most noble and valiant of God's children. You are capable of such obedience, and can become worthy of all these blessings. Just set your heart on a course of obedience, and you will accomplish all of this much more quickly than you anticipate. As has been stated many times in this book, a commitment to total obedience will blast you off so fast and high that it will be breathtaking, the height unimaginable, and the promised blessings very near.

THE SECOND COMFORTER—A VISITATION OF CHRIST

Mormon calls the process of arriving at the blessing of the rebirth "faith, hope, and charity." He taught us how to obtain the great joy of charity, and yet there was something greater he wanted us to understand. He wanted to tell us how to progress beyond the rebirth and how to qualify to enter into the presence of the Lord. His faith was in Christ, whom he had seen, yet he knew others might doubt, and desire a personal visitation to prove Christ's reality. To those who might unrighteously desire such a witness, He issues this command:

> And now, I, Moroni, would speak somewhat concerning these things; I would show unto the world that faith is things which are hoped for and not seen; wherefore, dispute not because ye see not, for ye receive no witness until after the trial of your faith. (Ether 12:6)

Faith is, he teaches us, in Christ, who is not seen yet is fervently hoped for. It is futile to dispute His existence because we have not seen Him, for He will remain unseen until after the trial of our faith. Or in other words, we may see Him, but only after we first have faith in Him, and have that faith tested and honed to near-perfect knowledge. Faith is a gift of the Spirit, received because of worthiness and righteous obedience. To have faith in Christ is to have faith in His voice. To know as Nephi knew that He will give us no commandment except He also prepares a way for us to accomplish whatever He commands (see 1 Nephi 3:7). Faith of this type motivates to greater obedience and greater blessings, until the greatest blessings become ours to claim. It was this type of faith Mormon knew brought these blessings to the ancient faithful.

> For it was by faith that Christ showed himself unto our fathers. (Ether 12:7)

Mormon is telling us that we may also kneel in the presence of the Savior of the world and behold His face if we will but have faith, hope, and charity, and endure the trial of our faith. He then testifies:

> But because of the faith of men he has shown himself unto the world, and glorified the name of the Father, and prepared a way that thereby others might be partakers of the heavenly

gift, that they might hope for those things which they have not seen. (Ether 12:8)

He testifies that the Savior of the world was born into the world and prepared a glorious way that others might be partakers of the heavenly gift. And what is the heavenly gift, that which we hope for and have not yet seen? It is that we might also see His face and worship at His feet. And what is the promised way? It is the gospel of Jesus Christ. It is faith, hope, and charity. It is the lesson of the tree of life, which is following the direction of the voice of the Lord until we qualify for these profound blessings.

Mormon calls other witnesses:

And there were many whose faith was so exceedingly strong, even before Christ came, who could not be kept from within the veil, but truly saw with their eyes the things which they had beheld with an eye of faith, and they were glad. And behold, we have seen in this record that one of these was the brother of Jared; for so great was his faith in God, that when God put forth his finger he could not hide it from the sight of the brother of Jared, because of his word which he had spoken unto him, which word he had obtained by faith [which word was the promise received when his calling and election was made sure].

And after the brother of Jared had beheld the finger of the Lord, because of the promise which the brother of Jared had obtained by faith, the Lord could not withhold anything from his sight; wherefore He showed him all things, for he could no longer be kept without the veil. (Ether 12:19–20)

How did the brother of Jared arrive at these glorious blessings? He did it exactly the same way we will. The brother of Jared was living the same gospel plan we are. His faith and knowledge were great because his obedience was great.

Hear again the words of Elder McConkie:

Faith [in Christ and His voice] and knowledge [gained through revelation] unite together to pave the way for the appearance of the Lord to an individual or to a whole people. The brother of Jared saw the Lord because he had a perfect knowledge that the Lord could and would show himself [which promise the Father had given him with his own lips]. His faith on the point of seeing within the veil was perfect; it had become knowledge. Because he knew, nothing doubting, he saw. (McConkie, *Promised Messiah*, 581)

> And because of the knowledge of this man he could not be kept from beholding within the veil; and he saw the finger of Jesus, which, when he saw, he fell with fear; for he knew that it was the finger of the Lord; and he had faith no longer, for he knew, nothing doubting. Wherefore, having this perfect knowledge of God, he could not be kept from within the veil; therefore he saw Jesus; and he did minister unto him. (Ether 3:19–20)

It is obvious that the key for the brother of Jared was his knowledge. He knew the Lord would reveal himself, and this near-perfect knowledge came to him because of the "word" which the Lord himself had spoken to him (Ether 12:19–20). The same verse informs us that he had received this word through his faith in Christ. This great faith was sufficient to call forth the finger of the Lord, which, after he had beheld, caused his knowledge to become absolute. Once the brother of Jared possessed this perfect knowledge, the Lord revealed himself and showed the brother of Jared all the workmanship of his hands.

See in this verse above the same sweet, simple, and pure gospel course we have discussed all throughout this book. This course is and has always been and will always be:

- Faith in Christ—*both* in His voice, and his Atonement.
- Repentance—as directed by the Lord through His spirit.
- Baptism—by authority.
- Hope—a revealed knowledge of acceptability and worthiness.

- Charity—gained through the rebirth—the most joyful and desirable above all things.
- Trial of faith—test such as Abraham triumphantly endured.
- Calling and election—the "word" of exaltation and promise of a celestial glory spoken by the Father. This includes the spoken promise that in due time the Savior will appear. It is this knowledge that gave the brother of Jared the knowledge he needed to pierce the veil.
- Second Comforter—the personal appearance of Christ in this life, the most transcendent experience to which mortal man may ascend while in mortality.

And in that day that they shall exercise faith in me, saith the Lord, even as the brother of Jared did, that they may become sanctified in me, then will I manifest unto them the things which the brother of Jared saw, even to the unfolding unto them all my revelations, saith Jesus Christ, the Son of God, the Father of the heavens and of the earth, and all things that in them are. And he that will contend against the word of the Lord, let him be accursed; and he that shall deny these things, let him be accursed; for unto them will I show no greater things, saith Jesus Christ; for I am he who speaketh. (Ether 4:7–8)

Therefore, sanctify yourselves that your minds become single to God [now comes the greatest promise of the gospel], *and the days will come that you shall see him*; for he will unveil his face unto you, and it shall be in his own time, and in his own way, and according to his own will . . .

Sanctify yourselves; yea, purify your hearts, and cleanse your hands and your feet before me, that I may make you clean; That I may testify unto your Father, and your God, and my God, that you are clean from the blood of this wicked generation; That I may fulfil this promise, this great and last promise, which I have made unto you [that you shall see me and know that I am], when I will. (D&C 88:68, 74–75, emphasis added)

And, who will ultimately see the Savior of mankind in this life? Elder McConkie explains:

> It is the privilege of all those who have made their calling and election sure to see God; to talk with him face to face; to commune with him on a personal basis from time to time. These are the ones upon whom the Lord sends the Second Comforter. Their inheritance of exaltation and eternal life is assured, and so it becomes with them here and now in this life as it will be with all exalted beings in the life to come. They become the friends of God and converse with him on a friendly basis as one man speaks to another . . . There are, of course, those whose callings and elections have been made sure who have never exercised the faith nor exhibited the righteousness which would enable them to commune with the Lord on the promised basis. (McConkie, *Promised Messiah*, 584–86)

The purest teaching we have on this exalted subject is from the Prophet Joseph. Part of this has already been quoted but bears repeating.

> The other Comforter spoken of is a subject of great interest, and perhaps understood by few of this generation. After a person has faith in Christ, repents of his sins, and is baptized for the remission of his sins and receives the Holy Ghost, . . . which is the first Comforter, then let him continue to humble himself before God, hungering and thirsting after righteousness, and living by every word of God [which is personal revelation], and the Lord will soon say unto him, Son [or Daughter], thou shalt be exalted. When the Lord has thoroughly proved him, and finds that the man is determined to serve Him at all hazards, then the man will find his calling and his election made sure, then it will be his privilege to receive the other Comforter, which the Lord hath promised the Saints, as is recorded in the testimony of St. John, in the 14th chapter, from the 12th to the 27th verses.

The Prophet Joseph then quotes verses 16, 17, 18, 21, and 23:

16. And I will pray the Father, and He shall give you another Comforter, that he may abide with you forever;

17. Even the Spirit of Truth; whom the world cannot receive, because it seeth him not, neither knoweth him; but ye know him; for he dwelleth with you and shall be in you.

18. I will not leave you comfortless: I will come to you.

21. He that hath my commandments, and keepeth them he it is that loveth me: and he that loveth me shall be loved of my Father, and I will love him, and will manifest myself to him.

23. If a man love me, he will keep my word: and my Father will love him, and we will come unto him, and make our abode with him.

Now what is this other Comforter? It is no more nor less than the Lord Jesus Christ Himself; and this is the sum and substance of the whole matter; that when any man obtains this last Comforter, he will have the personage of Jesus Christ to attend him, or appear unto him from time to time, and even He will manifest the Father unto him, and they will take up their abode with him, and the visions of the heavens will be opened unto him, and the Lord will teach him face-to-face, and he may have a perfect knowledge of the mysteries of the Kingdom of God; . . . (and will hold) communion with the general assembly and Church of the Firstborn. (Smith, *Teachings*, 150–51)

How do we arrive at such an exalted station? It is done by attuning and yielding ourselves to the voice of Christ through the Holy Spirit. It is done by living so we can enjoy the full measure of the gift of the Holy Ghost, which is the constant companionship of that member of Deity. Then the process of spiritual maturation will begin in earnest. The doors of heaven begin to swing open, and the views inside are glorious. Miracles become commonplace, our prayers powerful and effective. Angels attend, teach, and protect. The time will come when the heavens will open, and the voice of God will echo in your soul, declaring your irrevocable right to enter into His presence and ultimately into

His kingdom. Your heart will burn with a desire to serve, and your life will become a blessing to everyone you touch. Your service will be meaningful, and lives will change forever because of your work. You will walk in the light of revelation day by day, and contend successfully against the snares and entrapments of the adversary. After all this and more, you will find the light of eternity brightening upon you, and you will be ushered into the presence of the Lord.

Hear the words of an apostle of God:

> After the true saints receive and enjoy the gift of the Holy Ghost; after they know how to attune themselves to the voice of the Spirit; after they mature spiritually so that they see visions, work miracles, and entertain angels; after they make their calling and election sure and prove themselves worthy of every trust—after all this and more—it becomes their right and privilege to see the Lord and commune with him face to face. Revelations, visions, angelic visitations, the rending of the heavens, and appearances among men of the Lord himself—all these things are for all of the faithful. They are not reserved for apostles and prophets only. (McConkie, *Promised Messiah*, 575)

This is the way, the *only* way. It is the way prepared by Christ Himself through the great plan of exaltation. Elder McConkie defines the straight and narrow path to exaltation as beginning with learning to attune ourselves to the voice of the Spirit, a subject we have discussed at length. Then we must continue faithful in that gift and mature spiritually until we see visions, and do mighty works, until we have our callings and elections made sure. After this and more, it becomes our right—not just our privilege, *our right*—to see the Lord face-to-face. *Knowing* that it was his covenanted right to enter the presence of the Lord was what brought the brother of Jared the necessary faith to claim the reward. The promise is so magnificently beautiful, and the way so plainly marked, that all those who truly seek will obtain it. We must not fear the price required to receive it.

The fact that these blessings are for *all* Saints is nearly impossible to impress upon the hearts of the would-be faithful. This single seed of truth is so precious that it is often stolen away by the evil one before it can take root. The delusion supplanted in its place is that only the prophets and apostles ever become sufficiently righteous to receive such profound blessings. Or that it is possible for common members to enjoy the profound spiritual experiences, but that it rarely, if ever, happens.

The truth is that anyone who makes exaltation his or her primary goal in life will succeed. The laws of God promise that those who flawlessly obey Him will be exalted—no exceptions. It does not matter how profound your flaws are. If you obey Him, He will make you all that you must be to be perfect. Satan does not want you to believe this. He wants you to content yourself with spiritual mediocrity. He would have you give up trying to stretch your soul into eternity and grasp the profound blessings of God. He does not want you to penetrate the veil with your faith and behold the face of God.

But this truth remains, if you have the faith and courage to believe it, it is not beyond your reach. You have only to reorder your thinking to achieve it. It requires a willingness to sacrifice the present course of your life. It requires you to change, to allow yourself to be directed and guided in a manner you never thought possible, into paths you didn't know were there, accomplishing miracles you never dreamed possible. It requires obedience on a celestial scale. Once we realize that every wholesome prompting coming into our mind day or night is revelation, is the voice of the Lord, is our opportunity to hear and obey, we will have the path in sight. Making this realization is the easy part. The hard part is to change our mindset to one of absolute obedience. Even this becomes a joy as we begin to experience the sweet fruits of our obedience. He will bless us with an increasingly obedient heart as we take hold of the rod of iron.

If you struggle with the apparent impossibility of these dramatic accomplishments in your life, it is because you have no idea how complete the changes are, or how empowering is the constant companionship of the Holy Ghost. The process, once entered upon, is joyful, soul-enriching, and awe-inspiring. Imagine living in a state of mind where you cannot even comprehend how much the Lord has blessed you, nor find words magnificent enough to praise and worship Him, except when they are given you by the Holy Ghost. Imagine at times receiving immediate answers to your prayers, daily revelation, priesthood power as potent as Enoch's, and faith sufficient to move mountains at His bidding if necessary. Imagine having your soul filled day and night with His love. Imagine having the revealed promise that you will be exalted. Imagine all this and a thousand times more, and ask again, is it worth the price of absolute obedience? Let me give you the answer tens of thousands will also give with tears of joy flowing down their cheeks. Oh yes, my sister, my brother, *yes—yes—yes*. There is so much to gain, and an eternity to lose. If you truly try, you will succeed. If you fail to try, you fail. If you succeed, you gain eternal life.

Again, Elder McConkie:

> If we keep the commandments and are true and faithful in all things, we shall inherit eternal life in our Father's kingdom ... And all who are now living those laws to the full which will enable them to go where God and Christ are, and there enjoy eternal association with them—that is, all those who are now living in its entirety the law of the celestial kingdom—are already qualified to see the Lord. The attainment of such a state of righteousness and perfection is the object and end toward which all of the Lord's people are striving. We seek to see the face of the Lord while we yet dwell in mortality, we seek to dwell with him everlastingly in the eternal kingdoms that are prepared. (McConkie, *Promised Messiah*, 578–79)

The single most important lesson you can learn to prepare yourself to be born again, elected, and ultimately ushered into the presence of the Lord, is the lesson of obedience: obedience to the voice of the Lord and written laws.

Note the power of these principles:

> Verily, thus saith the Lord: It shall come to pass that every soul who forsaketh his sins and cometh unto me, and calleth on my name, and *obeyeth my voice*, and keepeth my commandments, shall see my face [in this life], and know that I am. (D&C 93:1, emphasis added)

The scriptures bear powerful witness of these truths.

The way we forsake sins is by qualifying for the rebirth. We come unto Him, qualifying for a place with Him through having our callings and elections made sure. We call on His name through mighty prayer.

We hear and *obey* His voice through obedience to the Holy Spirit. We keep His commandments by living by every word that He speaks, and after all this, we may see His face and know His glory and infinite love firsthand.

> And if your eye be single to my glory [which is a spiritual enhancement beginning at the rebirth], your whole bodies shall be filled with light, and there shall be no darkness in you; and that body which is filled with light comprehendeth all things. Therefore, sanctify yourselves that your minds become single to God, and the days will come that you shall see him; for he will unveil his face unto you, and it shall be in his own time, and in his own way, and according to his own will. (D&C 88:67–68)

The following touching description of what it is like to behold the Savior is so precious that no discussion of this type could be complete without it. These are the words of Melvin J. Ballard, who was ordained an apostle in 1919. He dreamed he was allowed into the presence of the Savior in the Salt Lake Temple.

If I shall live to be a million years old, I shall never forget that smile. He took me into His arms and kissed me, pressed me to His bosom, and blessed me, until the marrow of my bones seemed to melt! When He had finished, I fell at His feet, and as I bathed them with my tears and kisses, I saw the prints of the nails in the feet of the Redeemer of the world. The feeling that I had in the presence of Him who hath all things in His hands, to have His love, His affection, and His blessing was such that if I can receive that of which I had but a foretaste, I would give all that I am, all that I hope to be, to feel what I then felt! (Melvin J. Ballard, quoted in Cannon, "Latter-day Visions," 127)

Chapter Six

Making It Happen

Your Pocket Journal

Those who have read under the influence of the Spirit thus far will know what they must do to continue their journey home. What they may yet lack is a concrete starting point. It is not uncommon to have a testimony of a principle without having a clue how to implement it. The spiritual pilgrim thus lifts a foot to move onward in the journey, and not knowing where to put it down, puts it back where it came from.

Keeping a pocket journal is a tool many people find of great worth in helping them begin to identify personal revelation in their lives, and to begin to live thereby. It has been the means of blessing many lives, and can have a powerful impact upon your own if you diligently apply it. Here are some suggestions on making this tool work for you.

Obtain a notebook small enough to fit in your shirt pocket or purse. On the inside of the front cover write "The Small Plates of" and your name. I suggest using just your first name. Begin carrying this with you at all times. At night, set it on your bed stand with your pen inside.

Each time you receive a prompting, write it down. Write them *all* down, no matter how insignificant they may seem. (In reality, no revelation is insignificant.) Leave a blank space after each entry.

At a later time, record in the blank space whether you obeyed the prompting, and the results of your obedience (or disobedience).

At times you may be prompted to record your prayers, and the answers you receive. In time these recorded prayers, and the Lord's responses, will become a significant blessing to you.

Record priesthood blessings (given or received) and special insights gained on doctrine or scripture.

Start and keep another, more complete journal. Periodically transfer the most significant of entries from your "small plates" to your larger journal, adding as much detail as the Spirit directs. Write this journal with the clear understanding that others will eventually read it—certainly your posterity, possibly many others. When you write about your frustrations and failures, also write about their resolution, and eventual conquest through your faith. Write only what is truth. Fill your journal with things that will aid those who read it in their search for righteousness. Bear testimony often, express faith and joy. Write under the influence of the Holy Ghost. Remember that the Book of Mormon started as a righteous man's journal. Let your greatest legacy be the life you live and record in your journal.

Periodically reread your journal. Remind yourself of your blessings, learn from your mistakes, and rejoice in your successes.

As time goes by, you will be amazed at how often the Spirit prompts you and you are blessed by the Lord. You will find that you receive direction in many things throughout the day. You will also begin to clearly see the direction you are being urged to go. The reason it is so important to write down all your promptings, even when you disobey them, is that it becomes a written record of the mind and will of the Lord for you personally. In a sense, it becomes scripture to you, and your "small plates" will become a jewel of incalculable value.

An additional blessing this exercise brings is that it lets us identify false promptings or ones attempting to deceive us into accepting them as from God when they actually are not. When one of these false or deceptive promptings comes, you will faithfully write it down. In time you will realize that it did not come true or was not divinely inspired. When you go back to record the results of the prompting, you will be reminded of how that prompting came, what its "flavor" was, and how you eventually uncovered its deception. When such a one comes again, you will be forearmed and not easily duped.

Another unexpected blessing from this exercise is that it casts bright light upon your progress. In the beginning you will record many things like:

"Received a prompting to drive the speed limit. I ignored it. Got a speeding ticket!!"

As time goes by, the power of the promptings will increase. You will begin to rejoice in the voice of the Lord as He leads you line upon line, precept upon precept. Your entries will begin to look something like this:

"Received a prompting to bear my testimony to my boss. Was afraid at first and procrastinated several days. Finally did it and had a marvelous experience."

As long as your obedience endures, and you faithfully act upon all you know to be from the Lord, in time your entries will become similar to this:

"I felt impressed to read Ether 12. Pondered and prayed mightily as the Spirit rested upon me, causing me to burn from head to toe. The Spirit whispered 'You shall also be blessed, for this is your promised heritage.' Could not keep tears from coming. For the first time I felt perfect hope and joy beyond my understanding. How I rejoice in the Lord, and the promises that are mine. For the first time in my life, I know what the scripture means 'my cup runneth over.'"

I believe all revelation is sacred to the Lord, and He is offended when we ignore it. I also suspect He is offended when we just plain forget what He has told us. Besides this, forgetting where we're going slows our forward progress to a painful crawl.

OTHER HELPS

Here are several other suggestions that may aid you in ordering your life to obedience. This is not a formula for achieving spiritual growth but suggestions on things that may prepare you for such growth. Prayerfully consider which may be of value to you.

- Obtain a picture of the Savior and hang it on your bedroom wall where you can see it when you awaken.
- Set aside fifteen minutes each evening, just before retiring, for studying the Book of Mormon and for prayer.
- Set aside fifteen minutes each morning for scripture study and prayer.
- Critically examine your television viewing. Eliminate shows that you would not watch if the prophet, or other general authority, were a guest in your home. Instead of watching TV, find a more wholesome and uplifting activity to take its place.
- Schedule a fast during the week (not a weekend). Ask the Lord to guide you to know for what you should fast.

- If you are not doing so already, begin to attend all your meetings.
- Get a temple recommend, no matter how difficult it is or how long it has been. Set your life in order and enter the house of the Lord.

Select a basic principle of the gospel such as faith, hope, repentance, baptism, gift of the Holy Ghost, rebirth of the spirit, charity, or something similar. Find the subject in the topical guide and look up every listed scripture. Make notes in your "Small Plates" of new insights you gain.

- Go to your local LDS bookstore and prayerfully select a book. Read it in addition to your scripture study. Write your spiritual insights into your pocket journal. There are hundreds of books that will bless your life. There are thousands that will not. Following is a list of books you may want to consider.

RECOMMENDED READING

- *A New Witness for the Articles of Faith* by Bruce R. McConkie
- *Spiritual Progression in the Last Days* by Blaine Yorgason
- *Life of Joseph Smith the Prophet* by George Q. Cannon
- *Teachings of the Prophet Joseph Smith* compiled by Joseph Fielding Smith
- *The Promised Messiah* by Bruce R. McConkie
- *The Millennial Messiah* by Bruce R. McConkie
- *The Mortal Messiah* by Bruce R. McConkie, volumes 1–4
- *Approaching Zion* by Hugh Nibley
- *The Triumph of Zion* by John M. Pontius

Fearlessly evaluate your life, and through prayer and fasting, ask Heavenly Father what you should do next to further your spiritual journey. Do whatever you are prompted to do.

Conclusion

The Book of Mormon was written specifically for us, the Saints of the latter days. Mormon, the great Nephite prophet who compiled the book, saw our time (Mormon 8:35). He knew us in great detail and chose the lessons from the history of his people that would parallel our dispensation. We may, therefore, apply these lessons to ourselves, knowing absolutely that they were written to show us the way to fulfilling our role in the latter days. We may read warnings to those ancient peoples as a voice of one crying from the dust, delivering that same warning to us. If we ignore the prophetic voice of warning, we do so at our own peril.

We know we live in the times immediately preceding the Lord's second coming. With this in mind, let us analyze the affairs of the ancient church of Christ in the days of Alma, the son of Alma, immediately preceding the advent of the Savior to those people, a time in their history that parallels our own.

The church had gone through a long period of spiritual growth and then had quickly fallen into decay. Alma, the chief judge and prophet of the Lord, gave up his position as judge, so that he could labor full time in strengthening the church. He went forth among the people, enunciating their sins and calling them to repentance. He was fully aware that if he failed to convince them of their wickedness, they would be destroyed. He bore down in powerful testimony against them. He called them "wicked," and accused them of "trampling the Holy One under their feet" because of their great sins. And what was this great sin for which the Lord was about to destroy them? It was pride and envy within the church, not caring for the needy, and setting their hearts upon riches. Note the following:

> And now my beloved brethren, I say unto you, can ye withstand these sayings; yea, can ye lay aside these things, and trample the Holy One under your feet; yea, can ye be puffed up in the pride of your hearts; yea, will ye still persist in the wearing of costly apparel and setting your hearts upon the vain things of the world, upon your riches? (Alma 5:53)

The reason this chastisement is in the Book of Mormon is because we are likewise guilty of these sins. We, meaning those of us within the Church, have become an affluent and wealthy people, and we can only wonder at how many of us have become lifted up in the pride of our hearts. Some Latter-day Saints read this accusation and inwardly wonder why Alma was getting so excited about it, or why the Lord would destroy them for such a seemingly insignificant thing as pride. They even wonder what is so wrong about having riches.

Pride, and pursuing riches, is not a spiritual sickness in and of itself, it is rather a symptom of a larger disease. It is the presence of this disease within the Church which is so wicked, and for which the Lord was willing to destroy the Nephites—and us. *This disease is the cancer of disobedience.* The most visible sign of someone abandoning the path of truth, and obedience to the Holy Spirit, is the setting of his or her heart upon riches and the vain things of the world, wearing costly apparel, and despising those who have less than they. For *this* the Lord will destroy us, not because we have nice clothes. Again, I quote Elder McConkie:

> Even in the true Church in the last days there will be some who do not believe the whole body of revealed truth; some who do not give full allegiance to the cause of truth and righteousness; some who are members in name only and who continue to live after the manner of the world. This also is one of the signs of the times. It shall be as it was among some of old whom Paul rebuked:
>
> "When ye come together in the church," he wrote to the Corinthians, "there be divisions among you." Contention, debate, and false views have no place in the Church and kingdom of our Lord. (McConkie, *Millennial Messiah*, 59–60)

Let us consider more of Alma's words to the church of his day.

> Yea, will ye persist in supposing that ye are better one than another. . . . Yea and will ye persist in turning your backs upon the poor and needy, and in withholding your substance from them? And finally, all ye that will persist in your wickedness, I say unto you these are they who shall be hewn down and cast into the fire except they speedily repent. (Alma 5:54–56)

Alma wants there to be no mistake about what the outcome will be. He calls these sins wickedness and issues a solemn warning to the people. Then, as now, there were envyings, strife, and malice in the church, even pride to exceed the pride of those who did not belong to the church of God. (See Alma 4:9)

> And the wickedness of the church was a great stumbling-block to those who did not belong to the church; and thus the church began to fail in its progress. (Alma 4:10)

Because of the wickedness of the church, which was pride and seeking wealth, the church slowed and finally failed in its progress. Their pride and arrogance was a stumbling block to those to whom they were trying to teach the gospel. Their investigators could not see the truth because the people who were supposed to be living it were arrogant and unsaintly. At times, this seems to be the case today. Any former missionary can testify that the existing members of the church can be a stumbling block for investigators. Investigators often believe the missionaries' message and wish to embrace it, but are sometimes repelled by the fact that someone they know is a "Mormon" and not living their religion. It is even the case that new members are occasionally rebuffed, not welcomed, or perhaps embarrassed by those who should be rejoicing with them in their new faith.

Alma successfully called his people to repentance and prevented their destruction. We need to carefully examine his message, which was so effective. In so doing, we will discover the precious key to the way in which we may likewise avert the just judgments of God.

Having defined the source of the condemnation under which the Church was laboring, Alma then taught them what they must do. He taught them about the rebirth of the Spirit and how to achieve it. He knew those who experienced the *mighty change* attendant to the rebirth would no longer desire prideful living and worldly possessions. *Remember, these were active church members who considered themselves worthy, yet had focused on the world, instead of upon Christ.* The Lord calls all such "workers of iniquity." Alma calls to them, and to us, with great passion:

> Yea, even wo unto all ye workers of iniquity; repent, repent, for the Lord God hath spoken it! Behold, he sendeth an invitation unto all men, for the arms of mercy are extended towards them, and he saith: Repent, and I will receive you. (Alma 5:32–33)

He then reminds them of the lesson of the tree of life, which represents Christ's everlasting love, of which we may be partakers through the rebirth. He offers them the waters of life that spring up from the fountain of living waters, even Jesus the Christ. And the waters flowing from this eternal fountain are His light and truth through the Holy Spirit.

> Yea, he saith: Come unto me and ye shall partake of the
> fruit of the tree of life; yea, ye shall eat and drink of the bread
> and the waters of life freely; Yea, come unto me and bring forth
> works of righteousness, and ye shall not be hewn down and
> cast into the fire. (Alma 5:34–35)

Alma continues his address by condemning the workers of iniquity. To make sure there is no mistake in who He was addressing, He identified them plainly. He was speaking to people of his time, and ours, who profess to know the ways of righteousness, but have gone astray, and become puffed up in the vain things of the world. He was not speaking to lost sheep, inactive members, or even nonmembers. He was speaking to those who thought themselves righteous and faithful.

His words speak to us too:

> O ye workers of iniquity; ye that are puffed up in the vain
> things of the world, ye that have professed to have known the
> ways of righteousness nevertheless have gone astray, as sheep
> having no shepherd, notwithstanding a shepherd hath called
> after you and is still calling after you, but ye will not hearken
> unto his voice! (Alma 5:37)

But we are *not* without a shepherd. He *is* calling after us, but we will not hearken to His voice. Oh, how spiritually deaf and willful we sheep can be. What is the voice to which they would not, and many of us will not hearken? It is the voice of the Lord that echoes endlessly in our minds. It is the voice of the conscience, which if obeyed will become a fountain of living waters springing up unto eternal life. It is pure, sustained revelation from the Fountain of All Righteousness, and it leaves us without excuse for our failure to heed His loving call.

The Fountain of All Righteousness is Jesus Christ (see Ether 8:26 and Ether 12:28 as examples). It is a beautiful metaphor because all truth flows from Him through the light of Christ. But still the shepherd calls, and if we will not hearken to His voice, to whose voice are we hearkening? It is the voice of the evil one that we list to obey. Hear the words of Alma as he continues to warn us:

> Behold, I say unto you, that the good shepherd doth call you; yea, and in his own name he doth call you, which is the name of Christ; and if ye will not hearken unto the voice of the good shepherd, to the name by which ye are called, behold, ye are not the sheep of the good shepherd. (Alma 5:38)

He calls to us day and night, and if we will not hearken and come to Him, then we are not His sheep, *even if we belong to His true church*!

> And now if ye are not the sheep of the good shepherd, of what fold are ye? Behold, I say unto you, that the devil is your shepherd, and ye are of his fold. (Alma 5:39)

The Lord's sheep hear His voice and obey Him. His sheep come to Him by faithfully walking the straight and narrow path, which He reveals to them through the still small voice. His sheep know His voice and love to hear Him call. His sheep are obedient to His voice and delight in following after Him. His sheep are the wise virgins who have taken the Holy Spirit to be their guide. *They are His sheep because they have made Him their shepherd.* And, as the above verse testifies, if we hearken not to His voice, then we have taken the devil for our shepherd and are of his fold! There is no neutral ground. We are in one kingdom or the other. We cannot hold citizenship in both.

Alma's final words to the members of the Church were given by way of commandment. He commands them to repent and partake of the fruit of the tree of life, which is achieved by diligently holding onto the iron rod of personal revelation.

> I speak by way of command unto you that belong to the church; and unto those who do not belong to the church I speak by way of invitation, saying: Come and be baptized unto repentance, that ye also may be partakers of the fruit of the tree of life. (Alma 5:62)

Alma's message to his people just before the advent of the Savior in their day sounds a powerful warning as we prepare ourselves for the second coming of Christ. Now is the hour of our greatest peril. Never before has the enemy of righteousness had greater power over the Lord's people. But his dark power is not because the Lord's people want evil, it is because some of them have been deceived. They have grown comfortable and complacent. Nephi, the son of Lehi, likewise saw our day and issued this warning to us. In words of unmistakable power, he warns us against exactly what we have partly allowed to occur.

> And others will he pacify, and lull them away into carnal security, that they will say: All is well in Zion; yea, Zion prospereth, all is well—and thus the devil cheateth their souls, and leadeth them away carefully down to hell. Therefore, wo be unto him that is at ease in Zion! (2 Nephi 28:21, 24)

How does Satan lull them away? He entices people to think they are righteous because they are safe and secure. In other words, they have a good job, they have insurance and retirement, the church has lots of money—yea, all is well.

Just as the Holy Spirit whispers truth to our hearts, the evil one whispers lies of carnal security to our ears:

> And thus he whispereth in their ears, until he grasps them with his awful chains, from whence there is no deliverance. (2 Nephi 28:22)

This threat is more real in these times of prosperity and relative peace than in times of privation and persecution.

It is tempting to believe that we are prosperous and at peace because we are righteous. After all, are not these things blessings from God? Would we be so blessed if we were not righteous? Of course these things are blessings. The problem is, Satan is using the security of these times to lull the Saints into spiritual paralysis. If we hear and believe Satan's voice, we are not hearing the voice of Christ instructing us in the course to eternal life. We simply cannot obey both masters. If we choose to be enticed into carnal security, then we are being "lead away carefully down to hell."

Those who fall into this trap have not learned how to take the Holy Spirit to be their guide nor understood that doing so is essential to their spiritual survival (see D&C 45:56–57). Because they have not experienced the mighty change, which is the fruit of the rebirth, they continue to vigorously pursue those things that bring pride and worldly success and that lead them into forbidden paths.

> Behold, there are many called, but few are chosen. And why are they not chosen? Because their hearts are set so much upon the things of this world, and aspire to the honors of men. (D&C 121:34–35)

The prophets of our own day have repeatedly warned us that we are under condemnation and must repent:

> Nevertheless, Zion shall escape if she observe to do all things whatsoever I have commanded her. But if she observe not to do whatsoever I have commanded her, I will visit her according to all her works, with sore affliction, with pestilence, with plague, with sword, with vengeance, with devouring fire. (D&C 97:25–26)

Elder McConkie joins in the warning voice:

> Zion in [Joseph Smith's] day did not keep the commandments and gain the promised blessings, nor have we, their successors in interest, risen to the standard set by them of old. The saints sought to build up Zion in Missouri and failed. Some of the promised scourging fell upon them, and more of it will yet fall upon us if we do not keep the commandments more fully than in the past. (McConkie, *Millennial Messiah*, 288)

The prophet Joseph Smith was given this solemn warning to issue to us. We are still laboring under the same sin as the people of his day. Note well the warning:

And I now give unto you a commandment to beware concerning yourselves, to give diligent heed to the words of eternal life. For you shall live by every word that proceedeth forth from the mouth of God. For the word of the Lord is truth, and whatsoever is truth is light, and whatsoever is light is Spirit, even the Spirit of Jesus Christ. (D&C 84:43–45)

We are commanded to give diligent heed to the words of eternal life. And what are these words? They are every word that proceeds forth from the mouth of God through the Spirit of Jesus Christ, which is the Holy Spirit.

And the Spirit giveth light to every man that cometh into the world; and the Spirit enlighteneth every man through the world, that hearkeneth to the voice of the Spirit. And every one that hearkeneth to the voice of the Spirit cometh unto God, even the Father. (D&C 84:46–47)

Every person who is born has this gift, and all are without excuse. In the day of judgment all will see how complete and loving His guiding influence has been. And we will see that any person who would have listened to and obeyed the voice of the Spirit would have achieved exaltation! The promise is universal and profound, and everyone who hears and obeys cometh unto the Father.

For whoso cometh not unto me is under the bondage of sin. And whoso receiveth not my voice is not acquainted with my voice, and is not of me. And by this you may know the righteous from the wicked, and that the whole world groaneth under sin and darkness even now. (D&C 84:51–53)

Any person, even one within the true church, who does not receive and know His voice is under the bondage of sin. And by this gauge of whether or not someone harkens to the voice of the Spirit, you may know the righteous from the wicked. The following verse amplifies this warning to us specifically within His church.

> And your minds in times past have been darkened because
> of unbelief, and because you have treated lightly the things you
> have received—Which vanity and unbelief have brought the
> whole church under condemnation. (D&C 84:54–55)

What things have we treated lightly because of unbelief, which vanity has brought the whole church under condemnation? Among other things, *it is the promptings of the Holy Spirit.* We know this because in the previous eleven verses, He has been talking about the light of Christ, and immediately thereafter accuses us of being "darkened" because of unbelief.

Some of us are too vain, and our hearts are too swollen with worldly pride to allow ourselves to be led by something as insignificant as a still small voice. Some of us just don't realize the power of obedience nor the blessings that could be ours. Some want flashes of divine light and trumpeting angels, and then they would obey. There are even some who think they should do it all themselves, and even when they receive a prompting, they worry that it infringes upon their right to choose and chart their own path.

The Lord declares in the first thirty verses of section 93 that He is the true light that lights the world and every person therein. He attests:

> Therefore, in the beginning the Word was, for he was the
> Word, even the messenger of salvation—The light of and the
> Redeemer of the world; the Spirit of truth, who came into the
> world, because the world was made by him, and in him was the
> life of men and the light of men. (D&C 93:8–9)

Then He makes this tremendous statement: "Behold, here is the agency of man." In other words, because of the light of Christ which permeates our souls, we have the ability to choose, and hence, we have agency. "And here is the condemnation of man" also flowing from the fact that we have this tremendous blessing of the light of Christ, which the scripture calls the "messenger of salvation, . . . because that which was from the beginning is plainly manifest unto them." The light of Christ, the Word of God, is so plainly manifest that *all* who live may hear it. And sadly, the scripture concludes, "They receive not the light. And every man whose spirit receiveth not the light is under condemnation" (See D&C 93:31–32).

When we ignore the sweet voice of our Savior, quietly guiding us along, "That wicked one cometh and taketh away light and truth." How? "Through disobedience, and because of the tradition of their fathers" (D&C 93:39). The evil one steals away our light through disobedience, first to the voice of God, and ultimately to the commandments of God. No person ever yet broke a commandment of God, except they first disobeyed many promptings warning against doing so.

Is it possible that as a church, as a people of God, we have forgotten how to hear and obey His voice? Could it be true that those who do obey mostly do it instinctively? We seem to follow our feelings and inclinations, scarcely realizing that these promptings we follow are actually coming from Jesus Christ. Without this essential realization, we feel free to disregard those promptings that do not appeal to us. In order to become the elect of God, we must learn to hear and obey *every* word which proceeds forth from the mouth of God.

Now is the time when this message must be shouted from the rooftops, written into songs of worship, and taught in plainness to everyone. It must be taught to children, new converts, and life-long members alike. Now is the time when we need His voice in our hearts more than ever before. If we are to meet Him at His coming and be welcomed at the wedding feast, if we are going to be the "wise virgins" who have taken the Holy Spirit to be our guide, then we must get "wise" with great haste.

The cry will soon go forth, "The Bridegroom cometh!" and it will be everlastingly too late to purchase oil with which to light our lamps. For the oil is the voice of Christ in our hearts, the still small voice, and thereafter, the greater gift of the Holy Ghost. It cannot be bought or sold but must be acquired through diligent obedience.

This book constitutes my witness that Jesus Christ lives, that through His Holy Spirit, He speaks to us night and day. I am profoundly indebted to Him, and my heart swells with love at the mention of His holy name. He is my Savior, my Redeemer, and the meaning of my life.

The way is straight and narrow, and indeed, few there be that find it. Not because it is impossible, or even hidden, but because they do not learn the lesson of the tree of life.

I urge you to ponder these stirring words of the Lord, and commend you to seek Him of whom the prophets testify, and of whom the Holy Ghost bears fervent witness:

> Behold, there are many called, but few are chosen. And why are they not chosen? Because their hearts are set so much upon the things of this world, and aspire to the honors of men, that they do not learn this one lesson—That the rights of the priesthood are inseparably connected with the powers of heaven, and that the powers of heaven cannot be controlled nor handled only upon the principles of righteousness . . . Hence many are called, but few are chosen . . . Let thy bowels also be full of charity towards all men, and to the household of faith, and let virtue garnish thy thoughts unceasingly; then shall thy confidence wax strong in the presence of God; and the doctrine of the priesthood shall distill upon thy soul as the dews from heaven. The Holy Ghost shall be thy constant companion, and thy scepter an unchanging scepter of righteousness and truth; and thy dominion shall be an everlasting dominion, and without compulsory means it shall flow unto thee forever and ever. (D&C 121:34–35, 40, 45–46)

With your new understanding of the light of Christ, and the ultimate joy of having the Lord lift up His countenance unto you, I close with this ancient and glorious salutation:

The Lord bless thee and keep thee: The Lord make his face shine upon thee, and be gracious unto thee: The Lord lift up his countenance upon thee, and give thee peace. (Num. 6:24–26)

May this literally come to pass in your life.

Bibliography

All Bible references are from the King James version.

Cannon, Donald Q. "Latter-day Visions of the Savior." In *Hearken, O Ye People: Discourses on the Doctrine and Covenants*, 119–31. Sandy, Utah: Randall Book, 1984.

Clark, James R., compo *Messages of the First Presidency of The Church of Jesus Christ of Latter-day Saints*, 18331964. 6 vols. Salt Lake City: Bookcraft, 1965–75.

Faust, James E. "The Voice of the Spirit." *Ensign* 34 (April 1994): 6–10.

Hymns of the Church of Jesus Christ of Latter-day Saints. Salt Lake City: The Church of Jesus Christ of Latter-day Saints, 1985.

Journal of Discourses. 26 vols. Liverpool: F. D. Richards, 1855–86.

McConkie, Bruce R. *Doctrinal New Testament Commentary*. 3 vols. Salt Lake City: Bookcraft, 1965–73.

McConkie, Bruce R. *The Millennial Messiah: The Second Coming of the Son of Man*. Salt Lake City: Deseret Book Co., 1982.

McConkie, Bruce R. *Mormon Doctrine*. 2d ed. Salt Lake City: Bookcraft, 1966.

McConkie, Bruce R. *The Promised Messiah. The First Coming of Christ.* Salt Lake City: Deseret Book Co., 1978.

Nibley, Hugh W. *Approaching Zion.* Ed. Don E. Norton.

The Collected Works of Hugh Nibley, vol. 9. Salt Lake City: Deseret Book; Provo, Utah: Foundation for Ancient Research and Mormon Studies (F.A.R.M.S.), 1989.

Smith, Joseph, Jr. *Lectures on Faith.* On LDS Collectors Library CD. Infobases, Inc., 1991.

Smith, Joseph Fielding. *Doctrines of Salvation: Sermons and Writings of Joseph Fielding Smith.* Ed. Bruce R. McConkie. 3 vols. Salt Lake City: Bookcraft, 1954–56.

Smith, Joseph Fielding, compo *Teachings of the Prophet Joseph Smith.* Salt Lake City: Deseret Book Co., 1974.

Yorgason, Blaine M. *Spiritual Progression in the Last Days.* Salt Lake City: Deseret Book, 1994.

Appendix A

For verily the voice of the Lord is unto all men, and there is none to escape; and there is no eye that shall not see, neither ear that shall not hear, neither heart that shall not be penetrated. (D&C 1:2)

Wherefore the voice of the Lord is unto the ends of the earth, that all that will hear may hear. (D&C 1:11)

And the arm of the Lord shall be revealed; and the day cometh that they who will not hear the voice of the Lord, neither the voice of his servants, neither give heed to the words of the prophets and apostles, shall be cut off from among the people. (D&C 1:14)

Yea, behold, I will tell you in your mind and in your heart, by the Holy Ghost, which shall come upon you and which shall dwell in your heart. Now, behold, this is the spirit of revelation; behold, this is the spirit by which Moses brought the children of Israel through the Red Sea on dry ground. (D&C 8:2–3)

For it is my voice which speaketh them unto you; for they are given by my Spirit unto you, and by my power you can read them one to another; and save it were by my power you could not have them. (D&C 18:35)

Who will gather his people even as a hen gathereth her chickens under her wings, even as many as will hearken to my voice and humble themselves before me, and call upon me in mighty prayer. (D&C 29:2)

And ye are called to bring to pass the gathering of mine elect; for mine elect hear my voice and harden not their hearts. (D&C 29:7)

And even so will I gather mine elect from the four quarters of the earth, even as many as will believe in me, and hearken unto my voice. (D&C 33:6)

And even so will I cause the wicked to be kept, that will not hear my voice but harden their hearts, and wo, wo, wo, is their doom. (D&C 38:6)

Wherefore, hear my voice and follow me, and you shall be a free people, and ye shall have no laws but my laws when I come, for I am your lawgiver, and what can stay my hand? (D&C 38:22)

But, behold, the days of thy deliverance are come, if thou wilt hearken to my voice, which saith unto thee: Arise and be baptized, and wash away your sins, calling on my name, and you shall receive my Spirit, and a blessing so great as you never have known. (D&C 39:10)

And again I say, hearken unto my voice, lest death shall overtake you; in an hour when ye think not the summer shall be past, and the harvest ended, and your souls not saved. (D&C 45:2)

Hearken, O ye people of my church, and ye elders listen together, and hear my voice while it is called today, and harden not your hearts. (D&C 45:6)

And at that day, when I shall come in my glory, shall the parable be fulfilled which I spake concerning the ten virgins. For they that are wise and have received the truth, and have taken the Holy Spirit for their guide, and have not been deceived—verily I say unto you, they shall not be hewn down and cast into the fire, but shall abide the day. (D&C 45:56–57)

And it shall come to pass that he that asketh in Spirit shall receive in Spirit . . . He that asketh in the Spirit asketh according to the will of God; wherefore it is done even as he asketh. (D&C 46:28, 30)

And if ye are purified and cleansed from sin, ye shall ask whatsoever ye will in the name of Jesus and it shall be done. But know this, it shall be given you what ye shall ask. (D&C 50:29–30)

Behold, thus saith the Lord unto the elders whom he hath called and chosen in these last days, by the voice of his Spirit. (D&C 52:1)

Behold, I, the Lord, utter my voice, and it shall be obeyed. (D&C 63:5)

Verily, verily, I say unto you, I who speak even by the voice of my Spirit, even Alpha and Omega, your Lord and your God. (D&C 75:1)

And I now give you a commandment to beware concerning yourselves, to give diligent heed to the words of eternal life. For you shall live by every word that proceedeth forth from the mouth of God. For the word of the Lord is truth, and whatsoever is truth is light, and whatsoever is light is Spirit, even the Spirit of Jesus Christ. (D&C 84:43–45)

And the Spirit giveth light to every man that cometh into the world; and the Spirit enlighteneth every man through the world, that hearkeneth to the voice of the Spirit. And every one that hearkeneth to the voice of the Spirit cometh unto God, even the Father. (D&C 84:46–47)

And whoso receiveth not my voice is not acquainted with my voice, and is not of me. And by this you may know the righteous from the wicked, and that the whole world groaneth under sin and darkness even now. (D&C 84:52–53)

Yea, thus saith the still small voice, which whispereth through and pierceth all things. (D&C 85:6)

Behold, that which you hear is as the voice of one crying in the wilderness—in the wilderness, because you cannot see him—my voice, because my voice is Spirit; my Spirit is truth; truth abideth and hath no end; and if it be in you it shall abound. (D&C 88:66)

Verily, thus saith the Lord: It shall come to pass that every soul who forsaketh his sins and cometh unto me, and calleth on my name, and obeyeth my voice, and keepeth my commandments, shall see my face and know that I am. (D&C 93:1)

Behold, here is the agency of man, and here is the condemnation of man; because that which was from the beginning [the Word, the light of Christ] is plainly manifest unto them, and they receive not the light. And every man whose spirit receiveth not the light is under condemnation . . . . And that wicked one cometh and taketh away light and truth, through disobedience, from the children of men, and because of the traditions of their fathers. (D&C 93:31–32, 39)

Verily I say unto you my friends, I speak unto you with my voice, even the voice of my Spirit, that I may show unto you my will concerning your brethren in the land of Zion, many of whom are truly humble and are seeking diligently to learn wisdom and to find truth. (D&C 97:1)

There is even now already in store sufficient, yea, even an abundance, to redeem Zion, and establish her waste places, no more to be thrown down, were the churches, who call themselves after my name, willing to hearken to my voice. (D&C 101:75)

And it shall be manifest unto my servant, by the voice of the Spirit, those that are chosen; and they shall be sanctified. (D&C 105:36)

And make proposals for peace unto those who have smitten you, according to the voice of the Spirit which is in you, and all things shall work together for your good. (D&C 105:40)

Therefore, let your soul be at rest concerning your spiritual standing, and resist no more my voice. (D&C 108:2)

Inasmuch as they shall humble themselves before me, and abide in my word, and hearken to the voice of my Spirit. (D&C 112:22)

And if my people will hearken unto my voice, and unto the voice of my servants whom I have appointed to lead my people, behold, verily I say unto you, they shall not be moved out of their place. (D&C 124:45)

But if they will not hearken to my voice, nor unto the voice of these men whom I have appointed, they shall not be blest, because they pollute mine holy grounds, and mine holy ordinances, and charters, and my holy words which I give unto them. (D&C 124:46)

Hearken and hear, O ye inhabitants of the earth. Listen, ye elders of my church together, and hear the voice of the Lord; for he calleth upon all men, and he commandeth all men everywhere to repent. (D&C 133:16)

And upon them that hearken not to the voice of the Lord shall be fulfilled that which was written by the prophet Moses, that they should be cut off from among the people. (D&C 133:63)

Therefore I did obey the voice of the Spirit, and took Laban by the hair of the head, and I smote off his head with his own sword. (1 Nephi 4:18)

I beheld the Son of God going forth among the children of men; and I saw many fall down at his feet and worship him. And it came to pass that I beheld that the rod of iron, which my father had seen, was the word of God. (1 Nephi 11:24–25)

And it came to pass that the voice of the Lord spake unto my father by night, and commanded him that on the morrow he should take his journey into the wilderness. (1 Nephi 16:9)

And it came to pass that the voice of the Lord said unto him: Look upon the ball, and behold the things which are written. (1 Nephi 16:26)

And it came to pass that after I, Nephi, had been in the land of Bountiful for the space of many days, the voice of the Lord came unto me, saying: Arise, and get thee into the mountain. And it came to pass that I arose and went up into the mountain, and cried unto the Lord. (1 Nephi 17:7)

Ye are swift to do iniquity but slow to remember the Lord your God. Ye have seen an angel, and he spake unto you; yea, ye have heard his voice from time to time; and he hath spoken unto you in a still small voice, but ye were past feeling, that ye could not feel his words; wherefore, he has spoken unto you like unto the voice of thunder, which did cause the earth to shake as if it were to divide asunder. (1 Nephi 17:45)

And it came to pass that the voice of the Lord came unto my father, that we should arise and go down into the ship. (1 Nephi 18:5)

And I, Nephi, said unto them: Behold they were manifest unto the prophet by the voice of the Spirit; for by the

Spirit are all things made known unto the prophets, which shall come upon the children of men according to the flesh. (1 Nephi 22:2)

Angels speak by the power of the Holy Ghost; wherefore, they speak the words of Christ. Wherefore, I said unto you, feast upon the words of Christ; for behold, the words of Christ will tell you all things what ye should do. (2 Nephi 32:3)

For behold, again I say unto you that if ye will enter in by the way, and receive the Holy Ghost, it will show unto you all things what ye should do. (2 Nephi 32:5)

And now, my beloved brethren, I perceive that you ponder still in your hearts; and it grieveth me that I must speak concerning this thing. For if you would hearken unto the Spirit which teacheth a man to pray ye would know that ye must pray; for the evil spirit teacheth not a man to pray, but teacheth him that he must not pray. (2 Nephi 32:8)

And he had hope to shake me from the faith, notwithstanding the many revelations and the many things which I had seen concerning these things; for I truly had seen angels, and they had ministered unto me. And also, I had heard the voice of the Lord speaking unto me in very word, from time to time; wherefore, I could not be shaken. (Jacob 7:5)

And while I was thus struggling in the spirit, behold, the voice of the Lord came into my mind again, saying: I will visit thy brethren according to their diligence in keeping my commandments. (Enos 1:10)

Mosiah, who was made king over the land of Zarahemla; for behold, he being warned of the Lord that he should flee out of the land of Nephi, and as many as would hearken unto the voice of the Lord should also depart out of the land with him, into the wilderness. (Omni 1:12)

And it came to pass that he did according as the Lord had commanded him. And they departed out of the land into the wilderness, as many as would hearken unto the voice of the Lord; and they were led by many preachings and prophesyings. And they were admonished continually by the word of God; and they were led by the power of his arm, through the wilderness until they came down into the land which is called the land of Zarahemla. (Omni 1:13)

For the natural man is an enemy to God, and has been from the fall of Adam, and will be, forever and ever, unless he yields to the enticings of the Holy Spirit, and putteth off the natural man and becometh a saint through the atonement of Christ the Lord, and becometh as a child, submissive, meek, humble, patient, full of love, willing to submit to all things which the Lord seeth fit to inflict upon him, even as a child doth submit to his father. (Mosiah 3:19)

And then shall the wicked be cast out, and they shall have cause to howl, and weep, and wail, and gnash their teeth; and this because they would not hearken unto the voice of the Lord; therefore the Lord redeemeth them not. (Mosiah 16:2)

And it came to pass that the voice of the Lord came to them in their afflictions, saying: Lift up your heads and be of good comfort, for I know of the covenant which ye have made unto me; and I will covenant with my people and deliver them out of bondage. (Mosiah 24:13)

And it came to pass that so great was their faith and their patience that the voice of the Lord came unto them again, saying: Be of good comfort, for on the morrow I will deliver you out of bondage. (Mosiah 24:16)

And he that will hear my voice shall be my sheep; and him shall ye receive into the church, and him will I also receive. (Mosiah 26:21)

Therefore I say unto you, that he that will not hear my voice, the same shall ye not receive into my church, for him I will not receive at the last day. (Mosiah 26:28)

And also the Spirit saith unto me, yea, crieth unto me with a mighty voice, saying: Go forth and say unto this people—Repent, for except ye repent ye can in nowise inherit the kingdom of heaven. (Alma 5:51)

Yea, and the voice of the Lord, by the mouth of angels, doth declare it unto all nations; yea, doth declare it, that they may have glad tidings of great joy; yea, and he doth sound these glad tidings among all his people, yea, even to them that are scattered abroad upon the face of the earth; wherefore they have come unto us. (Alma 13:22)

And the voice of the Lord came to Ammon saying: Thou shalt not go up to the land of Nephi. (Alma 20:2)

And it did work for them according to their faith in God; therefore, if they had faith to believe that God could cause that those spindles should point the way they should go, behold, it was done; therefore they had this miracle, and also many other miracles wrought by the power of God, day by day. Nevertheless, because those miracles were worked by small means it did show unto them marvelous works. They were slothful, and forgot to exercise their faith and diligence and then those marvelous works ceased, and they did not progress in their journey; Therefore, they tarried in the wilderness, or did not travel a direct course, and were afflicted with hunger and thirst, because of their transgressions. And now, my son, I would that ye should understand that these things are not without a shadow; for as our fathers were slothful to give heed to this compass (now these things were temporal) they did not prosper; even so it is with things which are spiritual. For behold, it is as easy to give heed to the word of Christ, which will point to you a straight course to eternal bliss, as it was for our fathers to give heed to this compass, which would point unto them a straight course to the promised land. And now I say, is there not a type in this thing? For just as surely as this director did bring our fathers, by following its course, to the promised land, shall the words of Christ, if we follow their course, carry us beyond this vale of sorrow into a far better land of promise. O my son, do not let us be slothful because of the easiness of the way; for so was it with our fathers; for so was it prepared for them, that if they would look they might live; even so it is with us. The way is prepared, and if we will look we may live forever. (Alma 37:40–46)

Nevertheless they did fast and pray oft, and did wax stronger and stronger in their humility, and firmer and firmer in the faith of Christ, unto the filling their souls with joy and consolation, yea even to the purifying and the sanctification of their hearts, which sanctification cometh because of their yielding their hearts unto God. (Helaman 3:35)

Therefore, blessed are they who will repent and hearken unto the voice of the Lord their God; for these are they that shall be saved. (Helaman 12:23)

But behold, the voice of the Lord came unto him, that he should return again, and prophesy unto the people whatsoever things should come into his heart. (Helaman 13:3)

And it came to pass that he cried mightily unto the Lord, all that day; and behold, the voice of the Lord came unto him. (3 Nephi 1:12)

But if they will not turn unto me, and hearken unto my voice, I will suffer them, yea, I will suffer my people, O house of Israel, that they shall go through among them, and shall tread them down, and they shall be as salt that hath lost its savor, which is thenceforth good for nothing but to be cast out, and to be trodden under foot of my people, O house of Israel. (3 Nephi 16:15)

And they hearkened not unto the voice of the Lord, because of their wicked combinations. (Ether 11:7)

For behold, my brethren, it is given unto you to judge, that ye may know good from evil; and the way to judge is as plain, that ye may know with a perfect knowledge, as the daylight is from the dark night. For behold, the Spirit of Christ is given to every man, that he may know good from evil; wherefore, I show unto you the way to judge; for every thing which inviteth to do good, and to persuade to believe in Christ, is sent forth by the power and gift of Christ; wherefore ye may know with a perfect knowledge it is of God. (Moroni 7:15–16)

And he became Satan, yea, even the devil, the father of all lies, to deceive and to blind men, and to lead them captive at his will, even as many as would not hearken unto my voice. (Moses 4:4)

And she again conceived and bare his brother Abel. And Abel hearkened unto the voice of the Lord. And Abel was a keeper of sheep, but Cain was a tiller of the ground. (Moses 5:17)

And Cain was wroth, and listened not any more to the voice of the Lord, neither to Abel, his brother, who walked in holiness before the Lord. (Moses 5:26)

And he also said unto him: If thou wilt turn unto me, and hearken unto my voice, and believe, and repent of all thy transgressions, and be baptized, even in water, in the name of mine Only Begotten Son, who is full of grace and truth, which is Jesus Christ, the only name which shall be given under heaven, whereby salvation shall come unto the children of men, ye shall receive the gift of the Holy Ghost, asking all things in his name, and whatsoever ye shall ask, it shall be given you. (Moses 6:52)

After the true saints receive and enjoy the gift of the Holy Ghost; after they know how to attune themselves to the voice of the Spirit; after they mature spiritually so that they see visions, work miracles, and entertain angels; after they make their calling and election sure and prove themselves worthy of every trust—after all this and more—it becomes their right and privilege to see the Lord and commune with him face to face. Revelations, visions, angelic visitations, the rending of the heavens, and appearances among men of the Lord himself—all these things are for all of the faithful. They are not reserved for apostles and prophets only. (McConkie, *Promised Messiah*, 575)

Appendix B

A Partial List of Scriptures on Rebirth of the Spirit

Jesus answered and said unto him, Verily, verily, I say unto thee, Except a man be born again, he cannot see the kingdom of God. (John 3:3)

For the natural man is an enemy to God, and has been from the fall of Adam, and will be, forever and ever, unless he yields to the enticings of the Holy Spirit, and putteth off the natural man and becometh as a child, submissive, meek, humble, patient, full of love, willing to submit to all things which the Lord seeth fit to inflict upon him, even as a child doth submit to his father. (Mosiah 3:19)

And they all cried with one voice, saying: Yea, we believe all the words which thou hast spoken unto us; and also, we know of their surety and truth, because of the Spirit of the Lord Omnipotent, which has wrought a mighty change in us, or in our hearts, that we have no more disposition to do evil, but to do good continually. (Mosiah 5:2)

And now, because of the covenant which ye have made ye shall be called the children of Christ, his sons, and his daughters; for behold, this day he hath spiritually begotten you; for ye say that your hearts are changed through faith on his name; therefore, ye are born of him and have become his sons and his daughters. (Mosiah 5:7)

And the Lord said unto me: Marvel not that all mankind, yea, men and women, all nations, kindreds, tongues and people, must be born again; yea, born of God, changed from their carnal and fallen state, to a state of righteousness, being redeemed of God, becoming his sons and daughters; And thus they become new creatures; and unless they do this they can in nowise inherit the kingdom of God. (Mosiah 27:25–26)

And according to his faith there was a mighty change wrought in his heart. Behold I say unto you that this is all true. (Alma 5:12)

And behold, he preached the word unto your fathers, and a mighty change was also wrought in their hearts, and they humbled themselves and put their trust in the true and living God. And behold, they were faithful until the end; therefore they were saved. And now behold, I ask of you, my brethren of the church, have ye spiritually been born of God? Have ye received his image in your countenances? Have ye experienced this mighty change in your hearts? (Alma 5:13–14)

And now I say unto you that this is the order after which I am called, yea, to preach unto my beloved brethren, yea, and every one that dwelleth in the land; yea, to preach unto all, both old and young, both bond and free; yea, I say unto you the aged, and also the middle aged, and the rising generation; yea, to cry unto them that they must repent and be born again. (Alma 5:49)

Now I say unto you that ye must repent, and be born again; for the Spirit saith if ye are not born again ye cannot inherit the kingdom of heaven; therefore come and be baptized unto repentance, that ye may be washed from your sins, that ye may have faith on the Lamb of God, who taketh away the sins of the world, who is mighty to save and to cleanse from all unrighteousness. (Alma 7:14)

That by reason of transgression cometh the fall, which fall bringeth death, and inasmuch as ye were born into the world by water, and blood, and the spirit, which I have made, and so became of dust a living soul, even so ye must be born again into the kingdom of heaven, of water, and of the Spirit, and be cleansed by blood, even the blood of mine Only Begotten; that ye might be sanctified from all sin, and enjoy the words of eternal life in this world, and eternal life in the world to come, even immortal glory; (Moses 6:59)

And this is my gospel—repentance and baptism by water, and then cometh the baptism of fire and the Holy Ghost, even the Comforter, which showeth all things, and teacheth the peaceable things of the kingdom. (D&C 39:6)

About the Author

John M. Pontius is a former businessman and oil industry consultant. He is very happily married to Terri Jeanne. Together they have eight wonderful children and eighteen grandchildren. They are both lifetime members of the Church of Jesus Christ of Latter-day Saints. After thirty-three years in Alaska, they recently retired and moved to Utah to be nearer to family, and to be able to write and speak full time. Brother Pontius may be reached through www.followingthelight.org.